KICKING GRASS

TAKING GAMES

By Maddi Davidson
With Murder You Get Sushi
Denial of Service
Outsourcing Murder

KICKING GRASS
TAKING GAMES

MADDI DAVIDSON

Some names and identifying details have been changed to
protect the privacy of individuals.

Cover in Barbatrick and Candara
Text in Adobe Garamond Pro

ISBN: 1983653322
ISBN-13: 978-1983653322

To Christine Nolan, beloved teammate. The warmth of the sun wanes as it begins to set and yet, we are ready for the game to begin. In that golden glow, once again my friend, I see you on the field.

Contents

Photographs follow page 112

Acknowledgments

This book would not have been possible were it not for the women who so generously shared their stories: the good, the bad, and the oh-so-embarrassing. In particular, I'd like to thank: Ruth Walton, the former commissioner of Fairfax Women's Soccer Association, who knows everything about the early days of FWSA and its struggles to find fields; Nona Marsh, the commissioner for soccer at the San Diego Senior Games, for helping me reach so many soccer players from California; and Christiane Wollaston-Jury for spreading the word about the book to players at the Veteran's Cup.

Although I played recreational soccer for thirty years before writing this book, I was woefully ignorant of the hard work and tenacity of the women who made it possible. To all of you, I am eternally grateful. Let's go kick grass.

INTRODUCTION

Women born in the United States during the 1940s and 1950s entered a world with a prescribed place for women. In advertisements and on television, women were portrayed as wives, mothers, and dutiful homemakers. Women were not expected to work outside the home, except as teachers or secretaries until they married. The idea of a woman playing a strenuous team sport was laughable.

The 1960s brought a change in attitude: women could do and be so much more. The push for women's rights came to fruition in 1972 when Title IX of the Educational Amendments was signed into law by President Nixon. Its enactment put an end to programs that openly discriminated against women in education, such as quotas for law schools and medical schools. Title IX also had a profound effect on women's sports: schools now were required to offer girls equal opportunities on the fields and courts. Nowhere was that impact more visible than the subsequent success of the United States women's national team, winner of three World Cups and four Olympic gold medals. Today across the country, millions of girls each weekend emulate their national team idols by lacing up soccer cleats and sprinting onto the field.

Women born too early to receive the full benefits of Title IX did not stay on the sidelines. They, also, wanted to play. In the 1970s and 1980s, tens of thousands of women took up the sport of soccer and discovered a passion that has endured into their fifties, sixties, and beyond.

Why did these women choose to play such a demanding sport? When no infrastructure existed to support women's soccer, how did they learn the game, establish teams and leagues, and find fields? What were their experiences as coaches, referees, and administrators in the male-dominated soccer establishment? Now at age when joints ache, vision has deteriorated, and running is difficult, why are so many of them still playing this game? *Kicking Grass Taking Games* is their story, in their words.

ONE
A Whole New World

I N THE COOL, near-perfect spring evening, a slight breeze carried the scent of early blooming flowers across the soccer field. Nearly twenty women, all of them over sixty years of age, gathered on the sideline wearing a mix of red and white jerseys. Sandy Thorpe, seventy-three, in her bright orange T-shirt watched as several women changed from white shirts to red to even up the numbers on each team. When the referee signaled it was time to take the field, Sandy plodded across the slightly springy artificial turf toward the goal she would defend.

Sandy had always thought of herself as a jock. In the 1960s when sports programs for women were rare, she had the good fortune to attend McLean High School. Most high schools in Northern Virginia had little in the way of sports programs for girls, but McLean was one of few that allowed its Lady Statesmen to play softball, field hockey, and basketball as varsity sports. Sandy relished the opportunity and lettered in field hockey and softball. After high school, she played softball in church leagues, but eventually the responsibilities of being a wife, a parent, and working full-time ended her playing days.

At age forty-eight, Sandy was embroiled in a painful divorce. Her eldest daughter Shelly, already married and out of the house, wanted to do something to lift her mother's spirits. Aware of Sandy's lifelong passion for sports, Shelly surmised that her mother might find joy in playing on a team again. A soccer player herself, Shelly signed her mother up to play in FWSA, the Fairfax Women's Soccer Association.

All of Sandy's five children played soccer, yet for years she'd done nothing more than occasionally kick a ball when it rolled off the field. Sandy was dubious of learning a new sport at such an advanced age. Nevertheless, the FWSA representative convinced her to give it a try. Sandy purchased a pair of soccer cleats and shin guards, and showed up at the field for practice.

She picked up the strategy of the game almost immediately; like field hockey, soccer is contested between teams of eleven players, including a goalie, with the objective to put a ball in the opposition net. Through her previous athletic endeavors, Sandy had developed excellent ball skills using her arms and hands. However, she was nearly helpless with her feet. Despite her clumsiness in dribbling and kicking the ball, Sandy instantly fell in love with soccer.

The camaraderie of her new team overwhelmed Sandy. The women became a support group as Sandy struggled through her divorce. Despite knowing Sandy only for a short time, her teammates pooled their funds to help her retain a lawyer.

Teams have different philosophies about where to place a new and unskilled player. One approach is to put them on offense where they may provide little in the way of scoring, but blunders do not result in the opposing team scoring. Sandy had a natural bent toward defending, so she was placed at fullback, responsible for stopping the opposing team attacks. During her second year with the team, the goalkeeper failed to show for one of the games. Goalkeeper is a position loathed by most soccer players. At the amateur level, when a goalie can't make a game it's not uncommon for two, three, or even four field players to split the ninety-minute burden.

Unhesitatingly, Sandy volunteered. She'd played goalie in field hockey and was eager to give it a try.

The movement on the field of the goalie is entirely different from that of her teammates. Ten players on each team play on the field: running, passing, dribbling the ball, heading, and shooting. The goalkeeper stays at one end of the expanse, usually within an eighteen-yard box where she can use her hands. She does little running, uses her hands more than her feet, and unless she has a cannon for a leg, never shoots. She wears special gloves and sometimes shirts with padded elbows and pants with padded hips and knees for diving. A goalie's *raison d'être* is to stop the ball from going into the net, whatever it takes: throwing oneself onto rock-hard fields or into mud, diving into a melee of players kicking at the ball, or standing up to fifty-mile-per-hour shots taken five feet away. There is (almost) no such thing as a particularly crazy goalkeeper: they're all crazy.

"You know how hard it is to get a good goalie? Someone who's willing to stand there and take it like a woman?" said Christine Nolan, Sandy's former teammate. After years and years of playing on the field, being told not to use her hands, Christine was so thoroughly indoctrinated that she couldn't play goalie. Nor could she play volleyball any longer. When a volleyball would come flying over the net, Christine's brain saw a soccer ball, and she either headed the ball or tried to kick it back. "I don't fault anybody who goes in goal, ever. I don't care if you let in twenty goals. You're standing there, and that's all that counts."

Sandy took to goalkeeping like a kid to a puddle. She wanted to play soccer every minute of the day and goalkeeper every second of the game. Her kids were grown and out of the house, she was no longer married, and soccer was her passion. It was everything. Whether her team played poorly or well, Sandy radiated the love of just playing, and her mood was infectious. Her commitment to the sport grew until Sandy was on the roster of three outdoor and two indoor soccer teams, playing five times a week.

Eyes bright and dancing, Sandy searched for the words to express her feelings for soccer. "I just love it. I don't know what it is. I know it sounds corny, but I like the ball. I like the shirts. I like the shorts. I like the field. I like the whole thing! I like the type of people who play soccer. I just love the game."

Soccer opened up a new world for Sandy. Her first airplane ride came when she flew to San Diego to attend a soccer tournament. She was enthusiastic and excited about all the new experiences: the plane ride, the hotel, and even the rental van. Sandy liked the adventure so much she put together teams for tournaments in Las Vegas, San Diego, Puerto Vallarta, Mexico, and closer to home in York, Pennsylvania. Sandy became known amongst soccer players from Northern Virginia as "The Great Organizer."

Occasionally, her organizing ability let her down, like at the infamous tournament in York. Sandy assembled a team of women to compete in the over-40 (years old) division. She informed the tournament director that her team was a collection of players, not a competitive tournament team. Perhaps she was hoping to be put in a less cutthroat bracket. Just before leaving for York, Sandy learned that there were not enough teams registered for the over-40 division and her group would be playing in the over-30 division. Sandy decided not to tell the team ahead of time lest some chose to back out. She waited until the women were in the car and well on their way before breaking the news. The women called Sandy unprintable names during the remainder of the journey. Sandy knew they did it in fun—they didn't blame her for the situation—but they were not happy about playing in a younger age group. At the tournament, the over-30 teams were organized into two brackets, with the winner of each bracket playing for the title. The tournament director, sensing an easy victory, placed Sandy's team in her bracket. "They just creamed us," Sandy said. Predictably, her team also was crushed by the other younger teams.

Christine summed it up. "We got our butts handed to us on a platter, and it was literally 110 degrees in the shade. There was nothing good about that tournament except we all had fun off the field. But on the field it was a nightmare. Oh God!"

On the ride home, the women continued to call Sandy a few choice names. Not wanting to risk a repeat of the massacre, Sandy never took another group to York.

Sandy acquired a reputation in the tournament circuit as a reliable goalkeeper. As old as she was, women from as far away as Washington and California were asking her to play on their tournament teams. One such call led her to the west coast for the California Senior Olympics, where nearly a dozen women's teams played in the over-50 bracket. No one on the team knew Sandy personally, but they'd acquired her name with a strong recommendation.

"You're the goalie?" was all that the team organizer could say when she met Sandy for the first time at the San Diego field.

"Because I'm short and old, I think they were mortified," Sandy said. Elite goalkeepers are typically five feet, nine inches tall or more. Sandy stands a mere five feet on a good day. And carrying 135 pounds, she didn't appear to be the athlete that she was.

Sandy saved her best for tournaments and was determined to show the team that they were lucky to have her. She threw herself at any ball that came her way, recklessly risking her body to keep the ball out of her net. Sandy admitted that she reached new heights (figuratively, not literally) during the tournament. Sandy's team finished third, winning the bronze medal. The team knew their good showing was in large part due to Sandy's heroics. She had won them over.

That weekend the California women discovered what Sandy's Virginia teammates, like Judy Jones, already knew. "Sandy may not have been the greatest goalie; she is awfully short, but she probably had the most heart."

Like many soccer players, Sandy developed knee problems: first a meniscus tear and then a torn anterior cruciate ligament (ACL), one of the knee ligaments that joins the upper leg bone with the lower leg bone. She returned to play soccer from both. Then she developed deep vein thrombosis (DVT), blood clots in her leg. DVT is a serious and potentially fatal condition. Blood clots can break loose, travel up to the lung, and partially block an artery, a condition termed pulmonary embolism or PE.[1] Complications of a PE include heart palpitations and heart attacks. Sandy's doctors tried numerous methods to dissolve the clots, but the situation persisted. As a last resort, they removed the clots and part of a vein in her leg. As a result of the surgery, the circulation in Sandy's right leg is extremely poor, and her knee is continuously swollen. She has difficulty ascending and descending stairs and can no longer run. When she is down on the ground, it takes Sandy a few moments to get back on her feet.

Unwillingly and with a heavy heart, Sandy stopped playing soccer. But she still loved the game and continued to organize tournament teams. One or twice a year Sandy would assemble rosters, register the players, arrange for the shirts and the hotel rooms, fly to the tournament, prepare the lineup, and cheer on the women. For thirteen years Sandy watched the game she loved from the sidelines.

Sandy recalled the year she organized a quite energetic group of women for an over-40 tournament. The entire team went out for dinner and returned to the hotel in time to get a good night's sleep for the next day's game. Sandy went to bed at her usual time, 9:00 p.m. The following morning she discovered her teammates had changed clothes and gone out again. "To do what?" she'd asked. Pole dancing and lap dancing was the reply. Sandy had never heard of either one, so the women explained. Sandy was shocked that older, married women would partake in such activities. She still shakes her head in disbelief.

Even though she was not playing, Sandy enjoyed the tournaments. After each tournament, she'd tell herself it was the best team yet and the most fun.

Often Sandy's teams included a blend of women from across the country: players she knew and the friends they brought. For one tournament, she assembled a mix of skillful players from California and Northern Virginia. Before leaving for the competition, Sandy told Tricia, a goalkeeper from Northern Virginia, that three others on the team also played goalie. Tricia said she was okay with that and would play on the field for part of the tournament.

Sandy's core belief in managing tournament teams was to give players equal opportunity to play. "You pay the same, you play the same," is her mantra. Jennifer, a keeper from California, played the first game in goal. Tall, agile, and athletic, Jennifer was a terrific goalie. Her booming punts traveled nearly the length of the field—a rare skill among older women.

In the second game, Sandy gave Tricia her chance. Although Tricia played well, she was not nearly as impressive as Jennifer: her kicks never came close to even reaching the mid-field line. At halftime Kris, one of the defenders from California, stormed off the field, apoplectic. She headed straight for Sandy with all the appearance of someone going to flatten an opponent.

"She screamed," Sandy said. "Her face was red she was so upset." Kris's screeching voice lambasted Sandy, accusing her of positioning the team to lose "by putting *her* in." Kris denigrated Tricia's abilities and Sandy's intelligence. The entire team, the opposing team, spectators, referees, and all living creatures within a two-block radius heard Kris's diatribe.

Sandy was embarrassed. Nothing like this had ever happened to her before. After a few moments, she regained her composure. Sandy had her methods and wasn't going to change them just because of Kris. Players would get equal time on the field, as always. Her team finished with a respectable record but did not win the tournament. Sandy had no intention of ever including Kris in another tournament team, a decision that was reinforced when two of the talented Virginia players informed her that they would never again play with Kris.

In the fall of 2015, Fairfax Woman's Soccer Association launched an over-60 division. In deference to the age of the players, the game would be only an hour long instead of the customary ninety minutes. And instead of playing a full field, the playing area would be adjusted for the number of women who showed up to play: fewer women, smaller field. When Sandy heard about the over-60 group, she felt as if she'd been given another chance to play soccer. "I just had to do it. I have such a passion for soccer and had to try it again, and they let me."

Friends and former teammates were thrilled to see Sandy on the field again, knowing how much it meant to her, despite their concern that Sandy could be jeopardizing her already poor health. Her good friend Karen Sharpe called it "fabulous. She's so happy doing it."

Because she couldn't dive and slide like before, Sandy expected to play no more than half of the game, but the other women insisted at the first game that she play goalie for the entire time, which she did in all subsequent games.

Each Thursday night after the game, Sandy drove home with a serene smile spread across her face. She admitted that there had been Fridays when she was so tired she couldn't drag herself into work, but she wouldn't stop playing.

Sandy returned for a second season in the over-60 league. As she approached the goal on that splendid spring evening, she felt apprehensive and excited to be on the field again. Reaching the nets, Sandy turned and faced the field, ready for battle.

Sandy's team, wearing white, dominated the first half of play. Sandy found herself with little to do, but her heart pounded faster each time the ball came across the half-field line. Would the red team take a shot? Would she have to make a save?

White scored in rather peculiar fashion. The red team was playing without a goalkeeper and twice their experienced defenders miss-hit the ball trying to clear it out of danger, only to see it squirt into the red net.

For the second half, the white team gave their extra player to red. Now the red team dominated. Sandy was called to action several times to make saves. Fortunately, the balls were weakly hit. Easily gathered in when Sandy was younger, balls moving slowly across the ground now provided more of a challenge because she needed to bend down or get on her knees to scoop them up. It was less difficult for Sandy to manage a waist-high ball, even if hard-hit. Sandy made two saves before a shot got by her. It was now 2-1 with her team still in front, but red was pressing for a second goal. With ten minutes left in the game, white took the ball into the red half. A red player intercepted the ball and quickly passed to a teammate bursting across midfield. The red forward barreled down the field on a breakaway, deftly guiding the ball at her feet. The nearest white defender was yards behind, fruitlessly chasing, and no one was between the red forward and the goal except Sandy.

Players on both teams watched as the play unfolded much like a kickoff return in football where the speedster has outpaced his pursuers and only needs to get by the puny kicker to score. The outcome was all but decided. Sandy came out of her goal to narrow the angle for the shot, her arms held wide. All the players watching knew it was a sure goal … except it wasn't. The ball shot off the forward's foot flying unerringly toward the corner of the goal, but somehow someway Sandy got a hand on it and the ball caromed wide of its target and over the end line.

Players on both teams cheered.

TWO
Title IX and All That

WOMEN BORN IN the 1940s and 1950s entered a world that offered few opportunities for them to participate in organized sports.

Suzanne Mahoney was born in 1946 into a military family. Her father displayed an enlightened attitude toward his daughter's athletic talents, teaching her along with her two brothers how to pitch, catch, field, and hit a baseball. While living in Virginia, her brothers were allowed to play Little League yet Suzanne, despite a skill level superior to many boys her age, was prohibited by the league "boys only" rule. She was relegated to the sidelines, watching her brothers.

Despite the liberal outlook of Suzanne's father and other men, a sports-loving woman did not fit into the prevailing myth of the all-American family. In the 1950s, the model woman was portrayed on TV and in print as a white, suburban housewife who cheerfully cared for her home, husband, and children while perfectly coiffed and immaculately dressed. TV series such as *Father Knows Best* and *The Donna Reed Show* epitomized this ideal version of womanhood. Girls were expected to aspire to be just like their mothers. In a 1953 print advertisement for Hoover, a housewife is sprawled elegantly on the floor. One hand caresses a vacuum cleaner, the other holds operating instructions, and the ad is captioned, "Christmas morning she'll be happier with a Hoover." Despite these depictions of women, the reality is that one in three women were in the labor force and 12 percent of mothers with young children worked outside the house, many for economic reasons.[1]

Women also were shown as weak in both mind and body. A 1953 Alcoa Aluminum ad shows a woman holding a ketchup bottle with a new easy-open cap exclaiming with delight, "You mean a woman can open it?" Hard to believe that only ten years earlier, Rosie the Riveter and her muscular biceps had been an icon.

Since a woman's place was in the home, institutes of higher education oriented themselves to serve that purpose. The President of Mills College, the oldest undergraduate college for women in the West, confidently proclaimed, "The curriculum for female students should prepare women to foster the intellectual and emotional life of her family and community."[2] Home economics was deemed an acceptable course of study. Civil engineering was not.

During this era, athletics were not entirely off limits for proper women, provided they engaged in a sport that was suitably refined. In Abercrombie & Fitch ads, women played golf in dresses. A Ski Colorado advertisement showed a young woman on skis wearing bracelets, a sleeveless blouse, and glamorous sunglasses. Lucky Strike promoted smoking using a shapely woman ice-skating while holding a cigarette in her black-gloved hand. Women in movies and ads played tennis or waterskied. Naturally, the women in such advertisements were always pretty and never sweating.

Notable were the women who defied the norm by playing sports and excelling. In 1950, the Associated Press voted Babe

Didrikson Zaharias the "Greatest Female Athlete of the First Half of the Century." Babe was a singular athlete: an All-American in basketball who also played baseball and softball, won Olympic medals in track and field, helped to found the Ladies Professional Golf Association (LPGA), and competed with men on the PGA Tour.[3]

The 1950s saw Marcenia Lyle Stone Alberga (aka Toni Stone) become the first women to play major league baseball, signing a contract with the Indianapolis Clowns in the Negro American League. Toni was brought in primarily as a gate attraction to counteract declining revenue as Negro League players joined Major League Baseball teams. She batted a respectable .243 while appearing in fifty games.

In 1956, tennis player Althea Gibson won the French Championship, becoming the first African-American, man or woman, to win a Grand Slam event. She went on to win eleven Grand Slam tournaments over her career.

By 1956, the Winter Olympics offered women medals in downhill, slalom, giant slalom, cross-country 10K, cross-country relay, and ice-skating. Seventeen percent of all participants that year were women. The 1956 Summer Olympics in Melbourne awarded medals to women in diving, swimming, gymnastics, fencing, canoeing, and nine categories in track and field. Thirteen percent of participants were women, up from ten percent in the 1952 games. A young Australian woman, Betty Cuthbert, became the "Golden Girl" of the games by winning three gold medals in track for her country.

Ever so slowly, the rules for women changed. Since the 1920s, female participation in sports had been regarded as a healthy and necessary activity although competition was discouraged. As a consequence, the governing body for women's sports in colleges promoted athletics as an intramural activity with outside competition taking the form of "play dates:" informal gatherings where teams would include a mix of players from different schools. This format ensured that school spirit and competition would not get out of hand. No prizes were awarded for winning, and the women might imbibe tea and cookies following contests. Similarly, track and field competitions, as well as swimming, could be contested through "telegraphic meets." Each school would conduct their races or field events and wire the results to its competitors. It's not known whether the schools would also wire the type of tea and cakes the girls consumed afterward.[4]

Despite these guidelines, women in colleges and universities did conduct head to head competition between schools. In 1957, the American Association of Health, Physical Education, and Recreation recognized reality and modified its decades-long opposition to women competing by stating that intercollegiate programs "may" exist. Six short years later, its position was again amended to note that intercollegiate programs for women were now "desirable."[5]

In the 1940s and 1950s, women's basketball was distinctly different from the men's game: six players took the court for each team—three on offense and three on defense—and the women were not allowed to cross the centerline or steal the ball. A significant rule change in 1962 permitted two players from each team to roam the entire court. In the spirit of greater competitiveness, women also were allowed to grab the ball from an opponent. Dribbling was still limited to three bounces—to slow the pace of the game—until 1966 when unlimited dribbling was permitted.[6]

Many still doubted women's ability to run long distances. Not until the 1960 games in Rome could women compete in the 800 meters. The Boston Marathon forbade women from running, but in 1966 and for the following two years, Roberta Gibb snuck onto the course near the start and ran the race with the men. In 1967, Katherine Switzer registered as K.V. Switzer. Assumed to be male, she received an official racing bib and number. Boston Athletic Association officials noticed her presence early in the race—perhaps because she wore lipstick—and one tried to grab her. Switzer's boyfriend racing alongside tackled the official, allowing Switzer to continue. She finished the race and received widespread media coverage. "I wasn't running Boston to prove anything," Spitzer wrote years later. "I was just a kid who wanted to run her first marathon."[7]

In the 1950s and 1960s, girls' sports in high school were predominantly intramural. Anyone could play, and occasional competitions were scheduled with other schools. However, during the late 1960s and early 1970s, changes were underway.

Lisa Teal, born in 1949, attended Rolling Hills High School in Los Angeles County, California. While today her high school offers girls' varsity competition in more than fourteen different sports, talented athletes like Lisa had little choice but to become cheerleaders.

Wendy Matalon, also from Southern California, is five years younger than Lisa and had the option in high school of playing badminton, volleyball, field hockey, softball, track and field, and basketball. The GAA (Girls Athletic Association) provided competitive opportunities with other high schools. Pia Parrish, two years younger than Wendy, earned letters in several varsity sports, although the girls were not allowed to have letter jackets. "We had these ugly cardigan sweaters that buttoned up—like old men wear," Pia recalled.

Still, for every Pia and Wendy who played competitive sports in high school, a dozen or more were shut out. In the early 1970s, only one out of twenty-seven girls played sports in high school.[8]

The situation in colleges and universities was improving, but like the high schools, few women played sports. In 1966, over 2.3 million women attended college in the United States but just one half of one percent—fifteen thousand—were reported as competing in intercollegiate sports.[9] That same year, the governing body for women's collegiate sports established a commission to assist in the development of competition for women. By 1970 national championships had been established in badminton, gymnastics, swimming, track and field, and volleyball. In 1971, the Association of Intercollegiate Athletics for Women (AIAW) was founded with a membership of 278 institutions and by 1972, participation by women in intercollegiate sports had doubled: to 32,000 or 1 percent of enrolled women.

The support for women's programs, in financial terms, was limited. In the early 1970s, Bev Vaughn attended Mary Washington, a private women's college replete with red-brick buildings overlooking historic Fredericksburg, Virginia. The school offered its women intercollegiate sports programs in field hockey, lacrosse, basketball, and tennis. Bev played on the varsity basketball team. "Our uniforms were kilts. They had these little panties that you wore, and the kilts came to mid-thigh, I guess. You bought your own [white] shirt, and then, depending on what the other team wore, we may have had to wear pinnies [colored mesh vests] over that." The kilts were used by the field hockey team in the fall and then passed on to the basketball team. Once the basketball season was over, the uniforms—presumably cleaned—were given to the lacrosse team for the spring season.

Title IX changes everything

In 1972, Title IX of the Educational Amendments was passed by the U.S. Congress and signed into law by President Nixon. One would be forgiven for believing that the purpose of Title IX was to give women equal opportunities in sports, for indeed, it is within the athletic sphere where the most controversy has occurred, and where women's gains are often cited. However, as noted in the title of the act, Title IX was one of many amendments to an education bill, and it makes no mentions of sports. It simply stated:

"No person in the United States shall, on the basis of sex, be excluded from participation in, be denied the benefits of, or be subjected to discrimination under any education program or activity receiving Federal financial assistance."[10]

The congresswoman who wrote the draft of Title IX, Edith Green, intended to put an end to programs that openly discriminated against women in education, such as quotas for medical schools and law schools limiting female enrollment to 10 percent. Support was far from universal as even the *New York Times* stated that ending quotas was "educationally unsound." The notion that collegiate sports might be affected was raised only once. When Senator Birch Bayh backed a similar amendment to the Senate version of the Education Bill, he was asked if the law would require boys and girls to share locker rooms.[11]

Title IX passed with little fanfare. The Department of Health, Education, and Welfare (HEW) bore the responsibility for writing the new rules, but it was under no pressure to hurry the process. Not until mid-1973 did the agency deal with the impact of the law on sports. The Secretary of HEW, Caspar Weinberger, knowing that schools spent millions of dollars on boy's sports and just pennies on girls' sports, stated that school athletics would come under the purview of the law. Thus, when proposed regulations were published for comment in 1974, most of the 10,000 responses were regarding athletics: primarily on how Title IX could harm male sports. Fearing that the protests by male-dominated sports organizations would lead to a watering down of Title IX, feminist groups joined together to support the proposed regulations. Ultimately they prevailed. Final regulations were published in 1975 and secondary and post-secondary schools were given until July 21, 1978 to comply.[12]

The rise in girls' sports participation that followed was nothing short of phenomenal. In 1971, the year prior to the passage of Title IX, 294,015 girls participated in high school sports in the United States. Ten years later participation had risen to 1,853,780.

Women playing varsity sports in college doubled over this period, and the NCAA took note.[13] Hitherto devoid of women's sports, the NCAA developed an appetite to take over the representation and potential profits of the thousand schools whose athletic programs were affiliated with the Association for Intercollegiate Athletics for Women.[14] The NCAA made their move in 1981, welcoming all programs to the organization. By 1982 the AIAW was out of existence.

Little League resisted the growing tide of feminism and in 1972 was sued to change the ruling on girls playing. In defense of Little League policy, the Executive Vice President testified, "A blow to the breast of a female, as by a batted or thrown ball, could cause cancer."[15] Arguments like these no longer were acceptable and by 1974 Little League succumbed: girls could play. The change came decades too late for Suzanne Mahoney and others like her.

In the decade of the 1970s, female athletes continued to chalk up "firsts." Billy Jean King beat Bobby Riggs in tennis, and Diane Crump became the first female jockey to ride in the Kentucky Derby. Junko Tabei from Japan conquered Mt. Everest, and Janet Guthrie qualified for the Indianapolis 500. And there were many, many more.

While not making the sports news, other women like Kerry Eddy were leading quiet revolutions. At UC Davis, Kerry and a few classmates started a women's intramural soccer program, which soon was playing women's teams at other colleges and universities. When a local high school started a girl's soccer team, Kerry and a few teammates volunteered to coach. With the support of the girls' parents, they fought the city of Davis for the team to be given a grass section of N. Davis Park for a field. At a city council meeting, the mayor stated that soccer was a fad and it didn't make sense for the city to designate space for girls' high school soccer. Kerry and others pointed out a few provisions of Title IX and the city relented: the girls got their field.

Although the passage of Title IX was game-changing, another breakthrough in the 1970s could be regarded as equally momentous: the invention of the sports bra.

The oft-told story begins in 1977 with the travails of Victoria Woodrow, an enthusiastic participant in the new sport of jogging. For advice on how to manage the bouncing of her chest, Victoria contacted her sister Lisa Lindahl who was a jogger. Reportedly, Victoria expressed astonishment that Lisa wore her regular bra and wondered out loud why there wasn't a better alternative for women. Lisa collaborated with costume designer Polly Smith to develop a few prototypes that would reduce the bouncing. When Lisa's husband walked around the room with a jockstrap on his chest proclaiming, "Here is your jockbra, ladies," he unknowingly set the direction for the bra. Starting with two athletic supporters, Lisa, Polly, and assistant Hinda Schreiber developed and patented the modern sports bra.[16]

Women athletes were off and running.

THREE
Not a Game for Ladies

THE LATTER HALF of the 20th century has seen soccer become one of the most popular sports for women in the United States. But women playing soccer is not new: it's just new in the United States. Under the disapproving eyes of men, women have played the game for years in the soccer-mad countries of Europe. Or should one say, football-mad? For across the Atlantic, and indeed most places in the world, the sport is known as football or some variation thereof: futebol, fodbold, fotbol, futball, voetbal.

British Football

While men and women have been kicking balls around over two thousand years, what we know as the modern game of football was not established until 1863, when the Football Association in London set out a standard set of rules.[1]

The first recorded instance of women playing the modern game comes from 1881. The organizer, the Scottish suffragist Helen Mathews, billed the game as an international match with a team representing Scotland hosting a team of English women.[2]

According to the *Glasgow Herald*, "The Scotch team wore blue jerseys, white knickerbockers, red stockings, a red belt, high-heeled boots and blue and white cowl; while their English sisters were dressed in blue and white jerseys, blue stockings and belt, high-heeled booted and red and white cowl. The game, judged from a player's point of view, was a failure, but some of the individual members of the teams showed that they had a fair idea of the game."[3] Over one thousand spectators watched as Scotland thrashed England, 3-0.

In a rematch one week later in front of 5,000 fans, the Scottish team—now including several of the supposedly English players—again had the upper hand until fans stormed the field and the players fled the pitch. The threat of violence and the public opinion that women's games were unseemly—not just because of the women's limited skill set—made it difficult to play another game in Scotland.

The teams scheduled their next several games in England. A series of matches over six weeks drew thousands of paying patrons to observe the spectacle, and spectacle it was. Newspaper after newspaper condemned the women's skills and one game precipitated another near-riot. Many of the women (including the organizers) had expected a negative reception and used aliases. Following the debacle, it took another fourteen years before women's teams again were recorded playing in Britain.

In 1895, Nettie Honeyball (an alias) initiated the British Ladies Football Club "with the fixed resolve of proving to the world that women are not the 'ornamental' and 'useless' creatures men have pictured."[4] The games were to be played under English Football Association rules but would last only sixty minutes versus the official ninety. Honeyball noted the girls were practicing diligently, including on days when the ground was frozen and snow covered.

In response to questions about the women's safety—from the roughness of the game, not the hooliganism of the spectators—

Miss Honeyball stated, "We do not attempt to fortify ourselves against accidents any more than men. We wear proper football boots, with the corrugated toe and heel. At first some of the girls wore high-heeled and pointed boots, but these have been abandoned. We also wear ankle pads and shin guards, shirts and blue knickerbockers after the style of the divided skirt. Red brewers' caps are worn on the head and the hair is securely fastened up with hairpins, so you see we are fully prepared for the fray."

Many did not think so. The *Pall Mall Gazette* published a letter, which averred, "A woman sometimes waddles like a duck and sometimes like a chicken—it all depends on her weight. She is physically incapable of stretching her legs sufficiently to take the stride masculine…the smaller a woman's foot is the prouder she is of it, and very naturally…I don't think lady-footballers will ever be able to 'shoot' goals. In order to score a 'point' they will find it necessary, I fear, to charge the enemy's goal in masse and simply hustle the ball through."

The first match took place in London. As before, newspapers felt the need to comment on the uniforms and gave mixed but predominantly negative reviews regarding the quality of the match. Again the games were judged spectacle rather than sport and the press roundly condemned the notion of women playing football. The medical establishment opposed women's participation in the rugged sport, a *British Medical Journal* editorial stating, "We can in no way sanction the reckless exposure to violence of organs which the common experience of women had led them in every way to protect."[5]

Despite the criticism, the British Ladies Football Club scheduled an additional thirty-four matches over the next six months in England, Scotland, and Northern Ireland. Games consistently drew between 2,000 and 10,000 fans. The following year brought dwindling crowds and fewer games as the novelty wore off. The British Ladies Football Club folded. Not until

World War I forced changes in the role of women did female football teams again take the field.

In the first years of the Great War, British factories were re-tooled to produce munitions. The production of shells and missiles was dangerous and physically taxing work, and the prevalence of toxic chemicals ruinous to one's health. Yet, as men left the production lines to join the front lines, hundreds of thousands of women heeded the government's call for help and went to work in munitions factories.

Gabrielle West, a young Englishwoman who worked in a factory, kept a diary. "Many girls fainted from in the T.N.T. room but I was not affected so was often exposed to that deadly poison. I did, however, begin to faint fairly often, mostly with trapped fingers between the largest shells. Not having enough to eat probably helped to cause the fainting." In 1917, Lilian Miles watched her nineteen-year-old sister die from her munitions work. Lilian tried to get help for her. "The doctor said she was under the influence of alcohol because she was falling about. She died in terrible pain and they said that they reckoned that the black powder burnt the back of her throat away."[6]

The women earned about half of what men did for the same job. By 1918, over one million women had replaced men in the labor force. Of these, 700,000 were in the munitions industry. These munitionettes, as they were called, often were both young and unmarried and factories appointed welfare supervisors to oversee their moral and physical health. Apparently, these supervisors thought women's football was an acceptable activity for their charges because munitions factory ladies' football teams soon proliferated.

By 1917, ladies' football games between rival munitions plants took place before sizeable crowds: 10,000 spectators for a match were not unusual. Viewers paid for admission, and the money raised supported war charities such as Red Cross hospitals, prisoner of war funds, and war-orphan funds.

Although the men's professional football league ceased operations for the duration of the war, the ladies' games were not marketed as a replacement. In fact, some women's games stressed the novelty factor by having the women dress in outlandish outfits or play under silly rules, e.g., with hands tied behind backs.

Mainly due to their work for charities, lady footballers did not see the same level of disapproval as the teams playing in the late 1800s. Still, Victorian attitudes were in evidence in the prevalent belief that such a rough game could severely damage women's health. For example, it was known that playing strenuous games during a menstrual period could seriously affect fertility. Meanwhile, women working in munitions were moving seventy-two-pound shell casings around the factory and hundreds were dying in explosions and accidents. The detrimental effect on women's long-term health from munitions work seemed to be less of a concern than the potential damage wrought by playing football

However, there were those who openly supported the women, observing that ladies who were aiding their country should be encouraged in their sport.

Dick, Kerr Ladies

The most famous of the factory teams to emerge during this period was the Dick, Kerr Ladies from Preston, Lancashire, England.[7] Founded by two Scotsmen, William Dick and John Kerr, to build locomotives and tram equipment, Dick, Kerr Co. Ltd was one of the many converted munitions factories during the war. In 1917, Dick, Kerr Company fielded a woman's team to play Arundel Coulthard & Co. in a charity match. Funds from ticket sales were pledged to the local Moor Park Military Hospital. Preston North End Football Club allowed the women to use their grounds. Ten thousand spectators attended the game, in which the women played in shorts, long socks with shin guards, striped tunics, and close-fitting hats into which they secured their hair. Dick, Kerr's won by a score of 4-0, and the match raised the equivalent of $58,000 in today's currency for the hospital.

Dick, Kerr Ladies continued to play games for charity throughout the next year. On November 11, 1918, Armistice was declared, and soldiers began to come home. Munitions factories retooled for peacetime production, and munitionettes were no longer needed. Nevertheless, the ladies' football games continued. A Dick, Kerr Ladies match at Newcastle in 1919 drew 35,000 spectators. In the fall of that year, men's professional football in England resumed.

Alfred Franklin was the enterprising force behind the success of Dick, Kerr Ladies. He poached the best players from other teams and brought them to work at Dick, Kerr. When WWI ended, Franken found employment for his players outside the factory and understood that a continuation of the team required looking beyond England's shores. At his most enterprising, Franken creatively accounted for the funds raised for charities.

In 1920 Dick, Kerr Ladies hosted a women's team from France. Alice Milliat had founded the *Fédération des Sociétés Féminines Sportives de France* (FSFSF) and ladies' football was taking its nascent steps. "In my opinion," Mme. Milliat wrote in *Le Football Feminin*, "football is not wrong for women. Most of these girls are beautiful Grecian dancers. I do not think it is unwomanly to play football as they do not play like men, they play fast, but not vigorous, football."[8] A series of games between Dick, Kerr Ladies and the French team drew crowds between 12,000 and 25,000 for each match with the French winning two games, drawing two, and losing one. Over the next few years, Dick, Kerr Ladies and the French team would travel to one another's countries for games, drawing similarly large numbers of fans.

By the end of 1920, Dick, Kerr Ladies had played 30 matches, scored 133 goals versus 15 for their opponents, and had lost only 2 games. Average attendance exceeded 13,000 per game. Their most notable, or infamous, game was the 1920 Boxing Day match in Liverpool.[9] The Dick, Kerr Ladies beat St. Helen's Ladies in front of a capacity crowd of 53,000 fans. Astonishingly, another 10,000 to 15,000 fans had to be turned away at the gate. Attendance that day easily eclipsed the largest crowd to ever view a men's football match, a mere 41,000.

Dick, Kerr Ladies was the foremost women's football team in Britain. Alice Norris, one of the players, remembered, "It was sometimes hard work when we played a match during the week because we would have to work in the morning, travel to play the match, then travel home again and be up early for work the next day. But I was proud to be a Dick, Kerr's girl: it was worth all the effort we put in."

The success of women's football was not welcomed by the English Football Association. The Football Association was expanding the number of men's professional teams while simultaneously struggling to draw crowds to matches between teams from smaller cities. Individual men's teams and footballers had supported the ladies in providing fields and encouragement, but the Football Association was less kindly disposed. Adding to their disapproval was the apparent inconsistency in gate receipts versus monies donated to charity, particularly but not solely in the case of matches played by Dick, Kerr Ladies.

In December 1921, the English Football Association passed the following resolution: "Complaints having been made as to football being played by women, the Council feel impelled to express their strong opinion that the game of football is quite unsuitable for females and ought not to be encouraged. Complaints have also been made as to the conditions under which some of these matches have been arranged and played, and the appropriation of receipts to other than charitable objects.

The Council are further of the opinion that an excessive proportion of the receipts are absorbed in expenses and an inadequate percentage devoted to charitable objects. For these reasons the council request clubs belonging to the association to refuse the use of their grounds for such matches."[10] Since nearly all football fields were under the management of an FA team, this was a devastating blow to women's football.

The women were outraged. Alice Kell, a Dick, Kerr player, stated, "Girls have a right to play football if they desire. We play for the love of the game and are determined to go on." And go on they did.

The English Ladies Football Association formed, and the women found fields as they could, often using rugby pitches. Franklin worked through a tour promoter to arrange for the team to play matches in the United States and Canada. In 1922 Dick, Kerr Ladies set sail, but upon landing discovered they'd been misled by the promoter: there were no women's teams in either country. The Canadian Football Association prohibited their men from playing any matches with the ladies. So, the women played against several highly regarded men's teams in the United States, compiling a record of three wins, two losses, and two ties. It's believed that despite the ladies' skill and determination, their admirable record is due in part to a few of the men's teams holding back.

For forty-eight years, the Dick, Kerr Ladies (renamed Preston Ladies FC in 1926) played football, losing only 28 games in 833 matches. All games were played to benefit charities, and the women raised the equivalent of more than $12m in today's currency. In 1965, the team folded.

In 1971, after fifty years of opposition, the English Football Association dropped their ban on women using FA fields and formally recognized that women could play football. Thirty-one years later, Lily Parr—who played for Dick, Kerr Ladies from 1919 to 1951 and scored over 900 goals—was inducted posthumously into the English Football Hall of Fame, the first woman to be so honored.

Other Countries

The French women received even less support than their English counterparts. Records of women's football games up until 1970 are scarce. The last game played by a women's Fédération football team was in 1932 against a team from Belgium. The league folded shortly thereafter. In the late 1960s, French women worked to promote the acceptance of women's football, including sending a team to a makeshift Women's European Cup in 1969, won by the Italians. The following year the Federal Council of the French Football Federation—the English Football Association equivalent—officially reinstated women's football, and the women played their first internationally sanctioned match in 1971.[11]

In Germany, women began to form football clubs in the 1920s but did not take to the field in numbers until the 1950s. In 1955 the German Football Federation (DFB) rejected the idea of women playing football and DFB teams were forbidden to let women use their fields for play: "The attractiveness of women, their bodies, and souls will suffer irreparable damage and the public display of their bodies will offend morality and decency."[12]

The women played on, despite the ban, and in 1957 German hosted a European championship under the auspices of the International Ladies Football Association. The competition included teams from West Germany, Austria, England, the Netherlands, and Luxembourg. The Manchester Corinthians, a club from England, won. The Corinthians followed up their victory with several international tours over the next few years, playing women's teams in Italy, Portugal, South America, Madeira, and Ireland.

Despite large crowds at the European championship, the DFB reiterated their opposition to women's football in 1958, declaring that "Football as a game is first and foremost a demonstration of masculinity as we understand it from our traditional view of things and as produced in part by our physical constitution (through hormonal irritation)." German doctors felt the women should not be allowed to play due to "special anatomical characteristics such as knock-knees" and the "diminished ability to reproduce." Ignoring them, women continued to play in recreational clubs. Not until 1970 did the DFB officially support women's football, and even then it was with the proviso that games take place only in warm weather, with a lighter ball, and for seventy minutes (versus the ninety-minute international standard). Also, women were not allowed to wear football shoes with studs.

Except for a few women's leagues in the 1930s, there is little evidence of any organized women's football in Italy until after World War II. Women began to form teams in earnest in the late 1950s and a short decade later were competing in multiple club competitions across Europe.

In 1970 the first global women's football tournament was organized in Italy and included teams from several nations. The competition—Denmark won by beating Italy 2-0 in the final—was not recognized by FIFA, the global governing body for the sport. The following year, the Women's World Championship was held in Mexico. The Danes won again by beating Mexico, 3-0.[13] Despite the apparent success of the games in drawing crowds, no more world championships were held for another two decades until the 1991 FIFA Women's World Cup in Guangdong, China.

No doubt, women played football informally in Central and South America, but there are no records of organized women's football in any of those countries until the latter part of the twentieth century.

Officially, the first women's football match in Brazil occurred in São Paulo in 1921. The local newspaper wrote that the game was "curious" when not "comical." Interest in the game grew among women in the 1930s, drawing strong condemnation from the male-dominated society. Instead of merely facing a ban from football fields, beginning in 1941 women were legally prohibited from playing the game. After all, women football players were known to be sexually promiscuous. The ban protected women from both moral and physical harm. Women's teams were disbanded (at times by force), and players were threatened with excommunication from the Catholic Church. The ban was not lifted until 1979, but societal disapproval of girls and women playing football continued.[14]

For the first half of the 20th century, women's soccer in the United States was almost entirely limited to gym class, pickup games, and college intramural competition. Not until the mid-1960s did a college invest in a women's varsity soccer team. That honor belongs to Castleton State College in Vermont.

The women's soccer explosion in the United States began after the passage of Title IX when school administrators realized that compliance with the new regulation required putting a lot of women into sports quickly and cheaply. Soccer, with its large roster and limited equipment needs, was particularly appealing.

FOUR
Riding the Wave

KATHY CAREY HAS spent most of her life in Hawai'i; the islands are where her heart lies and where she has deep, deep roots. For Kathy growing up in the 1960s in O'ahu, playtime meant grabbing a surfboard and hitting the waves. There was little in the way of organized sports for kids—less for girls than boys. Kathy grew up right by the beach and surfed most days after school.

Kathy's parents raised their five children (four girls, one boy) without any preconceptions on the roles of men or women. They wanted all their children to grow into strong-minded, independent adults. Kathy's father, Richard, taught his children to surf at a time when most girls just sat on the beach. When Richard took hunting trips to Moloka'i, Lāna'i, and the Big Island of Hawai'i to shoot pheasants, wild pigs, and sheep, Kathy would accompany him. He also took Kathy and her brother on several trips to Canada for duck hunting. Kathy's parents believed that women should have control of their finances; Kathy's mother had her own checking account and managed her own money.

Kathy's mother was the epitome of the self-confident, capable woman. In an era of few women pilots, Jane Kelley flew planes and earned multiple licenses and certificates. This included an Airline Transport Pilot certificate, the highest level of aircraft pilot certification. Jane performed aerobatics at air shows, became the first female aerobatics instructor in Hawai'i, and judged contests for the Aerobatic Club of America.[1]

On O'ahu in the early 1970s, young women watching their boyfriends and husbands play soccer decided they wanted to play, too. Thereupon the women founded a league with five teams. One of Kathy's friends who played with her older sister persuaded Kathy to attend a practice.

Many surfers, particularly those taking up the sport as adults, vividly remember the pure ecstasy of catching their first wave. As one paddles frantically to catch the surge, one's surfboard is suddenly picked up by the rolling water and pushed along. The surfer struggles to her feet, precariously maintaining her balance as she speeds toward shore. The rumble of the breaking wave surrounds her, and she is overwhelmed with the joy of flying across the surface of the sea. All too soon, the wave diminishes, the surfboard slows, and the rider plops down on the board. Still filled with wonder and awe, all she can think about is paddling out to catch another wave to recapture that magical feeling.

Much the same feeling came over Kathy the first time she played soccer. Speaking of those memories, as intense as if they'd occurred just a few hours ago, Kathy's voice thrums with excitement. "The minute I went to that first practice and started running around, I was hooked. It was instant love. It changed my life. That one day changed my life forever. Soccer became all-consuming for me."

Kathy was fifteen when she began playing. She noted that in today's world many soccer players of that age have already had a lifetime of training. The elite players have traveled to tournaments too numerous to count and been exposed to college and national team coaches through the U.S. Olympic Development Program.

"Back in those days, soccer wasn't segregated by age group the way it is now. There was nothing for kids; everyone was playing with adults. Some of my guy friends played soccer in the men's adult league. When you are fifteen, sixteen years old, playing with twenty and thirty-year-old … they are grown up: college students, working in the real world, married."

Kathy attended Punahou, the premier college preparatory school in Hawai'i. The school offered a few sports for girls, but soccer was the only athletic endeavor that held any interest for Kathy. Soccer was considered one of the lesser sports. "It was for the short boys to play in the winter, instead of basketball," Kathy said. Several of the boys encouraged Kathy to try out for the Punahou team. The coach, Bob Clague, and the athletic director of the school endorsed the idea of girls playing on Punahou's soccer team. In 1974, the fall of her senior year, Kathy and another girl tried out for and made the squad.

The other girl decided she couldn't play due to schedule conflicts, so Kathy was the only girl on the team. She loved each and every single second. "I know people in various fields who have had a hard time because they were [the first] women. I was fortunate: it was a really positive experience."

Being the only girl in an all-male environment, however, does have its little inconveniences. The soccer team practiced in reversible shirts: blue on one side and yellow on the other. For drills or scrimmages, the coaches would divide the group into teams, then label one team yellow and the other blue. The boys with the wrong color would strip off their shirts and flip them. Kathy was more often than not in the wrong color, and there were no changing facilities or bathrooms at the fields. She had to duck down behind the nearest car or palm tree to change her shirt to the right color.

When it was unusually warm, the coach might opt for shirts versus skins. Because the division was arbitrary, often based just on where players were standing, Kathy frequently was placed on the skins team. There would be a few laughs and comments before the coach realized what he had done and made a switch. For Christmas that year Kathy's mother gave her a beige T-shirt with "Skins" emblazoned on the chest.

Kathy recalled the absence of sports bras. "Kids nowadays don't even realize there was a time we didn't have those. They were a game changer for women's athletics."

She insisted that playing on the boys' soccer team was in no way a political statement. "I was never trying to prove anything. I was never trying to earn anything for anyone else. I just wanted to play soccer."

Kathy graduated from Punahou in 1975 and enrolled in Stanford University in September. That fall Punahou School became one of 500 high schools across the United States to offer a girls' soccer program.[2]

Stanford offered varsity, junior varsity, and freshman soccer, but no women's teams. The freshman team accepted almost anyone who tried out, so Kathy and several of her friends from Punahou made the team. Kathy called it a fantastic experience where she first met several life-long friends. Another young woman, Ellen, was also on the freshman team. A talented athlete, she later played with Kathy on the Stanford women's club soccer team. Sadly, Ellen died suddenly a few years after graduation.

Kathy was self-effacing about her pioneering role at both Punahou and Stanford and gave credit to her coaches and teammates for the support she received. If she reveals any pride in her accomplishments, it is about her success in organizing and promoting the first women's soccer team at Stanford. During her freshman year, Kathy met other women at Stanford who loved playing the game. Together they formed a women's club team.

Club sports provide an opportunity for competition with other colleges and universities.

The Stanford women contacted other schools in the area and formed a Northern California soccer league with teams from Humboldt State, Chico State, San Francisco State, UC Berkeley, and UC Davis among others. The league organized a schedule, had referees for each game, and maintained standings. The women also participated in local soccer tournaments. Other than allowing the team to represent Stanford in competitions officially, the university provided no support. "It wasn't like today. We didn't get any money or uniforms: just us creating the opportunity because we loved to do it." And the women owned their success: it was their hard work that created a team and the league.

The women's coach, Phil Wright, was also the men's assistant coach and arranged for the women to borrow the men's jerseys for games. "You really, really hoped that if the game was on the same day, your guy didn't play in the game. You hoped he was on the bench because [the smell] could be pretty bad. Sometimes we had time to wash the uniforms but not always. Some days we could wash them but didn't have time to dry them." The women once drove to a game at Davis—a distance of 105 miles—with wet, red jerseys hanging from the windows, air-drying at fifty-five miles per hour.

The women were fortunate to have Phil as their coach. A former Stanford player, Phil was a "phenomenal, phenomenal coach." He received no remuneration for his work, coaching the women merely for the love of the game. His advice to "be creative and to use their imaginations in solving problems on the field," spurred the women to success after success. After his time at Stanford, Phil Wright became an attorney but remained an active force in soccer.[2]

The women believed that their club team accomplishments could influence the university to offer soccer as a varsity sport for women. They pestered the administration, even marching into the office of the athletic director where they plopped armfuls of trophies they'd won on his desktop and told him that he needed to support women's soccer. "Now!" The sport was going to grow, they argued. Stanford needed to get in early. Despite their pleas, Stanford University did nothing.

In 1977, the women's club team at the University of North Carolina petitioned their athletic director to offer women's varsity soccer. He listened, and UNC fielded a team for the 1978 season. Six years later, by which time the UNC program had secured three national championships, Stanford finally offered a women's varsity soccer program. Stanford did not win their first NCAA women's soccer championship until 2011, by which time UNC already had celebrated twenty-one national titles. Today, Stanford regularly fields one of the top teams in the country.

Kathy graduated in 1980 and that fall began a two-year MBA program at Santa Clara University. The school had just instituted varsity soccer for women. (The Broncos won their first NCAA Women's Soccer Championship ten years before Stanford.) When a school only offers club soccer, participation tends to be open to undergraduates, grad students, and even employees. The goal is to build momentum for instituting a varsity program. The establishment of a varsity team is often accompanied by a more restrictive policy regarding club team members, as was the case at Santa Clara. The club sport was limited to undergraduates, which meant Kathy had to look outside the university for a team.

Fortunately for Kathy, California's youth soccer system had been around for many years. A group of young women who had played together on a youth team graduated from high school in June. They formed a women's team. Kathy joined them and played on the San Jose Bobcats during her two years in business school, making several life-long friends.

After obtaining her MBA, Kathy returned to Hawaiʻi to work in her family's travel and tourism business. Within a month of her return, she fielded a phone call from her old Punahou coach. After a few pleasantries, Bob Clague mentioned that the coach of the girl's junior varsity soccer team had just broken her leg and would be unable to coach the fall season. Practice was starting in three days, and he wanted Kathy to coach the team. Kathy couldn't envision herself in such a role and politely declined. She assured Bob that he would find someone else.

But in the early 1980s, it was not easy to find someone who knew the sport of soccer and was willing to coach girls, particularly when practices were held several days each week in the middle of the afternoon. The next day Bob called again to plead with Kathy to take the position. Practice started in two days. He was stuck and Kathy was his only hope. Kathy turned him down.

Perhaps Bob Clague knew that as a teenager, Kathy had to be nagged by her friend to try soccer, or that Kathy tried out for the Punahou team only after repeated encouragement from different people. The next day, Bob called again. "It starts tomorrow. We're desperate. Can you please help us?"

Kathy agreed just to get Bob off her back. She assumed that she'd do just the one season, Bob would find somebody else, and he'd leave her alone after that.

Since youth soccer was still not widespread, Kathy's junior varsity team included many girls new to the game. There was no high school league for JV teams, so the girls' team competed in the same women's adult soccer league in which Kathy had played. The team had its growing pains, reflected in a rather poor record for the season. However, Kathy realized at the end of the season that she'd thoroughly enjoyed coaching.

While girls' soccer was a fall sport, the boys' teams still played during the winter season. Kathy shouldn't have been surprised by what happened next: Bob Clague called. "We really need a coach for the intermediate boys' team," he said. (Intermediate at Punahou includes the 7th to 9th grades.) Kathy declined, but by now, Bob knew he had a winning formula. He continued to call Kathy until she gave in.

Coaching intermediate-school boys versus high-school girls was a day versus night experience, but Kathy loved them both. She coached soccer at Punahou for the next eleven years, even without Bob Clague begging each season.

In 1994, the University of Hawaiʻi initiated soccer as a varsity sport for women: the Rainbow Wahine—women in Hawaiian. The university hired Kathy as an assistant coach. The head coach, Pinsoom Tenzing, encouraged Kathy to take advantage of the national licensing program for soccer.

In the 1980s and 1990s, the U.S. Soccer licensing system included levels A through F. The lowest level, the F license, consisted of a two-hour course and was enough for teaching the game to young children. The licenses progressed up the alphabet, with the C and B licenses offered for coaches of elite players, and the A license the pinnacle of achievement for any coach. Armchair coaches were not allowed at the A level: they had to be able to execute all the skills they were teaching. Kathy Carey became the first woman in Hawaiʻi (and one of a handful of women in the nation) to earn an A license.

Kathy was much in demand. In addition to her stints with Punahou and the University of Hawaiʻi, she coached with the American Youth Soccer Organization and the Hawaiʻi Olympic Development Program—a U.S. Youth Soccer program that identifies high-potential players and provides opportunities for them to compete with other elite players and receive quality coaching.

So highly regarded was Kathy at the University of Hawaiʻi that when the university hired a new head coach in 2010, she was the lone assistant to be held over. In 2016, Kathy turned fifty-nine and decided it was time to retire from coaching. "I never thought I'd coach for a lifetime," she said. "I've had a lot of great kids. Some of the kids I coached in the early years are now coaching their kids. It's a whole generation that has gone by. It's so cool to see them growing up and feeling like I had this little bit of something in their lives. It's very rewarding."

Forty plus years after kicking her first soccer ball, Kathy still plays. A natural midfielder, Kathy understands the game tactically, foresees her teammates' moves into open space, and delivers pinpoint passes. She's always maintained a high level of fitness, ideally suited to a position that requires one to run the length of the field. By not playing on the front line where one is subject to harsh tackles, nor being a defender and having to lunge in for the ball, she has avoided major knee problems and remained relatively injury free.

In addition to her recreational team in Hawai'i, Kathy makes time for tournaments where she reconnects with the women she's met over the years. Thirty-six years after playing with the San Jose Bobcats, Kathy still plays with former teammates on tournament teams. In the 2016 Adult Soccer Fest tournament in Denver, Colorado, Kathy's team (including a Bobcats contingent) won the title for over-55 women. It was Kathy's tenth national championship as a player.

Kathy is grateful for the fantastic friends she has made through soccer. "And the breadth and depth of people that it brings to my life. They enrich my life because it is so broad. There are people I might not have stayed friends with if not for this common bond. We don't have that much in common in the rest of our lives. Yet, we have stayed close, and I love these women deeply. They have brought so much to my life." And each tournament brings opportunities to make new friends with one or two new people on the team who, in turn, bring their friends. "That pot of gold keeps getting bigger."

While on the Stanford freshmen's soccer team, Kathy met David Carey. "If it were not for soccer, I don't know if I would have met my husband. He was an engineer and we might not have connected if we hadn't had that in common, if I hadn't recognized him from the soccer fields. He's been a tremendous gift for my life."

When Kathy was told that Punahou wanted to induct her into its Athletic Hall of Fame, she protested. Punahou honorees had set records, led their teams to state championships, and competed in the Olympics. She'd only played one sport for one season. But Punahou insisted on recognizing Kathy who had not only served as a catalyst for change but had returned to the school and coached a generation of young men and women.

As a coach, Kathy told her players to be open to opportunities and experiences. "Don't ever close a door because you don't know what is on the other side." It is a tenet she developed through personal experience. "That first day when I went out for soccer, I would never have guessed how it would impact my life. Soccer has been a blessing."

FIVE
Not To Be Denied

IN THE 1970S, soccer participation and interest multiplied in the United States fueled in part by the nascent North American Soccer League. The NASL New York Cosmos featured the Brazilian Pelé who was widely considered to be the greatest soccer player of all time. Other NASL teams also signed international stars. Though on the downslope of their careers these players lifted the profile of the league, attracting fans and media coverage. Children began playing the game in growing numbers: in 1974, only 100,000 players registered with U.S. Youth Soccer, but by 1980 the number exceeded 800,000.[1]

Adults too were inspired to take up the game. A patchwork of men's teams and leagues already existed, comprised of soccer-loving immigrants and former high-school and collegiate players. Men wishing to learn the game tapped into this existing infrastructure. But for women there was nothing. So across the country, virtually simultaneously, women created teams, found coaches, begged and borrowed fields, and formed women's soccer leagues.

Eastern Massachusetts Women's Soccer League

Launched in 1978, the Eastern Massachusetts Women's Soccer League today includes more than sixty teams with 1,200 players. The success of the league owes much to the perseverance of its founders and early leaders.

Born in 1945 and raised on Long Island, Ellen Simons was exposed to a surfeit of sports. "I played inter-school everything: lacrosse, field hockey, softball, volleyball, and basketball—although I'm really too short." Ellen's high school also offered inter-school badminton, fencing, and modern jazz dance. A rarity at the time, the school awarded letters to girls for sports participation. In college, Ellen played both varsity field hockey and lacrosse.

Several years out of college, Ellen moved to Boston and searched for an opportunity to continue playing field hockey and lacrosse. But at age twenty-five, Ellen was already on the back end of the age curve. Most of the players on the association field hockey and lacrosse teams were less than twenty-three years of age, and Ellen didn't fit the association mold: "They were all [expletive deleted] super jocks. It's true I played on my college varsity team, but I was not like these people: super athletes, really skilled."

So Ellen contented herself playing coed drop-in volleyball offered by the Boston Ski and Sports Club. When she read an ad in the newspaper for Max Spector Club Atlantic soccer, she thought she'd give it a try. She already had experience with and enjoyed field sports and, since her brother had played soccer in high school and college, Ellen was familiar with the game.

Ellen began playing soccer one day each week at the Salvation Army gym in the fall of 1977. She soon realized that Spector was taking the women's money and providing T-shirts, but offering virtually no instruction. Many of the women were not happy; for $75, they had expected more. The prevailing sentiment was, "This is bullshit. We could do better than this." So Ellen collected the names of women in the program who were interested in playing the following spring outdoors. Among those was Joan Quinzani who attended Spector's program on a different day of the week. Ellen and Joan agreed that each would recruit enough players for a team, and they would play one another.

Ellen arranged the first game to be played at Daly Field in Brighton. Following the game, the women planned to watch a soccer game on television at Ellen's house and have a picnic.

Bob Friedman, an assistant soccer coach at Harvard, agreed to coach Ellen's team. Bob had been the one bright spot in Spector's program, occasionally attending sessions and teaching the women the basics of the game. He had also encouraged them to form outdoor teams. At the initial game, no one on Ellen's side wanted to play goalie, so she volunteered. Ellen received a few instructions from Bob about diving for the ball and then took her place between the goalposts. During the game, Betsy, a player on Joan's team, broke through and charged Ellen's goal with the ball at her feet. With the instructions from Bob fresh in her mind, Ellen confidently dove for the ball. Betsy was caught off guard; no goalie had taken a dive on the gym floor. She had been powering full steam toward the goal, and now Ellen was stretched out in front of her. Betsy attempted to vault over Ellen's prostrate body and failed. She plowed into Ellen and broke her wrist. Ellen received a fractured eye socket.

One would think that such early injuries would cast a pall over the game, but Ellen remembers the day as an utter success. The women were ecstatic.

Later that spring, Joan discovered an opportunity for the women to play in the Boston Area Youth Soccer (BAYS) Summer Twilight League. Teams consisted almost exclusively of high-school teens, but the league had agreed to allow the women to participate. Games would be played on Monday and Wednesday nights. Neither Ellen nor Joan had enough players to field a full team for both nights. They decided that Ellen's team would provide the core players for one night with extra players from Joan's team. The other night, Joan would provide the core with subs from Ellen's group. Neither woman suggested merging the two groups. Ellen noted, "We wanted to remain separate, so we'd have someone to play against."

That fall, the teams again competed against each other outdoors at Fresh Pond in Cambridge on the Lusitania Field. Many of the women thought the field was named after the RMS Lusitania—a passenger liner sunk by a German submarine in World War I—because after heavy rains the area would be under water. Indeed, Lusitania Field had been built on wetlands. However, the field got its name from the local Portuguese Lusitania Social Club that had developed the soccer pitch. Ellen recalled, "When we had games in the early days, we'd collect money to give the referees a bottle of Two Buck Chuck and a bag of Quinzani rolls as payment." For non-Bostonians, that translates into a $1.99 bottle of Charles Shaw Wine from Trader Joe's and bread from Joan Quinzani's family business, a highly respected Boston bakery.

In the winter the women moved inside, playing at Jackson Mann School in Alston, Massachusetts. The gym bleachers were pulled up and used as walls by the women. (Indoor soccer allows the ball to be played off the walls, much like hockey). The next spring the women returned to playing outdoors, and by the second summer, both teams had enough players to compete independently in the BAYS Twilight League.

The women placed notices in the *Boston Globe* sports calendar about the soccer, welcoming all who were interested. When the teams played outdoors, it was not unusual for other women to stop by the field and ask to join in. The newcomers were encouraged to create their own teams to increase the pool of competitors. Although many had never played before, a few of the women had played in high school or on club teams in college.

One woman was a recent graduate of Brown University and had played on the school's inaugural women's varsity soccer team.

Once a third team was in place, the number of players sky-rocketed. "None of us from that initial group that left Max Spector's indoor had any idea what we were doing," Ellen said. "We were just collecting people to play with. We weren't forming a league. We had no big vision." Perhaps not a vision of the outcome, but Ellen had a clear idea of what it wouldn't be: a situation like association field hockey and lacrosse where only young jocks could play. She wanted an environment in which any woman who showed up could play, regardless if she'd ever played soccer before, or played any sport. It was to be a place to learn soccer and enjoy the game.

Sue Spencer is self-effacing about her role as one of the founders of the Eastern Massachusetts Women's Soccer League. "I got them organized and then stepped away."

Sue grew up on Long Island. There were no organized sports for girls, so she played kickball in the neighborhood. Her high school offered field hockey, volleyball, and gymnastics. Although Sue tried out for sports teams, she was not selected. In college her roommates were athletes, but not Sue. Not until she attended graduate school at the University of Texas did she play her first organized sport. Sue's master's degree program was offered under the auspices of the Institute for Latin American Studies. The Institute fielded a women's soccer team, and Sue joined.

After completing her degree, Sue returned to Massachusetts and searched for a place where she could continue playing soccer. She found Max Spector's program in Cambridge, a forty-five-minute drive (with no traffic) from her home in Lawrence. "It was the only place for women to gather and play, but very quickly there was dissatisfaction with that," Sue said.

Sue organized the women to form a league. Since her husband was a doctoral student at MIT, Sue had access to an office at the university where she hosted the women. Sue provided some helpful documentation to start the process. "I don't know why I even did this, but when I had come back from Texas, I brought the league organization paperwork." With the Texas documents in hand, the women created a constitution and bylaws for a soccer league. "And then my job was done," Sue said. "I never held any league positions after that."

Ironically, despite the disgruntlement with Max Spector, it was through his indoor soccer program that many of the founding members of the Eastern Massachusetts Women's Soccer League were introduced to soccer, and to each other.

Lois Kessin has been one of the driving forces behind the growth of the EMWSL. Born in a small town amongst the mountains and lakes of New Hampshire, Lois as a young girl played and competed with the boys. "You had to be able to swim across the lake by the time you were ten," she said. Her first exposure to soccer was through a junior high gym teacher, a woman devoted to ensuring that girls had a chance to play team sports. She organized an after-school program for the girls two nights each week: one night for soccer, the other for field hockey. Lois doesn't remember learning much in the way of soccer skills—the games were little more than running after the ball and kicking it. Nevertheless, the chance to play was more than most girls had in the early 1960s.

Lois attended Laconia High School and was on the girl's ski team for four years. While the boys had uniforms and bus transportation to all the meets, the girls had neither, and Lois resented it. The girl's coach "was very good, but on Sunday afternoons we got ourselves to the ski area, and we practiced, and then our parents drove us to the ski meets. Not my parents; they didn't approve of it. My senior year, we were allowed one afternoon a week on the boys' bus to go up to the ski area if we did not make trouble." Given Lois's subsequent history with the soccer establishment, one suspects that Lois may indeed have caused trouble, but was crafty enough not to be caught.

In her senior year in high school, Lois's boyfriend was a soccer goalie. Lois would kick the ball at him so he could practice, and she attended his games. A nearby town hosted a pickup soccer game, which Lois and her boyfriend would join regularly. Like Lois's junior high games, the level of soccer was little more than kickball and the other players, intimidated by the skill level of Lois's boyfriend, asked him not to wear his cleats to the pick-up game.

At New York University, Lois played basketball. "I'm 4'11½" and made NYU's basketball team, which is frightening. Although I did have a twenty-inch plus jump." This was in 1967, and the women still wore skirts for the game and the rules prohibited most players from crossing the half-court line. In her spare time, Lois hung around the soccer field where only men played. She joined in when she could, and was tolerated because it was "cute that this little kid loved soccer."

In 1969, Lois left college and moved to Cambridge, Massachusetts. As others drove to church each Sunday, Lois religiously headed for the broad expanse of Harvard's playing fields to join a 9:00 a.m. coed pickup soccer game. As the amateurish game wound down, a men's game would start on an adjacent area. Lois noticed the men were all highly skilled. She knew to improve her game she'd have to compete against more talented players so Lois joined the men's game. Most of the players didn't want her there, and a few told her to go home. But she wouldn't. She stuck around and forced her way into the game, despite the insults, locker room talk, and general hostility.

Lois would not be denied. "I took a lot of crap. I did not, I did not back down! You get in there and play, and you don't cry. You take your lumps. I've broken probably every finger on my hand, and I don't think I cried once. I've sprained ankles over the years ... I can't think of any time I've cried in front of a man in an athletic situation. It just won't happen."

Several of the men berated newly married Lois for playing soccer rather than being at home making dinner for her husband. Her response was to invite them to have dinner at her home after the game. Over time a number of them accepted Lois's invitation and gradually became friends. Many of the men who objected to Lois playing soccer later had daughters of their own who played soccer. Years afterward they made a point of telling Lois that they admired her bravery and because of her and women like her, their daughters were now able to play.

But not all the men changed their tunes. One of them was Max Spector who particularly disliked Lois. When she tried to join his indoor program, he wouldn't take her money nor let her stay to watch. Lois eventually got wind of the nascent women's outdoor teams and joined the effort to form a league.

For Lois, establishing a women's sports league was nothing new; she had created a women's volleyball league a few years earlier. While playing pickup volleyball with men in 1973, Lois and three other women decided to form a women's league. The women scoured the gyms for female players and established the first women's volleyball league in New England. Initially, the women were forced to play in decrepit gyms. It wasn't good enough for Lois. "I started fighting with the powers that be, and we got the good gyms for our tournaments. I just wasn't going to be slighted."

The new women's soccer league encountered a similar problem: finding decent fields for games. Open space in the Boston metro area has always been at a premium. Women's sports were for many years last in line for securing playing fields; even Frisbee games were assigned better fields. For decades, Lois has been in charge of getting Cambridge's soccer fields for use by the women's league. Year after year the field director would tell Lois that she didn't get better fields because "you are the new kids on the block." Lois pushed back. "Kevin, we've been playing in Cambridge for ten years; we're no longer the new kids." Ten years became fifteen, became twenty. But her complaining did little good.

Sue Spencer recalled that one of the Cambridge fields had no grass, just dirt, and it glittered from all the broken glass. Her team left Cambridge and moved to Weston, Massachusetts thirteen miles to the west. Because Sue was on the soccer board in Weston, she was able to secure fields for team practices and games. For years the town accommodated the women, but as its budget tightened and the fields became more expensive to maintain, Weston revised its policy. Henceforth, if the team roster were not 50 percent Weston residents, the team would be charged an out-of-town fee. Women's athletic teams, by and large, are aligned around who one knows rather than where one lives. The women couldn't meet the residency rule and paid a small fortune to use the fields. The men, generally the soccer dads in the community, used the fields for free. Sue squawked, and Weston rescinded the ruling after one season. Despite the ongoing competition with youth and men to get quality fields, Sue feels her team has been lucky; at least it has a place to play. Not all women's teams in the league have a home field.

When Cambridge appointed a new field director, he'd barely found his office before Lois approached him with her field requirements. She found him much more accommodating than his predecessor, and the women have been pleased with their assigned fields. As in most locales, adult soccer is shunted aside for youth soccer, and in the fall, high school sports come first. Lois has no problem giving up fields to high school games, but she won't tolerate the women being at the end of the line.

Lusitania Field at Fresh Pond, the field where EMWSL began, is no more. Lois recalled that for many years one could watch "international matches there. On Sundays, you could go by the field and see families picnicking and doing whatever they wanted. The West Cambridge people who have the big houses decided they did not want foreigners in Fresh Pond—I'm sure they wouldn't say that. They made it a butterfly field. We fought it tooth and nail. I went around finding all these old, old men in the Portuguese bars in East Cambridge and dragging them to the City Council to speak. But we lost the field there, and it was a field women were allowed to play on during the week. It was a huge, huge fight." And a huge loss.

Model Café Steamers

Peggy Ueda is another of the EMWSL founders. Growing up in Los Angeles, Peggy played soccer in her school physical education classes and loved it. In the mid-1970s she moved to the Boston area, saw an ad for Max Spector's program, and joined. She too was dissatisfied with Spector and asserted, "We can do it better."

When playing at the Jackson-Mann Middle School during the winters, the women would often adjourn to the Model Café located just across the street. While discussing how to fund the teams—pay for uniforms, referees, balls, fields—Ellen suggested someone talk with the management of Model Café about supporting the team. The establishment had a good record of sponsoring sports teams. With Ellen's concurrence, Peggy approached the owners. They agreed to provide shirts and equipment for her team. Even though Peggy was on Joan's, not Ellen's team, Ellen was fine with the arrangement. She felt the important thing was that one of the women's soccer teams now had a sponsor.

Joan Quinzani came up with the idea of calling the team Model Café Steamers. The team logo could be a partially opened clam with "a soccer ball in its mouth." Although she was informed that clams don't have mouths and the Model Café did not serve steamers, both the name and the logo were adopted.

Charles River

Ellen's team chose the name Charles River. Each year the team had a banquet celebrating their accomplishments and traded gag gifts. Often the coach would add a few nice remarks about each team member. Forty years later, a Charles River team still plays in the Eastern Massachusetts Women's Soccer League. The women still have annual banquets sans gifts, but they no longer have a coach.

In the early years, Charles River had regular practices. Ellen recalled being told by the coach to be vocal on the field. She took it to heart. Garrulous by nature, Ellen talked more than ever before. She offered encouragement and gave instructions throughout the game. Finally, one of her teammates was fed up. She told Ellen to be quiet; she was doing the best that she could. Ellen heeded her teammate's advice and, not for the last time, ignored the coach.

It was a mystery to the women why anyone would want to coach a bunch of opinionated women. Through its long history, Charles River has been committed to the tenet that everybody plays. No matter the skill level, everyone was to have equal playing time. If the game was on the line, the coach was not allowed to sub in the best players. She had to put in those that had played the fewest minutes. The team endured seasons where the women lost much more often than they won. Surprisingly there were other years Charles River did well. Eventually, the women concluded they didn't need anyone telling them what to do and, like most of the teams with older players, opted to proceed with neither a coach nor practices.

Sue recalled that for a time the women of Charles River would travel to tournaments. "Then it got to the point where the team would be saying, 'Man, if we win this next game, we got to come back tomorrow. I wonder if we want to do that.'" The women did like to win, but it wasn't just about that; camaraderie, belonging, and having a good time were much more important to them.

Sue played briefly with other, more competitive teams and traveled to national tournaments. She found it wasn't the life for her; she preferred to play with friends just for the pure joy of the game. Sue is still on the Charles River roster. "I went from my twenties to my sixties on the same team, and there are plenty of people right behind me that joined in the 1980s and are still playing. Of course, people come and go. But a core group has been there for a very long time. It's a team not based on geography, but based on connections. Someone who knew someone invited someone to play. If people got along, if they were of the same spirit, they stuck around. If they didn't, they moved on."

When Sue's daughter turned eighteen, she joined Sue on Charles River. "How many things can mothers and daughters do on a team sport? Of course, my teammates were thrilled when she showed up: she was a great soccer player." Sue's daughter played varsity soccer as a freshman in high school and found her mother's team a fun, relaxing way to play. High school soccer was stressful, wondering who was going to take your spot and worrying about what the coach thought. Charles River allowed her just to play the game.

In the early 1990s, Ellen owned a summer home in New Hampshire and was helping her partner raise children. She schlepped back and forth to Cambridge for Monday and Wednesday games in the summer, then only went one night a week, and then stopped playing in the summer entirely. Ellen played a few times in the spring and fall before drifting away from the sport, but not her teammates. Almost all of Ellen's friends and significant relationships have been soccer players or the neighbors or friends of soccer players she knows. Two decades after leaving the game, Ellen is still regularly having dinner with a handful of her long-time soccer friends.

Among Charles River alumnae are women who have become coaches at the youth, high school, college, and national levels including: Lauren Gregg who was the Assistant Coach for the

U.S. Women's National Team when they won the World Cup in 1999; and Linda Grant who became chair of the Women's Committee for the Amateur Division of U.S. Soccer and a representative on Women's Committee of soccer's global governing body, FIFA.

For their track record of promoting women's soccer for all and providing leadership to the soccer community, the Charles River Soccer Team was inducted into the Massachusetts Soccer Hall of fame in April 1999.

Still Searching for Respect

At an early organizational meeting for the Eastern Massachusetts Women's Soccer League, the women determined that each team would assume a portion of the responsibility for managing league operations. One team would handle referee assignments, another would find fields for games, yet another would manage the schedule, and so forth. The lone man attending the meeting declared that no one ran leagues that way; it would never work. Lois Kessin ripped him apart. "We're not bimbos," she said. "We are all well-educated women with careers, and we'll get it done." The league operated and prospered under that system for many years.

Soccer is played on a field twenty yards longer and wider than an American football field. Hence, referees must run several miles to monitor the action effectively. Lois remembers that as a sign of disrespect or laziness some referees for the women's game in the early years couldn't be bothered to move from the center of the field to call the game. At least there were no incidents of referees propositioning the women that Lois could recall. They were better behaved than that. However, one referee sought her permission after a game to ask out one of the players. "The ref says to me, 'Hey, this is much better skill than I expected.' Then he said, because he knew I was a big deal in the league, 'Would it be inappropriate to ask that woman on the other team out for a date?' And I said, 'You go right ahead.' I knew she would just laugh at him; we were playing an entirely gay team." That was her worst experience with a ref. Today, Lois believes that the referees, male and female, are at a much higher professional level and more respectful than they once were.

Unlike Ellen and Sue, Lois did not remain with Charles River. She was interested in playing with women who, as she puts it, "have a sense of game," a deep level of understanding, almost preternatural, of how the game should be played. On the field, a player with a sense of game sees how a play will develop before it happens, and positions herself accordingly. When players of similar understanding play together, the game is elevated to a much higher level and at times can appear as an elegantly choreographed dance. The soccer coach at Boston University told Lois that she didn't believe that sense of game could be taught; players either had it or they didn't. As a coach, she had discovered that all she could do was to hone it.

Lois coached girls' soccer for twenty-five years: recreational, club, and high school. She also started a girls soccer program in Dorchester, a large Boston area with significant minority and foreign-born populations where a nearly a quarter of the households live in poverty. Although Lois has coached elite players, she prefers players who just want to play and be with their friends. Of her current team Lois said, "I have kids who can't walk and talk at the same time. It's like, 'Lock your ankle. Don't kick it with your toe.' That's my skill level, but they are out there having fun."

In 2003, Lois was inducted into the Massachusetts Soccer Hall of Fame for her "outstanding contribution to soccer in the state" and "exhibiting integrity, sporting conduct, and character." At the induction ceremony, Lois was about to take a seat in the front row when a gentleman huffily informed her that the seats were reserved for inductees. Lois pointed to one of the large poster boards with her photograph on it. "See that picture over there? Look at this face." Lois shakes her head at the memory. "That kind of stuff still happens."

Lois's parents never quite understood her love of sports. "My parents were ninety-one and eighty-nine when I got elected into the Massachusetts Soccer Hall of Fame. I looked over and my father finally got it, and he's sobbing. My mother… I'm not sure she got it."

In 2007, the New England Soccer Hall of Fame recognized Lois for her contributions to the sport. Much like the Massachusetts Hall of Fame induction, the evening was not without unintended insults. Seamus Malin, an announcer for ESPN for many years, was inducted the same year. The master of ceremonies at the event was thrilled and spent the time before the ceremony chatting to Seamus, and neglecting Lois.

After dinner, the time came to introduce the honorees and the master of ceremonies realized he had no idea who Lois was. "He said, 'Well, and soccer moms have done so much for soccer,'" Lois said. "I look over at Seamus, and he is doubled over looking at his plate laughing, wondering what I am going to do to this man." In the audience were many who coached with, played with, and played for Lois. "My high school team is going, 'Oh, my God. She's going to kill him.' I looked at him and said, 'Actually, I was never a soccer mom. I was a player.' He said, 'Oh. So then …' and he covered himself well. 'So your mom is the original soccer mom.' And I said, 'Okay, sure.' That was so annoying."

"It's just a male world still, and I hate it. I hate that nobody watches women's soccer even though American women's soccer is better than Major League Soccer. I hate that [in] the *Boston Globe* … a young woman at MIT, a Division III school, won the NCAA athlete of the year award. Where is it? In a little two-sentence blurb on the sports page that says Miscellaneous. Or in the *Boston Globe*, 'The U.S. Women win the World Cup,' and it's below the fold. Above the fold is, 'Red Sox Lose Again.'

Really. The Head of the Charles [the world's largest two-day rowing event] was this weekend and nothing. Nothing. I had to look for it. Minor sports and women have always taken it in the shorts."

"I've just been around so long and seen so many changes. Sometimes I get very frustrated with my little girls and tell them, 'When I was your age I couldn't do what you are doing.' It's a privilege. I don't know that it should be, but doing anything is a privilege."

The unintended insults keep coming. "I had my U-14 [Under 14] Cambridge team on a field. The ref comes over. I said, 'Oh, I'll get my coaching card.' He said, 'Oh, you don't need it. You look like a kindly grandmother.' My kids started to laugh at him. I took him aside and said, 'Do you know who you are talking to? I am not a grandmother. I've got licenses out my wazoo. I'm a three-time member of the Massachusetts Soccer Hall of Fame and member of New England Soccer Hall of Fame. Be careful the next time you insult an older woman.' I let him have it privately. He could have carded me for what I said to him."

But there have good times, too. Lois was in a pub in Ireland, and on the TV the Irish men's soccer team was playing a World Cup Qualifying Match. Sitting between two men, Lois talked to herself, critiquing the action. "One guy turned around to me and said, 'Wow, you know what you are talking about.'" Lois laughed at the memory. "That was kind of refreshing."

Lois recently retired from the soccer field, but not from sports. "I've had medial meniscus and lateral meniscus [procedures], and I need two knee replacements. I'd rather ski for a few more years than risk my knees anymore. I've always had fun playing sports. I've always had a sense of camaraderie. You think about six women who still get together from 1973 from a volleyball team. That's pretty impressive. It was a sense of— and that was true with the Charles River Soccer Team—look at what we've done. We formed a league. We got equal rights for volleyball players in New England. We did something. We made it possible for women to play. I wouldn't trade that for anything."

"It's funny as years go by you forget the insults and remember only, 'I got to play.' People did make it up to me by saying, 'Thank you. My daughter is playing because of you.' I'm not sure it makes it all worthwhile, but … I wanted to play. That was the big thing. And to play at our age, you had to start everything or play with men. And you know what a drag that is: the worst man on the pitch will tell Mia Hamm how to play. If I thought about how hard it was at times, standing on that field with men yelling at me, I probably now would say, 'Nah, not going to do it.' But I just wanted to play. That's all I ever wanted to do. And I wanted to play on my terms. So I did."

SIX
Kicking in the Rain

THE PACIFIC NORTHWEST has long been a hotbed of soccer and one of the first locations in the United States where adult women gained a significant foothold in the game.

<u>Oregon</u>
In 1975, soccer fever overtook Portland, Oregon. The Portland Timbers, a new, professional, men's team in the North American Soccer League, finished the year with the best record in the league. They stormed through the playoffs only to lose in the championship game. Despite less than stellar play in subsequent years, Portland was enamored with the Timbers and assumed the moniker, "Soccer City, USA."[1]

Janice Hellyer's eleven-year-old daughter, bit by the soccer bug, came home one day and announced she'd signed up to play and had volunteered her mother to help with the team. Janice assumed that meant she'd bake cookies, bring drinks, or perform another traditionally female task. At the first team meeting, the parents learned that the team didn't have a coach. Nobody seemed anxious to volunteer for the role. Janice had free time and was confident of her ability to learn what she needed to know, so she spoke up and said she'd do it.

Fathers who had coached their children's teams helped out. "They didn't try to take over," Janice said. "They were just real supportive." The first season, Janice's team won their division.

On Sundays, Janice would hold practice for the girls and allow the parents to participate. During scrimmages with the children, the parents had to play one-touch: control and pass the ball with one strike of the foot. The nucleus of the Sunday parents spawned the first Gresham women's soccer team.

A small town of about 20,000 at the time, Gresham sits fifteen miles from downtown Portland. Here and there other women's teams were forming but as yet no women's leagues. The Gresham women had no coach and no experienced players and sought out high school girls' teams from Portland for competition. Their first game took place against a team of girls that would become the high school state champions that year. Gresham lost 18-0. Undaunted, the women continued to practice and play whomever they could.

In 1978, Gresham's high school formed a girl's team and Janice became the coach. As was all too common, the athletic director for the school was also the football coach. He had little use for girls' athletic programs. Instead of purchasing soccer uniforms for the girls, the athletic director gave them the old boys' soccer uniforms and purchased new jerseys, shorts, and socks for the boys.

Janice credits soccer for teaching her how to cuss. No, she didn't swear at the high school athletic director, wayward high school girls, overly aggressive competitors, or teammates, no matter how much the aforementioned might have deserved it. Her swearing was confined to the field and directed toward herself, or to no one in particular.

In a reversal of the norm, the enjoyment on display by the women during their games (aside from Janice swearing) inspired the men of Gresham to learn the game. Janice and others put together a coed league. While the overall skill level in the league was dismally poor, the league was a great success. The men and women soon formed coed teams to travel and compete in tournaments up and down the west coast. Over the years, soccer became a staple in Janice's life. Soccer also helped her cope with life's vagaries.

Janice's younger daughter, the one who had lured Janice into soccer, became a highly skilled player and earned a place on the First Team All-Stars for the State of Oregon. While a senior in high school, she was diagnosed with a brain tumor. She fought a courageous battle for three years before finally succumbing. Janice averred that she didn't know how she would have made it through that awful time without the physical release of playing soccer. In the same year that Janice lost her beautiful daughter, another woman on the team also lost her child, and another lost her husband.

"Soccer is a metaphor for life," Janice said. "You have to keep going, even if you're tired, sore, and discouraged."

At age seventy, Janice splits her time between her homes in Tucson and Eastern Oregon. She no longer plays soccer regularly, but joins a game now and then in Tucson. Occasionally Janice makes the four-hour drive from her home in LaGrande, Oregon to Portland to meet with old soccer friends and play indoor soccer.

And if there is a tournament team needing a player, Janice is the girl. "Have soccer ball, will travel," she said. Her Tucson team uniform is aptly emblazoned with: "You don't stop playing because you get old; you get old because you stop playing."

Washington

Bernadette Noonan grew up in Ireland, near the northern border where soccer was reviled as an English sport. She moved to Seattle as a young woman, married, and started a family. As her children grew and participated in soccer, Bernadette struggled with ingrained admonitions about this game of the English. Eventually, she overcame her reservations and tried the game herself. She joined a group of women calling themselves the Red Hot Mamas. Initially, the women competed against their children's teams.[2] Interest grew, and soon thirty-two women were playing informally. In a stroke of brilliance, the women approached Mike Ryan, the highly regarded coach of the University of Washington men's soccer team, to ask his help in forming a women's league. Mike enthusiastically agreed.[3]

Born in Dublin, Ireland, Mike Ryan developed an early love of soccer. By age twelve he was already coaching local teams. As a young man, Ryan was unable to find work in Ireland, and at twenty-three he immigrated to the United States. Ryan enlisted in the U.S. Army and, for one of his postings was sent to Ft. Lewis, Washington, forty-five miles south of Seattle. Leaving the Army in 1962, Ryan moved to Seattle and immediately became immersed in the local soccer scene. By 1966, when he was asked to be the coach of the University of Washington men's soccer team, Ryan had already started several soccer teams, helped to form the Washington State Youth Soccer Association, and served as its first president. During his eleven-year tenure with the Washington Huskies, the team garnered over one hundred wins and four NCAA tournament appearances. Ryan's participation in the establishment of the Washington State Women's Soccer Association (WSWSA) brought a slew of contacts and instant credibility throughout the soccer establishment.

The women placed ads in local newspapers, and would-be players appeared in droves. "We had nine teams from Bellingham and Tacoma the first year," Mike said. I was elected the first president, for one year. After one year they were … ahead of the guys in terms of organization."

Mike Ryan's involvement with women's soccer did not cease after his year as president. In the early 1980s, he coached selected women's teams in the league's open and over-30 divisions. He took his teams to tournaments, winning five national championships. While coaching a team at the 1985 Olympic Sports Festival in Baton Rouge, Louisiana, Ryan was asked to take a group of women to represent the U.S. at the Mundialito (Little World Cup) tournament in Italy. There was but a small catch: U.S. Soccer had almost no funds for a women's team. Ryan secured support from the airline Alitalia and other benefactors so the first-ever women's national soccer team for the United States could attend the tournament. Playing in jerseys borrowed from the men's team, the women lost their first game to Italy, 1-0. In subsequent games, the women tied Denmark, lost to England, and then lost to Denmark in the third-place match.

Meanwhile, the WSWSA continued to grow. Its success was due to the sustained efforts of many women, such as Bernadette. Despite having her playing career cut short by knee problems, Bernadette unflaggingly promoted and supported the league over many years. She organized fundraisers, established tournaments, recruited unceasingly, found teams for those who wanted to play, secured fields, and was on the board of WSWSA as it grew to serve thousands of women.

In 1994 the men's World Cup was played in the United States for the first time in its history. MasterCard, a sponsor of the tournament, developed a program to honor foreign-born U.S. residents who had made outstanding contributions to the growth of soccer in this county. Bernadette was selected to represent Ireland. She was one of twenty-four chosen from across the United States and the only woman so honored. Her good friend and WSWSA stalwart, Maj Surowiecki, was the runner-up for Sweden. Tears of joy streamed down Bernadette's face as she met the all-time soccer great Pelé. She also attended the Ireland/Italy match.[4] In Bernadette's honor, the WSWSA annually bestows the Bernadette Noonan Award upon those who "reflect the very best of what a WSWSA volunteer gives back to the game through her or his efforts."

Janet Slausen was another key figure in the growth of WSW-SA.[5] A born and bred Seattleite, Janet played field hockey at the University of Washington in Seattle. She served as the WSWSA vice president in its first year and president the following year. Although Janet's playing career ended after ten years due to hip problems, she continued to work on behalf of WSWSA and soccer. Janet served WSWSA twice more as president, ran youth soccer camps for youngsters in conjunction with the University of Washington and the Seattle Sounders, refereed youth games, and held many positions in soccer administration in the state of Washington. The Washington State Soccer Association recognized her contributions by giving her the Barney Kempton Award for volunteers, conferring upon her Life Membership, and in 2004 inducting her into the Hall of Fame. In 2009, Janet was selected for the United States Adult Soccer Association Hall of Fame.

One of the most significant issues faced by Bernadette, Janet, and others was securing adequate field space. Field use was near capacity in the league's inaugural spring season, and the women had to beg, borrow, and steal playing space for their nine teams. In only its second year, the league grew to thirty-six teams, making it even more of a challenge to find fields. Incredibly in 1976, the third year of its existence, WSWSA fielded seventy-two teams. As Mike Ryan noted, "Pretty soon we ran out of fields. The parks department told us we couldn't add any more teams." But they did. Time and again the women were told there was no place for them to play even when fields were wide open. Relegated at times to Little League baseball fields and other non-soccer venues, the women learned to rely on portable goals they could lug to and from the fields. To continue playing, the women had no choice but to move scheduled games from weekends to weeknights. These and other struggles during the early years spawned the WSWSA informal motto that "Ladies don't play soccer, women do."

For the first few years of its existence, WSWSA held games only in the spring. It wasn't enough for Wendy Fletcher. Originally from Michigan, Wendy was a physical education teacher and track team coach in the Seattle area when she discovered the nascent WSWSA. Age twenty-eight, Wendy had never played an organized team sport before, but loved soccer from the start. She played her first game during a heavy rainstorm, and by the end was "covered head to toe with mud" and euphoric. After a few years, Wendy began organizing summertime leagues for women who wanted to play more soccer. Wendy rented the fields from the parks department, scheduled games, and held a Sunday morning pick-up game for all comers. Then she organized a fall season for a half-dozen teams in her local area, Issaquah. Seeing the success of Wendy's efforts, the WSWSA added summer, fall, and eventually frostbite seasons to their calendar. At the same time, Wendy began her long association with league administration, including stints as secretary and vice president.

Now sixty-nine, Wendy manages and enjoys playing over-60 on Monday nights with women she has known for decades, but she is by no means the eldest on the field: women in their seventies and even one eighty-year-old play regularly.

Lynne Clewell collaborated with Wendy in creating the over-55 and over-60 playing opportunities for women on Mondays. Lynne and her good friend Joyce Trader, in touch with tournament directors across the country, were at the forefront of pushing tournaments to adopt over-50, over-55, and then over-60 divisions for women's soccer. Lynne and Joyce both served many years on the board of WSWSA.

Born and raised on a farm in Ohio, Lynne honed her quickness and endurance chasing pigs through rows of corn. Having dairy cows try to rub her into the wall prepared Lynne for the same behavior by the more aggressive players in indoor soccer.

Lynne particularly enjoys the glory of scoring goals. Joyce, a sprinter from Jamaica and natural goal scorer, taught Lynne the secrets to scoring. Lynne made it her specialty, scoring winning goals at tournaments. She's proud of once scoring a winner in front of a watching Michelle Akers, famed goal scorer for the women's national team. Still competitive with the over-60 age group, Lynne can from time to time be found playing in the over-50 division as a substitute. No matter where she is in the world, Lynne is ready for a game of soccer, with or without soccer cleats. "I've played soccer in the Cape Verde Islands on the beach with a squashed water bottle with young people. I was the only older woman playing on the beach with these kids, the only white person if you will. And then again in the Andes." In high mountains, the residents play soccer with a deflated ball since a fully inflated ball bounces too high and travels forever in the thin air. "Soccer is a universal language. Those people spoke no English. It was a remote village, but they understood soccer. They were astounded I wanted to run and play in that atmosphere, way up high, in a poncho."

Maj Surowiecki is another of the many foreign-born women who populate Washington's soccer fields. Born in Sweden in 1941, Maj's first encounter with the Seattle area was in 1968 when as a nurse she spent nine months in a training program for delivering home dialysis. Returning to Sweden, a country with socialized medicine, she was dismayed to learn that budgeted funds for dialysis had been reduced. Maj returned to the United States in 1970, married, and had four children. Maj had never played sports in Sweden, but her American-born daughter began playing soccer. Like many soccer mothers, Maj thought the game looked like fun and joined other women learning to play in the early 1980s. At age forty-three she was one of the oldest on the team, but she was also one of the fastest runners. In 1994 she learned about a soccer tournament in California and joined other older women in traveling to their first tournament.

The women surprised themselves by winning the trophy for the over-50 division. They were hooked, and many of them, including Maj, have been traveling to (and winning) tournaments ever since.

Recently Maj played on a tournament team from Washington that included Myka from Indonesia, Olga from Brazil, Jytte from Denmark, Jillian from Wales, and assorted American-born players.

Despite being "a little bit loud-mouthed on the field," Maj has formed deep bonds with soccer teammates. "They know my deepest secrets," she said. Those friends and soccer give meaning to her life. "Without soccer, I think I would go crazy. It's my number one interest. As long as I can play, I'm happy. I just live one day at a time. I don't know what tomorrow is going to be like. Right now I'm happy."

Alaska

Liz Lauzen is another Pacific Northwest native, having grown up in Bremerton, Washington. Located on Puget Sound just a one-hour ferry ride from downtown Seattle, Bremerton is a beautiful city of 46,000 inhabitants. Liz was always athletic and swam for the YMCA, but did no sports in high school. In college she completed the necessary physical education requirements, but nothing more. Liz graduated from the University of Washington in 1968. Her son, born in 1972, was caught up in the soccer tidal wave and began playing at age five. Her daughter was born in 1976, and shortly afterward, the family moved to Alaska. Growing up in the 1950s and 1960s, Liz never thought about girls playing organized sports. "Never crossed our minds there might be something girls could do," she said. But by the time her daughter was born the world had changed. Liz and her husband "expected everything the boys had the girls would have." However, in Alaska they discovered that the boys and girls clubs were not equal. The boys club actively enlisted fathers to coach soccer. The girls had to wait for someone to volunteer. For two years Liz watched "dismal, dismal coaching" of the girls' teams. She knew she could do better so for the next decade, Liz coached or managed her children's teams. Not until she was forty-two did she step on the field to play.

Anchorage boasted a women's league with an upper and lower division based on skill, not age. Liz was often one of the oldest on the field. The weather-limiting outdoor season ran officially from April through August. As there was no women's league for indoor soccer, Liz played coed throughout the fall, winter, and spring.

Liz soon took over as manager for her indoor and outdoor teams. "People were asking to be on my team," she said, "not because we were good, but because we were organized. Many teams were slapdash." The other teams didn't have shirts, were lax about collecting money, and didn't communicate well. When her son left for college, his friends begged to be part of Liz's team.

Liz and her husband were still living in Alaska in 2000 when they retired. Although she stepped away from her job in April, Liz refused to leave the area until after the state soccer championship held in August. Her team won the four-day tournament. She and her husband then spent several months traveling before settling back in her hometown of Bremerton. Excited to discover that the local parks department ran a summer soccer league for women, Liz called them at Christmas time. She was told the league didn't start for five months, but she insisted on paying her fee then; she wanted to guarantee a spot for the upcoming season. Liz later learned of the WSWSA and its over-40 and over-50 divisions. For the next twelve years, she joined the tide of women from the western side of Puget Sound riding the ferry on weeknights to downtown Seattle and making their way to the playing fields—a journey that could take two hours each way.

Now seventy-one, Liz no longer plays on a team in WSW-SA, but will occasionally take the ferry on Monday nights to play with the over-55 or over-60 groups that Wendy Fletcher organized. On Wednesdays and Sundays, Liz plays indoor soccer on an over-50 team in Bremerton. This past October her husband broke his leg on a Tuesday and was told he would have to wait until Thursday for the operation to set the bone. Despite being virtually immobile on that Wednesday evening, he urged Liz to play the game she loved. "You go, you go," he said. Of course, she did.

For the women in WSWSA who can no longer run due to injuries or age-related deterioration of hips, knees, and ankles, soccer is still an option thanks to Sue Boettcher. A native of Seattle, Sue began playing soccer as an adult on a coed recreational team. Her next-door neighbor, one of the many foreign-born engineers hired by Boeing, started a neighborhood soccer program for children that soon encompassed interested adults. Like many of their neighbors, Sue, her husband, and their children all played soccer. "We played co-rec soccer on Friday nights," Sue said. "There is a place called Sixty Acres, and they have sixteen soccer fields. The men and women would play, the kids would play on the sidelines, and the hot air balloons would fly over. It was a great Friday night activity for everybody."

Sue played for decades until the stress on her joints led to a hip replacement in 2013. Distraught to think her playing days were over, Sue was ecstatic to learn of a program in England called Walking Soccer. The game is played by older men who have lost the ability to run the miles required for a full soccer game. Sue realized such a program could attract a large following among the women she knew. "A lot of people I've played with have stopped playing because of one physical issue or another, or health issue. We've all become isolated with our physical issues and are missing the game." Sue's research uncovered a woman in Oregon who had started a walking soccer program.

She sent Sue the rules and Sue began a program in her area, which she called Ultimate Soccer. Teams play thirty-minute halves using a futsal ball—a smaller and much heavier ball than a regulation soccer ball. The ball stays on the ground because it is too difficult to loft. Far from being a static game, players are constantly moving during Ultimate Soccer and easily log about five miles of walking during a one-hour game. The game attracts women recovering from injuries and those who want to improve their skills and technique. However, the greatest joy is displayed by those women who, after thinking their playing days are over, have returned to the field to play once again the game they love.

For years Sue had worked with the University of Washington women's team on coaching programs and events for the team. She contacted the women's coaches, Leslie Gallimore and Amy Allman Griffen, about staging a video on Ultimate Soccer. After one of the UW practices, the players took the field for a seven vs. seven Ultimate Soccer game. The U-20 National Team of Papua New Guinea, in the midst of a tour of the United States, was practicing with the UW women and formed one of the teams. The video demonstrated the constant motion and great fun of the game and has become a successful recruiting tool.[6]

Tony DiCicco, the most successful coach in U.S. Women's National Team history, had an opportunity to see Sue's video. "That is so cool! I've never seen that before!" he said. The U-20 Papua New Guinea team, after completing its time with the UW women, flew to the Washington, DC area to practice with and play against the Washington Spirit, a women's professional team. At the urging of the U-20 squad, the Spirit engaged in and enjoyed an energetic game of Ultimate Soccer.

With such positive responses to the game, Sue envisions that in the next few years Ultimate Soccer will become a regular event at adult soccer tournaments.

In 2017, Sue received the Washington State Adult Soccer Association (WSASA) Barney Kempton Award for her volunteerism. She is currently on the WSASA board as the Ultimate/ Walking Soccer Director.

SEVEN
Finding the Game

IN 1967, FEWER than 100,000 people played soccer in the United States. By 1984, more than four million were playing.[1] Soccer moms, professional women, girlfriends, and graduate students found their way onto the soccer field and into women's leagues with the help of children, boyfriends, husbands, teachers, and pure luck.

Lisa Teal was introduced to soccer by actor Kurt Russell. In his younger years, Russell was a child TV, movie star, and an accomplished athlete, even playing minor league baseball for several years. Lisa and Kurt were neighbors in Aspen, Colorado. When the 5'11", dimpled, blue-eyed Kurt invited Lisa to watch one of his soccer practices, she responded enthusiastically. While observing the men play on the Aspen High School field, Lisa was overcome with the urge to stretch her legs and ran several laps around the field. The coach of a women's team, observing this exhibition of athleticism, approached Lisa and asked if she'd be interested in joining the women's side. Lisa replied in the affirmative but noted she was thirty-nine, had never played, and knew almost nothing about the game. Immediately the coach assured her she could play fullback. Indeed, Lisa was positioned on the back line for her first game and instructed to at every opportunity kick the ball out of bounds—a basic but safe tactic for an inept defender. Lisa has been playing ever since that day, and—fortunately for her teammates—her skills have improved. Now in her late sixties, Lisa plays in recreational leagues and on competitive tournament teams, all thanks to Kurt Russell.

Wendy Matalon graduated from her southern California high school in 1972 and started college that fall at the University of La Verne, a private university thirty-five miles east of Los Angeles. While pursuing her degree, Wendy worked for the Community Services Office coaching youth soccer and refereeing boys' soccer games, although she didn't play. For her senior project, she wrote a manual for coaching children's soccer. A natural athlete, Wendy competed in multiple sports in high school. As a junior in college she walked onto the women's varsity volleyball team. Tall, she was adept as a hitter and was offered a stipend to stay at La Verne for a fifth year and play volleyball. She took the opportunity to secure a second major.

After graduation, Wendy couldn't find any women's volleyball teams and joined a mixed team. "Coed volleyball really sucked," she said. "I wasn't a setter, and I couldn't be a hitter because the net was too high so I just got pounded in the back row." Working full time and enrolled in a master's degree program at Cal State Long Beach, Wendy heard about an adult women's soccer league from a classmate. She jumped at the chance to try a new sport and has been playing on recreational and tournament teams ever since. Wendy has been with her current soccer team for more than twenty-five years.

Diane Lieberman grew up in a small town in California. "We had a woman coach who had all these club teams," Diane recalled. "I swam, and I played tennis and volleyball, but I never played soccer. I graduated in 1968 from high school. I was definitely pre-Title IX." Decades later, at age fifty, Diane was chauffeuring her children and a friend's son to various activities. While dropping the boy at an indoor soccer facility, Diane was approached by a member of a coed soccer team. He explained the team was preparing to play a game, but it was short of female players. Would Diane play with them? Attired in jeans and sans appropriate soccer footwear, she hesitated. Her children however clamored for her to give it a go. "Yeah, Mom. You can do it." Diane surrendered to their pleas and played. She enjoyed it so much that she acquired the appropriate shorts and shoes and played indoor coed soccer for the next several years. After awhile, Diane grew tired of the men "beating you up and throwing you against the wall." Her daughter, who had played in high school and college, discovered a women's outdoor league and urged her mother to join. At age fifty-eight, Diane played her first outdoor soccer game. Since she'd always been a runner, the larger field suited her well. Eight years later Diane plays outdoor soccer regularly and travels to tournaments. Instead of yelling at her soccer-playing children from the sideline, which she did for many years, Diane is now the recipient of their sideline encouragement (and instructions). She intends to play as long as she can drag herself onto the field.

Alice Moore also discovered soccer when recruited to play for a coed team. Male members of the team asked Alice and her friend Margaret—both accomplished softball players—to join their over-30 soccer team as they had difficulty finding female players. Alice noted that she and Margaret easily met the age requirement—they were both over forty-years-old—but neither had ever played soccer. However, if the team needed them, they'd give it a whirl. Twenty plus years later, Alice and Margaret are still playing in the over-30 coed league. Soccer long ago supplanted softball in Alice's affections, although she still plays both sports. "I can't pitch anymore because I blew my arm. I can still throw ... so I play first base now." And she hits. Alice, one of only four women in the men's league, can pull the ball to either field and maintains a high batting average. She's a darn good goalkeeper in soccer, too.

Another softball player, Connie Bunch, played fast-pitch in college and continued when she moved to Sacramento. When the fast-pitch league folded, Connie gave slo-pitch a try and hated it—too dull. In her thirties, Connie and several of the other women on the softball team tried soccer. Connie was en-amored with the game. Unlike Alice, Connie never felt the need to pick up a softball glove again, and she's been playing soccer for over thirty years.

On a beautiful fall day in Virginia, Suzanne Mahoney took her two young sons to visit a local park where she chanced upon the Thunder Thighs, a women's soccer team, practicing. Although she'd taken physical education classes through high school and college, Suzanne hadn't done anything athletic in a dozen years. The opportunity to run around a soccer field with other women her age appealed to her. She asked one of the women how she could learn the game and was given a contact name and number. Since she was pregnant with her third child, Suzanne waited until after the delivery and the advent of spring to make the call. She was placed on a soccer team with women, like her, who did not work full time (except for motherhood). Team practices were held twice each week during work hours. Suzanne soon established her practice routine: mid-morning she would pack lunches for her two boys, load up the car, nurse her daughter, pick the boys up from nursery school, and then drive to practice. Upon arriving at the field at Ft. Belvoir, Suzanne would set up the playpen, get the boys' lunches out, nurse her daughter again, put the children in the playpen, and then put on her cleats and shin guards. The first game Suzanne ever saw was one she played in. Over the years the women on the team grew close as they watched each other's children grow, attend school, and begin playing soccer. Suzanne first played in 1978 and remained with the same group of women up to the 1990s. When the team folded, many of the women, like Suzanne, moved on to other teams.

Tran Diem Kratzke, born in Viet Nam, grew up in an environment where girls' sports were neither expected nor supported. In Tran's family, extracurricular activities were not permitted. When Tran was not in school, she would help her mother in her bookstore, do housework, or study. "Physical activities and anything outside of core subjects, such as music or arts, were not encouraged or even were prohibited. We were scolded for singing, even though our bookstore sold lyric sheets. Singing did not bring honor to the family, as an A+ report card would." Tran secretly dreamed about learning how to swim and play tennis. She never thought of soccer, having zero knowledge of the sport. In 1975 Tran arrived in Chicago, Illinois with her family and, although she hadn't finished her last year of high school, started at a local community college. Later she transferred to Northern Illinois University where she met and married her husband. After completing their undergraduate degrees, the couple moved to Washington where he had secured a job.

Tran's new home sat at the confluence of the Columbia and Yakima Rivers in the tri-cities of Richland-Kennewick-Pasco. The metropolitan area of 150,000 is home to the Hanford nuclear site and a center of nuclear power research and production. Most employment opportunities at the time were with the U.S. Government or government contractors. Tran hoped to find a job, but it was difficult as most positions required U.S. citizenship. Had Tran stayed in Illinois for another year, she would have been eligible for citizenship, but by moving to another state, she had to wait an additional two years for eligibility. Tran scoured the help wanted ads in the local newspaper, desperate to find something where she could use her skills. One day by chance she saw an advertisement for women's soccer. Tran had no idea what soccer was. She asked her husband who encouraged her to give it a try. She did. "I called, and they took me. I played for about a year. I had the time of my life; I didn't want to quit." But Tran had become pregnant. She and her husband moved back to Illinois for graduate school. It was sixteen years before she played soccer again; full-time work and motherhood left her no time for sports. When her last child was born, Tran took a part-time position and then quit working altogether. She then found a soccer team and fell in love with the game all over again. Tran enrolled all her children in soccer. Since she regretted never having had the opportunity to play sports as a child, Tran encouraged her children to try other activities: swimming, skating, ballet, T-ball, gymnastics, scouting, music, and arts. Now adults, none of Tran's children have continued with soccer, but Tran, nearly sixty, plays on. "I am grateful for the team that took me in when I was uncertain in a new town. I love soccer."

Soccer Moms

In 1974 Judy Jones and her family moved from Lansing, Michigan to the Virginia suburbs of Washington, DC. Her son, a second-grader, came home from school one day and told his mother about a great new game he'd discovered: it was played with a ball, but you couldn't use your hands, only your feet to kick the ball. Judy knew nothing about soccer. Her husband knew a little more, just that it had been a men's recreational sport at his college. Her son was so enthused that Judy signed up both him and her daughter for organized soccer. Another woman whom Judy had met through Girl Scouts mentioned to Judy that it would be great if the moms learned how to play. Soccer was terrific exercise, cost a lot less than golf, and would give the women a proper perspective on what their children were struggling to master. Judy was game. The women enjoyed the experience and wanted to continue playing. Judy became one of the founding members of Fairfax

County Women's Soccer Association, an organization that would grow to encompass over a thousand women.

At age six, Carrie Hood's daughter brought home from school a flyer about playing soccer. Carrie enrolled her daughter and, when she was old enough, her younger daughter also. When a few soccer moms decided to form a women's team, Carrie jumped at the opportunity. "It was the most out-of-character thing that I have ever done," she noted. At first, Carrie didn't know how to fit soccer into her other obligations: full-time career, marriage, and motherhood. However, she so loved the camaraderie, the competition, the satisfaction of learning new skills, and the delight of shedding the labels of teacher, wife, and mom that she was determined to make it work. Carrie's daughters understood their mother's soccer mania, but her husband was slower to accept it. Over time he realized Carrie was a happier person when she was able to run around on the soccer field and fully supported her soccer career.

Born in 1955, Gene Forsythe grew up in Canada playing hockey. Years later and living in California, she learned about the sport of soccer when her children began to play under the auspices of the American Youth Soccer Association (AYSO). Gene remembered her children's AYSO coaches as predominantly American men who brought the American football mentality to the soccer field. Tactics were to kick the ball down the field then have the kids run for it. Not until one of her boys had a coach from India did Gene begin to see that there was more to the game than brute force. Watching her sons' team learn from a coach who knew the game, Gene discerned that good soccer required finesse, tempo, accurate passes, and creativity. It was a lot like hockey.

As in many other locales the soccer moms, many of them athletic, wondered why their children were having all the fun. One mother volunteered her husband, Larry Webb, to teach soccer moms like Gene how to play. In addition to playing soccer in college, Larry had coached numerous youth and adult teams in the area across various skill levels. However, this would be his first women's team. Larry started from scratch, teaching the women how to stop or trap a ball, how to pass, how to send long passes, and other basics. The women, on average about forty-years-old, hoped to form a team and play in the YMCA women's over-25 league. After conducting a few practices and watching the YMCA women's league games, Larry informed his trainees they were not ready to compete at that level. He would hold practices for another year before recommending they join the YMCA league. Gene realized that coming into the sport late she'd have to practice, practice, and practice more just to attain a decent skill level. Not one to shirk a challenge, Gene spent endless hours working alone on her skills. She would "go to the handball court and kick against the wall. I would draw circles on the wall and then kick and kick and kick and kick until I could hit the circles every time no matter where I was … working it and working it and working it. And working angles so you could curve the ball. All those things you had to practice and learn at a late age." And she learned to do it with both feet.

The women finally joined the YMCA league and were immediately disappointed. They played on "a crappy little dirt field," often without nets. When nets were provided, they were full of holes: discards from the men's league. At the time though, the women had no other option.

While picking up uniforms for her son's team at Zama Sports in Costa Mesa, California, Gene was astonished to see stacks and stacks of uniforms in the store. She inquired as to the purpose all the uniforms and learned they were for teams in a men's league in Long Beach. The owner of the store ran the league and was committed to the growth of soccer in the area. "How'd you like to run a women's league?" Gene asked him. He thought it was a great idea and the Newport Beach Soccer Association for women over-25 was created. Gene played in the league for ten years before joining the over-50 division of the Orange County Women's League where she still plays.

Kathy Bomar's sons played youth soccer in Chantilly Youth Association (CYA) in Chantilly, Virginia. A born organizer, Kathy was soon in charge of the CYA soccer program. Kathy knew women who played soccer and decided she'd like to learn the game. But rather than join an existing team, Kathy organized her own. Bev Vaughn was one of the early fish caught in Kathy's net. While signing her daughter up for CYA soccer, Bev was told by the registrar that her daughter's team needed an assistant coach. Would she take the position? Bev protested that she knew nothing about the game; she'd never played before. From the other end of the table, Kathy's voice rang out. She was starting a team to play indoor soccer. It would be a great way to learn the game, make new friends, and Bev should join them.

An avid athlete, Beth had played varsity basketball and several club sports at Mary Washington, a women's college in Virginia. Her love of sports began by playing baseball as a child with other children in the neighborhood, and her first baseball glove came from saving S&H green stamps. "I was so proud to have that glove. When I was in the fourth grade, I lobbied my teacher to be able to play baseball with the boys at recess instead of kickball with the girls. I bugged her so much that she finally let me do it. And that meant I got to bring my glove to school every morning." Soccer was an opportunity to learn new sport. Bev was in.

While the basics of indoor soccer are the same as outdoor, there are fundamental differences. In the early days, almost all indoor fields were small areas bounded by low walls and included rounded corners. (Larger fields with no walls are now more prevalent indoors.) As in ice hockey, players bounce the ball off the low walls in making passes to teammates. Indoor soccer could be played with five, six, or seven on a team. The fast-paced game is non-stop, unless someone scores, the ball is kicked over the wall, or a foul is committed. At the time Kathy formed her team, fields were covered with an early version of artificial turf that resembled carpet more than grass. The turf/carpet overlaid a hard and unforgiving concrete floor. Players frequently caught the soles of their shoes on the turf, leading to many a fall. However, for Kathy's team carpet burn was the least of their worries.

Kathy knew from the practices that her team was weak, but she had hopes. The roster included former field hockey players who were quick on their feet. They had a good sense of where the ball should be played, if not the skills to put it there. The team's only experienced soccer player was the goalkeeper. From the nets, she could provide leadership and a sense of calm during the game. Or so Kathy thought.

With great excitement and anticipation, the team took the field for their first indoor game. The goalie broke her femur, and the team lost 16-0.

Bev and the other women were shell-shocked at how fast and rough the game could be. Over time, a few women dropped out. Kathy's force of personality was no small part of why many remained. After several months of indoor soccer, Kathy proposed that the team play outside. Bev had doubts; she wasn't confident she had the stamina to play on the larger field. In her usual manner, Kathy convinced Bev and others it would be okay, and they took to the great outdoors. As one of Kathy's former teammates noted, "Kathy could persuade a hungry squirrel to give up his winter stash of nuts and be happy about it." Bev and many of Kathy's other recruits played soccer for years.

Andrea Wessel, an active fifty-something who looks barely forty, was drawn to soccer because the female coach of her children's team played. To learn the game, Andrea attended a soccer camp for women held under the auspices of the Fairfax Women's Soccer Association. Despite attending the weeklong camp, Andrea couldn't find a team that would give her a chance. Stars, a team that spent many years as bottom dwellers in their division, was known for accepting new players. Tired of always losing, Stars changed their long-standing policy and decided to strengthen their team with experienced players. They rejected Andrea's petition to join. Nevertheless, Andrea registered to play, hoping FWSA would find a place for her. The league put together a group of newbies, like Andrea, with the remnants of a team that had just lost many players to retirement. Thus was born Genesis. "A group of women who had never played soccer before, who didn't know the rules," Andrea said. "Didn't know how to throw in, didn't know how to kick the ball, didn't know anything. And then you had a group of women who … were more competitive. The experienced players were very patient with us. They taught us all the rules, taught us everything." For many seasons the women rarely won, but the one team they could beat was Stars. When Andrea scored her first goal against Stars, "I just wanted to say, 'See, you should have taken me.'"

School Teachers

Señor Hernandez, a Spanish teacher in a southern California junior high school, introduced Janice Akridge and her classmates to soccer. Janice spoke fondly of him. "He used to take us out and just play. He obviously loved soccer. He nicknamed me Scooter. I just always loved that sport, but we didn't have it in high school." Athletic girls like Janice opted for the Girls Athletic Association (GAA). "That basically meant that you had PE the last period of the day. You played all the sports whatever the season was. I played field hockey, volleyball, and basketball."

Fifteen years later Janice was having her hair cut when her stylist mentioned that she played soccer. Janice thought it crazy that such an old woman—she estimated her stylist was between thirty-five and forty-years years of age—could play such a demanding sport. Janice reasoned that if such an old woman could play then she, a mere twenty-eight, could certainly handle it. Janice announced to her husband that evening that she was going to play, but suspected he didn't believe it would last.

Janice played Sunday mornings in a large women's soccer league in Northern California. Years later her husband wanted to move the family to Northern Virginia. Janice didn't want to go, fearing there would be no soccer. Her husband investigated the area and found both indoor and outdoor soccer for women. Janice made the move and joined not one but several soccer teams. "At the peak, I was probably playing five days a week: two indoor teams and however many outdoor teams. It got to be a joke with my husband, but he was very accommodating." Señor Hernandez would be proud. (Janice no longer believes her hair stylist was too old for soccer.)

Pia Parrish, a Southern California girl like Janice, learned the game from her fourth-grade teacher who was British. It was still the era when girls were required to give up baseball and play softball in its stead. Pia liked playing with the boys, but girls couldn't participate in organized sports. Her teacher introduced the children to soccer and Pia played pickup with the boys. She continued to play in pickup games through high school, college, and afterward until women's soccer leagues formed in her area.

Rose Noga, Michigan born and bred, was told when she signed her children up for soccer that she had to volunteer for something. "I'll make cookies," she said. However, the league didn't need bakers; they needed coaches. Rose was given a video and book, attended training classes, and assigned to coach her kids. She "loved it, loved it, loved it." At one of her children's games, a schoolteacher asked Rose if she'd like to join a woman's team. Rose responded, "Well, I don't play. I just kick the ball around with the kids." The woman persisted, and Rose joined a team in the Great Lakes Women's Soccer League. Since then, she's traveled the world playing soccer, up to six tournaments each year in such far-flung places as Puerto Vallarta, Virginia Beach, Sydney, Las Vegas, Turin, and Palm Desert.

Friends and Boyfriends

Christine Nolan's boyfriend brought her to soccer. He played on a coed team and asked if Christine would like to give it a try. She'd played a lot of kickball as a child and had kicked a soccer ball around at the field house in college, but had no idea about how soccer was played. Although it looked like fun, Christine didn't want to embarrass herself on the field, so she didn't immediately sign up. Attending a stage play one night with friends, Christine met Melissa who mentioned she attended informal soccer practices for women where they learned the necessary skills and the rules of the game. Christine was delighted to have an entrée to the game where she could learn without humiliating herself.

At one of her first practices, Christine was invited to an indoor soccer game to watch. Christine had never even heard of indoor soccer but thought the experience might be fun. "They didn't have enough players," she recalled. She was pressed to join in. "I was not even wearing soccer clothes or soccer shoes, and I ended up on the field, playing indoor soccer. I had no idea what the rules were for that either because I had just been playing for a few weeks at that point. I fell in love with indoor." Christine's outdoor practice group then formed a team to play in the Fairfax Women's Soccer Association. Christine became part of the team and signed up to play on her boyfriend's team. In no time, she went from never playing to being on three teams: two outdoor and one indoor.

Playing coed with other couples seemed like a great idea until two of the couples, including Christine and her boyfriend, broke up. Nevertheless, she continued to play coed for a time. During one memorable game a male opponent was "extremely physical," and "pounded me into the ground." Christine hurt all over from the hip checks, elbows, and tumbles on the hard ground. At the conclusion of the game, Christine's assailant approached her. Expecting a handshake and "good game," Christine was gobsmacked when he asked her out on a date. Attractive and outgoing, Christine had experience in fending off unwelcome advances. "Are you out of your mind?" she responded. "You just tried to kill me, on purpose! You think I would go out with someone who just did that to me?" The next day revealed the extent of Christine's wounds with the blooming of massive purple and blue bruises. Shortly after that, Christine quit coed but continued to play on women's teams for many years.

Growing up sandwiched between two brothers, Karen Sharpe was the quintessential tomboy: riding mini-bikes, climbing trees, and playing all kinds of sports including football. However, she never was part of a team. Her family was too poor to pay for lessons, membership fees, or uniforms. They couldn't even afford to let Karen join the neighborhood swim team or the Girl Scouts. "I never played any [organized] sports. I just didn't," she said.

In her twenties, married, and working, Karen at times would join a friend in watching a soccer game in which her friend's mother was playing. Eventually, the young women and several other friends participated in the soccer practices, then joined teams in a women's league. Karen's competitive streak, dormant since childhood, reawakened. Her friends, finding better things to do with their time, dropped out of soccer, but Karen played as much as she could, thriving on the camaraderie and athleticism. "I was addicted," she said. Karen raised three boys but never became a soccer mom. Because their father had played basketball, the boys eschewed the soccer field for the basketball court. That was okay with Karen, as long as she could play as much soccer as she could handle.

Ruth Walton was signed up for soccer by a tennis friend, Lynn Gaaserud. In the fall of 1976, Lynn and others created the Fairfax Women's Soccer Association. Lynn recruited women she knew to the league by signing them up and informing them later. Lynn found a woman to coach the team and organize practices. Ruth noted that the coach had the women run sprints in their first practice, which in retrospect was a huge mistake. Ruth among others pulled her quadriceps muscle. But determined to play through the pain, she continued. "The first time I went out on the field I couldn't believe it. It was so exhilarating." In her late seventies, Ruth has given up playing, but not the game. She's an official recruiter for the Fairfax league, but unlike her friend Lynn, she won't sign up new players without asking, even though it might be good for them.

EIGHT
All the Wrong Moves

Learning a new sport as an adult is challenging. Fortunately, tennis, golf, surfing, snowboarding, skiing, and other individual sports have infrastructures to help the beginner learn through group and individual lessons. Team sports like volleyball and softball have adult leagues where newcomers can play. When women began playing soccer in the 1970s, there was no support infrastructure: no leagues, clinics, nor pickup games for women. Into the void stepped husbands, boyfriends, lacrosse and field hockey coaches, male soccer coaches, referees, and even children. Together, they helped the women learn how to play the beautiful game. However, this patchwork of support generated the inevitable odd bounce or two along the way.

Coaches and Referees
Sue Pratt Brown, one of the early players in the Fairfax Women's Soccer Association, played goalkeeper on a team coached by a former college All-American soccer player. He may have been immensely talented on the field, but she remembered him less than fondly. When Sue arrived early one day for practice on a

muddy field, the coach informed her that she was going to learn how to stop shots by diving. Following his instructions, Sue repeatedly launched herself to one side or the other, stretched out as if to parry away a ball, and rolled when she hit the ground. Poor Sue, ever the fashionista, had worn her favorite pair of "really cute" white soccer shorts. By the end of practice, a thick layer of mud encased her lower body. Soaking the shorts in bleach and repeated washings removed much of the dirt, but shredded the seams. Her once adorable shorts weren't even salvageable as rags. The following week Sue donned shin guards, goalie gloves, and one of her many, many prom dresses. She stared down the coach at practice, daring him to try and make her dive one more time. He didn't, and Sue's prom dress was saved.

Many coaches had no idea how much to push the women. For that matter, the women didn't know, either. Californian Lynn Naftel was in her thirties when she attended her first practice. She had signed up for soccer at the local YMCA, and the husband of another beginning soccer player had volunteered to coach the women. At the first practice, the women went straight into sprinting and kicking, without any warm-up activities. "After what seemed like hours," Lynn said, "practice ended, and I hobbled to my car. By the time I drove the five miles home, I could hardly get out of the car. My thighs were so sore! Thought I'd have to call my husband to carry me up the stairs. Three days later both of my thighs were purple; I had severely torn my quads. But, I wrapped them and kept going to practice." Following weeks and weeks of training, the women thought they were ready for their first game. On the day of the game, Lynn walked to the edge of a large bowl and stopped in shock as she gazed down to the field below. Soccer practices had been held in a small grassy area. The soccer field below was regulation sized, nearly 120 yards long and 80 yards wide—an American football field measures only 100 yards (excluding end zones) by 54 yards. Lynn was aghast at the thought of running the length and breadth of such an expanse. "I don't even remember the score. Just the image of that enormous field remains burned in my memory."

The Aztecs, an early Fairfax team, included a field hockey coach on the roster who volunteered to run practices. She tried, unsuccessfully, to get the women to warm up by running laps around the field. Judy Jones recalled tearing the thigh muscle in her right, dominant leg at an early practice. It turned out to be a blessing in disguise, as Judy then had to learn to kick with her left foot. Even at elite levels, fewer than 20 percent of soccer players are comfortable kicking the ball with either foot.[1] Despite the challenges faced by the field hockey coach, Judy would rather have her, or any female coach (or even no coach at all) rather than a male coach. She believed too many of the men were imbued with a dictatorial approach and were clueless in handling women. "They would tell their [male] players jump, and they would jump," she said. "They'd say go right, go left, and they did it exactly. Tell women to jump and they ask how high or why. Or say 'go left' and they'd say how do you want us to go left? They weren't sure what to do with us."

The Tidal Basin Blues, one of the best women's soccer teams for years in the Washington DC area, had hiccups with their first two coaches. One man whose coaching experience was limited to children had difficulty communicating with the women. His successor was controlling to the point of making bed checks: calling each player the night before a game.[2]

Jim Givargis, a highly regarded soccer trainer in Northern Virginia, was one of those adept at instructing women. Kathy Bomar persuaded Givargis to open his indoor training facility in the evenings so she and her friends could practice during the cold months. She later convinced him to retain his staff for several days after his summer youth soccer camp concluded in order to run a weekend camp for adults. Each year these training sessions at Sweet Briar College in Central Virginia were almost exclusively filled with women, thrilled to be attending their first ever sports camp. For many, the inducement to attend was not just learning soccer skills, but three days when they didn't have to cook, clean, or run errands.

Located in the foothills of the Blue Ridge Mountains, Sweet Briar typically experiences August temperatures in the middle to the high eighties with humidity to match. Christine Nolan, a regular attendee at the camp, recalled a newcomer, Vicki, from outside the circle of Virginia women. Vicki had never, ever played soccer and her training attire for the weekend consisted of a blouse, tights, and a field hockey skirt. An odd choice for any occasion, it was incomprehensible to Christine why Vicki continued to wear the tights as the temperatures soared into the upper nineties and afternoon practices were in sauna-like conditions. Christine, never bashful, posed the question directly to Vicki who responded that she needed to cover her legs because she was allergic to grass! At the time, artificial turf soccer fields were few and far between, and none of the women at the camp had ever played on one. Grass, or dirt, was the only option. Although she didn't voice it, Christine wondered, "Why in the hell would you pick soccer as your sport if you were allergic to grass? It's like being lactose intolerant and bathing in a pool of milk."

Perhaps Vicki's reasoning was the same as the two young women from Maryland who showed up at the camp the following year. They admitted their interest in learning soccer was that it provided a venue to meet men; they planned to join a coed league that fall. To the amusement of the mostly older and married women from Northern Virginia, while Givargis's male staff was teaching the women how to trap the ball, the Maryland women were practicing their man trapping skills on the staff. Givargis was not pleased when it appeared the women were having more success with his staff than with the soccer ball.

Like the Maryland women, male soccer players often chose to coach women to improve their social lives. One woman recalled her first coach, a divorced man from Guatemala with custody of a two-year-old parrot and eight-year-old daughter. "He was definitely on the make, but I don't think anyone minded since most of us were married or engaged already. I think he was less concerned about finding a mother for his child than someone who would be okay taking care of a parrot for its sixty-year life span. But, he was a decent coach and taught us basic skills. Before a game he would tell us to 'go rip their lips off,' but never told us how to do that without getting a red card."

Referees in the early days were often bemused by the women. In the early years, the women could be like five-year-olds in their understanding of the rules: a referee would make a call and face a sea of incomprehension. In Sue Pratt Brown's early games, the referee would blow the whistle and call for a corner kick. (When the ball, last touched by a defender, travels over the end line, the attacking team kicks it back into play from the nearest corner of the field.) None of the women had the least idea what a corner kick was, so the referee explained the rule and then physically positioned the women for the ensuing kick. The next time he blew his whistle for a corner, women still didn't understand what to do.

The first time Kathy Straight played soccer, she fell down laughing. "It was so much fun. The next week I went into play, and the referee said, 'there will be no laughing on the field.'" In their governance role, FIFA has laid down seventeen laws or rules for the game. Laughing is not mentioned.

As part of managing the games, referees may hand out disciplinary cards: yellow for unsporting behavior, including dissent and persistent fouling; and red for dangerous fouls, violent contact, spitting on opponents, deliberate handballs to stop a goal, and offensive or insulting or abusive language. A red-carded player is immediately banned from the remainder of the game and may not be replaced with a substitute. She also is banned from the next game. In recreational adult women's games, disciplinary cards were rare: women might play over a hundred games without seeing anyone receive a yellow card. Red cards were almost non-existent.

Shirley Metzger was on the board of the Fairfax Women's Soccer Association when she received a red card, was tossed from the game. Shirley claimed the referee had been unpleasant during the entire game. One of Shirley's teammates picked up the ball before it rolled entirely over the out of bounds line—a common mistake by new players. Uncommonly, the referee gave her a yellow card. The woman protested that she had just been picking it up to throw it in. Shirley's anger got the better of her. "We'd all have more fun if you had a better attitude," she told the referee. Shirley laughed retelling the story and remembering just how quickly the referee whipped out his red card.

Penny Schulstad, Shirley's sister and teammate, acknowledged that the women sometimes want it both ways. They become upset when the referees are patronizing and don't take the women's game seriously. "There are plenty of refs who act bored, don't call much, and act like it's too much trouble to call something." Penny would prefer that referees called the game by the rules instead of giving the women a pass.

The quality of the referees for women's games has improved dramatically over the last forty years. Perhaps because the U.S. lacked a strong soccer tradition, the early years were a mixed bag and too many referees were not just bad, but terrible. In Texas, Martha Dinwiddie played soccer, refereed youth and women's games, and was a linesman for high school games. She knew poor refereeing when she saw it. "We had one referee who was really, really bad. We had him for several games. He wasn't biased; his attitude was horrible."

Martha took her five-year-old golden retriever and beagle mix, Chivas, to games where someone on the sideline would always keep an eye him while Martha was on the field. During one game, Martha and her teammates bitched and moaned about the referee. Following the game, the women gathered up their gear and walked toward their cars. Chivas, trailing behind, perhaps thought there was unfinished business that required his attention. "All of a sudden he turned around," Martha said, "ran back to the bench and peed in the referee's bag. He had never ever done anything like this. We all tried to run and not laugh, fearing we'd be red-carded and out of the next game." The women made their escape, and Chivas was rewarded with treats.

Learning Through Experience

From the beginning, Sue Pratt Brown was a goalkeeper. When the coach put her in the game as a field player for the first time, she had little idea of her responsibilities. He told her to "mark" a particular opponent, i.e., keep close to the player to stop her from getting the ball and scoring. Stick to the opponent "like a shadow," were her instructions. This Sue did, faithfully. When her opponent subbed out of the game, Sue dutifully followed as the woman trotted off the field and up the hill, looking for a place to relieve herself—there were no portable toilets in the area. When Sue realized her error, she turned a bright shade of red and hustled back onto the field to a chorus of laughing teammates.

Since many of the women had never played football as children, they didn't know how to punt a ball. It's not an essential skill unless one is playing goalie. While the women envisioned themselves routinely kicking the ball halfway down the field—as is oft seen on televised games—many goalies in the early years were more apt to miss-hit the ball such that it squirted sideways, traveled only a few feet, or went straight to an opponent. The ultimate embarrassment was to strike the ball so weakly into a headwind that it flew backward, over the goalkeeper's head and into her net. Punting blunders were frequent.

Shirley Metzger began playing in 1984. Since all the players on the team were over thirty, the team asked to be in the Masters Division. The league noted the players were all inexperienced and instead placed the team in the lowest level of the Open Division, which included women of all ages, including young women who had played in college. That first season, Shirley's team lost all their games and never scored a goal. They rarely were able to take the ball over the midfield line. The league moved the team into the Masters Division for their second season. Again the team didn't score a goal, although their losses were less lopsided as the season progressed. In their third season, they finally scored and celebrated as if they'd won the World Cup, screaming and yelling and high-fiving all around while their opponents looked on, bewildered. There have been countless goals in the thirty years since then, but it's that first goal that Shirley remembered so vividly.

When Janice Akridge first moved to Virginia, she played indoor soccer in Manassas where all the games were held at night, some starting as late as 11:00 p.m. "We were a tight team," Janice said. "We didn't switch teams [and] a lot of people didn't like us." One of Janice's teammates, Leslie or Nasty Pants as she was known, was a dirty player, the type who would push people from behind when the referee was looking the other way. Eventually, Janice and her teammates kicked Leslie off the team, but not before she'd created many bad feelings on the field. Janice missed a game where Leslie had provoked an opponent into responding with an unprintable word. Janice heard about the incident the next morning. Later that day Janice was waiting on the street with other moms who were picking up their sons from Cub Scouts. Janice admitted she was proud that the Cub Scout mothers thought it was "so cool" that she played soccer. Janice glanced down the street and saw a woman walking purposefully and quickly in her direction. As the woman drew closer, she recognized her as the one who had blown up at Leslie the previous evening. The woman began to yell at Janice, her voice carrying to all the Cub Scout moms in the vicinity. She accused Janice of playing on a dirty soccer team that should be kicked out of the league and added a few imprecations. Janice was embarrassed and finally blurted out, "I heard you called Leslie a &*#%." At the time, Janice had no idea what the word meant, but her accuser clammed up. The Cub Scout moms, many suddenly red-faced, pretended they had to be some-where else. Janice longed to sink into oblivion. Later, when she learned the meaning of the word, she was mortified.

In her first game, Rita Wilkie's team lost to a team from Holliston, Massachusetts by a score of 3-0. The loss didn't bother Rita one iota. "I went home and couldn't even sleep all night. I was so excited. I was going to quit my job and play soccer!" Hundreds of games later, Rita is no less enthusiastic about playing. She loves the game and all its elements: the camaraderie, which she'd never had as a kid, the patches the teams used to trade, and the opportunity to play in all kinds of field conditions including large mud puddles and virtual lakes. During one long-ago game on a muddy field in Framingham, forty-something Rita was playing with a highly skilled young woman sporting nice makeup and a perfect hairdo. As always, Rita gave the game all she had, so when the young woman avoided contesting an opponent for a ball, Rita called her on it. "Why didn't you go after that? You could have got it!" The young woman replied that she didn't want to risk being hurt. "You know, your life may be over, but mine isn't." First shocked, then angry, Rita picked up the woman and threw her into the mud.

Mud was not usually an issue in Southern California where the women play year-round. Lynn Naftel recalled that when she first started playing, the women were not accustomed to hot days and would experiment with different ways to keep cool. One opponent made a habit of putting ice cubes in her sports bra. Even if Lynn had her back to this player, she knew of her approach by the sound of clinking cubes.

In contrast, women in the Seattle area, before the installation of artificial grass, oft contended with water in front of the goals. More than one goalkeeper dove into a puddle to block a shot and emerged with a mouthful of muddy water, but not the ball.

In many locales, women took responsibility for ensuring the soccer fields were playable. In the Boston area, the local park authorities lined the fields, but the team captains were responsible for ensuring their home fields were ready for play. If a referee said the area was not correctly lined, he could cancel the game, and the team would forfeit the game. Women carried bags of flour in their cars in case the lines had faded or disappeared. They bought their own nets and stepstools. If the nets at the field were not in good shape, the women were prepared to change them out.

In Fairfax County, Virginia, wet or muddy goals were frequent in the spring and women would bring hay bales to their games to soak up the water. One player, Jeanne Farris, eschewed hay bales for kitty litter. She didn't mention if stray cats near the goalmouth were ever a problem. Teams in Fairfax County were also responsible for lining the fields. Judi Whitestone recalled lining several times with the help of her dear friend Pat Ryan. The women sat on the sidelines and chatted while their children did the work. A pre-school teacher, Pat wouldn't worry how the lines came out as long as they were there. Judi was not as casual and worried when the lines were wavy, as they often were. However, the Glasgow Middle School field was so infamously bad that no one cared how it was lined. The surface was rock hard and rock filled, and the ground tilted from northeast to southwest. Instead of being parallel to each other, the goals were often askew. When teams scored, it was just as often due to the capriciousness of the wind or a strange bounce as to the skill of the women.

A Woman's Touch

The dawning of women's soccer introduced new team names to the age-old sport of men. Instead of time-worn names such as Savage, Venom, Outcasts, or Generals followed by an FC for Football Club, early women's teams bore such monikers as Violet Vipers, Sunshine Girls, Moms on the Run, Hot Flashes, and Burgundy Belles. Uniform colors were at times unconventional, such as the aforementioned burgundy plus fuchsia, neon yellow, hot pink and mauve. Like their children, the women had their names marked on their shirts. Shirley Metzger blushed a deep red when she recalled that her first jersey was emblazoned with Shirley across the back in huge, red letters.

She should not be embarrassed. The United States Major League Soccer (MLS) teams established in the 1990s also took odd names and wore unconventional jerseys. One MLS team was called the Kansas City Wizards and sported five-colored sine waves across jerseys and shorts. Dallas, Texas was home to the Dallas Burn and their jerseys were festooned with fire-breathing, leaping stallions. What's a Burgundy Belle amongst such kitsch?

For years finding decent soccer cleats was a challenge for women. Those with longer feet, size eight and up, could purchase men's shoes, although they might be too wide. Women with smaller feet bought cleats in the children's department and hoped not to be asked by the clerk if the purchase was for a son or daughter. When Carrie Hood and her friend began playing, they were thrilled to discover women's cleats in white for $15 in Payless Stores at a time when better quality cleats cost $50 or more. Her teammates rushed to take advantage of the bargain. When the ball rolled into a puddle during one of their games, the women refused to go after it. "We just stopped, none of us were going to get our new white shoes dirty!"

General athletic wear for women also was limited in quantity and style in the 1970s and early 1980s. In cold weather, women could be found practicing in long winter coats, hats, and gloves. Soccer players Pat Ryan and Judi Whitestone, recognizing the need, opened a women's athletic clothing store The Fhysical Female to serve their sisters on the field and other athletic women.

Changing Family Roles

In the 1970s, Judi Whitestone participated in a university panel examining the effect on the families of women playing soccer. While women in the past might have belonged to garden clubs and book clubs and volunteered in many capacities, these activities usually were confined to school hours. Soccer practices and games were more apt to take women away from the family several times each week during evenings and weekends, leaving the men to care for the children. More than a few marriages groaned under the stress.

Some husbands embraced the change. A men's soccer team from Hockington, Massachusetts attended their wives' games and served as cheerleaders. Spouses and significant others became coaches with a few discovering the difficulty of ordering around their partners. Bernie Hylinski and Ripley Forbes coached their wives' team in the Arlington Women's Soccer League. It wasn't clear that their wives always appreciated their hard work; there was a high level of back talk and irritation directed toward the husbands. However, the men knew what they were doing. After a so-so season under the previous coach, the women went undefeated. All the players' husbands and boyfriends pitched in and bought the women plaques to commemorate the season. Although they compiled a successful record, Bernie and Ripley lasted only a few seasons with the women, perhaps deciding to retire for the good of their marriages.

For other husbands, coaching became a long-term commitment. Howard Walton coached his wife Ruth and her team for many years. When Ruth retired at age seventy from playing,

Howard continued to coach the team, much to the delight of the players.

Spouses who didn't coach could still provide support when needed. Judi Whitestone heard of a team in her area looking for players for a California tournament. She had no plans to join until her husband pushed her to attend tryouts. Judi made the team and traveled to California with her husband. During one of the games, her tooth was knocked out. "I came out of the game. My husband said, 'Is it hurting you?' I said no. He said, 'Well, go back in the game then.'" She did.

In contrast to Judi Whitestone, Judy Jones did not want her husband at games despite the fact he coached their daughter's team and understood the game. Judy didn't want him offering any criticism or even helpful suggestions. However, when teammates put together an indoor coed team, Judy joined them and asked her husband to play. Many of the men had never played before. Judy's husband took his turn in goal during a game played against college-age players home from school. A highly skilled young woman "hauls off, whoosh, and kicks that ball. Knocks him flat. Glasses went flying." The coed team lasted one season.

Women's teams would have friends or spouses tape their games. One team took their tape to Kilroy's, a favorite sports bar and restaurant in Northern Virginia, and persuaded the bar to play the tape on the overhead TVs. The women watched the game while downing a few beers. The taped game was incredibly dull: the women seemed to be moving in slow motion, and nothing much happened. Nevertheless, the occasional moments of skillful play, few and far between, were met by shouts from the women of "Yeah, look at that! Look at that!" The men at the bar were furious; they wanted to watch something else, anything else.

In one league a woman used soccer to express support for feminism by playing through her entire pregnancy. There is no record of her husband's reaction, but other women on the field resented being in a position where they felt like they had to hold back. They dare not be aggressive around her lest they cause a dreadful injury.

Women with young children brought them to games and teammates or husbands babysat on the sidelines. Those still breastfeeding might have to run off the field in the middle of a play to attend to basics, so a substitute always had to be ready.

Debbie Greenlit is proud her son learned that women could be as passionate about soccer as men. During one of Debbie's games, he was walking behind the goal with his father when the goalie let loose with a loud "What the f%$#." Old enough to be familiar with the expression, he was nonetheless surprised that "she said that!" Soccer and swearing: not just for men.

Debbie Mowry, a single mother, brought her son to soccer games and practices. If he wandered out of sight, a sharp whistle from Debbie would bring him running, or he'd be in big trouble. Debbie supported her son throughout his athletic career attending his football, baseball, and competitive soccer games. Her son is now grown and returning the favor. He will still come out and watch Debbie play, even without the commanding whistle.

NINE
Characters, Crazy and
Otherwise

LIKE OTHER SPORTS, soccer has its memorable characters: women exhibiting a larger than life presence touched by a hint of craziness.

<u>Alice</u>

It's a soccer truism that goalies are an odd breed. They throw their bodies in front of screaming projectiles; a hard-struck ball in women's recreational soccer can travel forty-five mph. Men's shots easily exceed fifty-five. Alice Moore has faced both.

Alice Moore and her good friend Margaret Danner are in her mid-sixties and play in an over-30 coed league, an over-40 coed league, and an over-30 women's league as substitutes. They would love to play with people of a similar age, but the Fresno, California area does not offer over-50 or over-60 leagues.

"Bakersfield has some senior leagues," Alice said. "I'm about an hour and a half drive from there, and I have friends that run the league. Every once in awhile we buzz up there. We go down and play tournaments. We play women and coed both. We go down and spend the whole day going from one field to another because we'll play coed then we'll go over and play women, then we'll go back to coed."

One noteworthy Saturday, Alice and a few friends played multiple women's and coed games at a Bakersfield tournament. Alice's legs cramped up on the journey home. The pain was so excruciating that she could no longer drive and had to pull off the road. "Couldn't even straighten my leg out." The other women in the car couldn't drive either: all had severe leg cramps. They limped into a nearby restaurant. While downing big platters of carbohydrates, they shared a tube of Bio Freeze––a topical analgesic with menthol. No doubt the pungent odor of menthol with French fries made an indelible impression. Alice recovered sufficiently to drive the women home. They returned to play soccer the following day. Sunday was a repeat of Saturday. Alice and Margaret "kept going from field to field because they needed people for coed. Some of the other players didn't show up." The two women were well known by the Fresno coed teams. Despite how tired they were, they didn't feel they could let their friends down. "We ended up playing the whole time, the whole weekend. It was a lot of fun."

Alice first played goalie when she joined a women's team. No one wanted to play goalkeeper, so Alice was told that was her position. Although she enjoys her stints as keeper, Alice is often stuck in the position on women's teams because she is good at it. She loves to run, so she'd like to play on the field more often. In coed soccer, Alice is typically a field player but has served as the goalkeeper in emergencies. In one game, the male goalkeeper on Alice's team mouthed off to the referee and was ejected from the game. Alice's male teammates begged her to step into the position. "We'll protect you," they promised. Reluctantly, Alice acquiesced for the good of the team. Ten minutes later she was ruing her decision. Three blue-shirted men from the opposing team were barreling toward her, one with the ball at his feet.

Not a single one of her teammates was chasing them. After a muted "Oh, my God," Alice prepared herself. She kept her eyes on the player with the ball and moved toward him to cut down the angle of his shot. With a quick fake and touch of the ball, he attempted to dribble around Alice for a clear shot on goal. Alice dove for the ball and knocked it away, collecting a hard kick for her trouble. Since her teammates—the ones who had vowed to protect her—had given up on the play, not a single one was in the area to collect the rolling ball. Alice lay on the ground, battered and bruised, and watched another man in blue calmly kick the ball into the goal. Alice and the other women vociferously castigated their male teammates. The men promised to do better, and Alice agreed to continue as goalkeeper. During the remainder of the game, Alice made a few more saves, but the defense was tighter and did not allow another three-on-one breakaway.

Her female teammates have also let Alice down on occasion. One time a wide-open forward shot a ball that Alice managed to parry away from the goal. It went right back to the forward who shot again. The ball was coming too fast for Alice to catch it, so again she knocked it away. Alice might have wondered what her teammates were doing because the same forward retrieved the ball. Five times in rapid succession Alice stopped her shots. On the sixth shot, Alice dived for the ball. She got a glove on it, and pushed it away, but not far enough. Ever so slowly the ball trickled towards the line and across for a goal. No doubt Alice would have been happier had she saved the last shot, but her teammates were duly impressed with her reaction saves.

In the World Masters Games in Turin, Italy, not a single opponent was able to score on Alice. However, her teammates did. The bane of goalkeepers is the errant ball off a teammate that flies into one's net—dubbed an own goal. Alice endured the heartbreak of an own goal not once, but once each game. Her team lost each and every game by a score of 1-0.

Goalies are in a vulnerable position on the field. Not only do they have to dive for the ball onto rock-hard ground, but they also risk injury from other players kicking or running into them, sometimes deliberately. Alice recalled when a "big gal" plowed into her hoping to jar the ball loose and score. "She just creams me," Alice said. "Then she tries to tell the ref that I hit her." The referee who was on top of the play gave the woman a yellow card. She was lucky not to get a red, and Alice was fortunate not to be seriously hurt. Because a referee was not protecting the goalkeepers during one tournament, Alice received her first concussion. She had made save after save, yet paid for it. Lying on the ground with the ball in her grasp, Alice endured repeated kicks from opposing players. The Laws of the Game state that if a player attempts to kick the ball while the goalkeeper is handling it, a penalty is to be called for dangerous play. Egregiously, the referee did not enforce the rule. During one of many goalmouth scuffles, a player's knee connected with Alice's forehead. She "saw stars" and came out of the game for the remainder of the first half to recover her senses. The trainers, at Alice's insistence, let her return for the second half. Near the end of the game, Alice leaped for a high shot and pushed it out of the goal only to have an opponent crash into her. Alice went flying past the goalpost, landed on her back, hit her head, and was knocked out. The referee, consistent to the end, didn't blow the whistle. Her teammates, certain that a foul had been committed and the play was dead, stopped playing. The other team scored and went on to play in the championship game. Alice, on the way to the hospital with a concussion, was distraught not so much at having been hurt, but because her teammates had let an opportunity slip away to play in the championship game. "We could have been playing for first," she said.

In another game with more kicking by opponents and a negligent referee, Alice took matters in hand. At halftime, she approached the referee. "'Can you put that whistle in your mouth?

Put it in your mouth please.' He finally did, and I said, 'Now will you please blow that whistle?' He blew it. He said, 'What's your point?' I said, 'I just want to make goddamn sure it worked.' The second half he started blowing it."

Like all goalies, Alice has had her share of injuries over the years. She admitted that at age sixty-six, she doesn't bounce back quite as quickly as she once did.

One of Alice's great joys is bringing her great-granddaughter to tournaments. Her great-granddaughter also accompanies Alice to softball games, as did her father, as did her grandfather—Alice's son. Alice has played softball with her sons and soccer with both her son and grandson. "That's something you can't replace, being out there with your children and grandchildren."

Christiane

Christiane Wollaston-Joury was persuaded to try soccer by a flyer in the Parent-Teacher Association newsletter that challenged mothers to get up off the sidelines. Christiane, who had competed in field hockey and still played tennis, was intrigued. How hard could this game be?

Per the PTA advice, Christiane and other women took to the soccer field and kicked a soccer ball around. And that was it. The flyer had mentioned neither a team nor a league. One of the more skilled players heard about the Eastern Massachusetts Women's Soccer League and suggested the mothers form a team and join. The women diligently practiced over the summer. When the team registered to play in the fall, Christiane and another woman were left off the roster; the team organizer had decided they weren't good enough.

Once off the sidelines, Christiane was not going back. "We were miffed, so we formed Purple Haze. I didn't know the reference; a teammate chose the name.[1] The first game we show up, and I've dyed my hair purple. We're on the sidelines, and somebody says, 'Well, who is going to play goalkeeper?' I hadn't thought of that. I go into goal: no gloves, no pads, and no knowledge. There's a foul in the penalty box during the game, and I stopped the penalty shot. I put the ball down, and we are all high-fiving each other and jumping around. My friend who is playing on the opposite team says, 'Christiane, the ball is still live. Either pick it up or kick it out. You have to do something.' Oops!"

One aspect of the goalkeeping position that has held particular appeal for Christiane is the independence. Since she plays the game at some distance from the sidelines, the coaches can't instruct her in what to do; or if they try, she ignores them. Christiane has been willing to learn from other soccer players but has never cared for coaches, or for anyone trying to direct her life.

Born in the United Kingdom at the conclusion of World War II, Christiane attended Catholic boarding schools and then an all-girls college of London University. She would occasionally watch a cricket or rugby match, but never soccer. In elitist Britain, soccer was entertainment for the working class. Thrown out of college for bad behavior (she didn't provide details), Christiane headed for France and then Austria. A friend bet she wouldn't move to Lebanon and enroll in the Armenian College. Perversely, she did just that, and it was there she met her husband. Christiane transferred to the American University to complete her work. She and her husband resided in Lebanon for a few years until civil war broke out, then lived ten years in Saudi Arabia before moving to Massachusetts. When her husband's job took him back to the Middle East, he commuted while the family stayed in Massachusetts, and Christiane found soccer.

When Christiane's nephew visited from England, he took it in stride when one cousin had a class at 9:00 p.m. and another had an appointment with a friend at 10:00 p.m. But when Christiane dragged him out to watch her in an 11:00 p.m. soccer game he regarded the situation as "bizarre."

"I suppose it is," Christiane said, "but that's when you can play." Her nephew wrote home of the experience and noted that Christiane and her teammates "play awfully well, but it's like watching a glacier."

Like all goalies, Christiane has been injured repeatedly. A collision required eighteen stitches in her head. She has broken fingers multiple times when players stepped on her hands. When Christiane's ankles were in bad shape, she thought of Robert Parish, the star center for the Boston Celtics, who played during one of Boston's championship runs with two heavily sprained ankles. If Robert could sacrifice for the team, then she could, too. Once on the field the adrenaline kicks in and one doesn't feel the pain. But it does return. The Tuesday following her Sunday game was the worst, but she got through it. "Wednesday I was playing another game, so it all started over."

Christiane sees her injuries as battle wounds, and herself as a warrior on the field. Sometimes she will play fullback and is a self-proclaimed hip checker who can be rough if the situation requires it. One summer she played fullback on a coed team that included her daughter, son-in-law, and another daughter and her boyfriend. The son-in-law played sweeper, the last line of defense before the goalie. He had a great time being able to yell at and instruct his mother-in-law. In that context, Christiane avowed that she didn't mind and loved playing with family members. After a while, Christiane's daughters dropped out, and only Christiane and her son-in-law continued to play. The coed team traveled to New Orleans for a tournament and surprisingly put Christiane in as goalie. Christiane admitted the soccer wasn't much fun because the men's shots were so hard and difficult to stop. She did not play up to her usual high standards. Nevertheless, she enjoyed the chance to play soccer with her son-in-law.

After two decades of playing in Massachusetts, Christiane moved to the Olympia, Washington area. Her husband had died, and she wanted to be near her daughter and grandchildren. Sadly, it meant leaving her soccer friends behind. Finding a team in her new home proved difficult. At seventy Christiane wasn't thrilled about joining an over-40 coed team. "I watched a few games. They play in the pouring rain. Oh, my God. I don't want to do that. I'm such a wuss. I'd rather play in snow than rain. I've played on frozen fields, and I've played through a bit of rain, but not this kind of rain. Just bucketing down." To play over-50 women's soccer, she would have to drive to Tukwila, a minimum one-hour trip each way.

Christiane met up with several of her old teammates to play in the 2016 Adult Soccer Fest (Vets Cup) in Denver. At the time, she was not sure whether she would try to play regularly in Washington, or whether this was her last time on a soccer field.

Debby

Debby Bowman's goalie career was short, but intense. When a neighbor asked Debby if she'd be interested in trying soccer, she thought the woman was out of her mind. Debby was thirty-eight; why would she want to play? In retrospect, she said it was a "stupid thing to think." Her neighbor persisted and cajoled Debby into playing pickup soccer for one summer. She enjoyed it so much that she signed up for two teams that fall. The Red Tops was one of the teams that selected her. Debby thought the team must be desperate to choose someone who didn't know how to play. She stayed on the team for years, and some of her ex-teammates are still her very good friends. Over more than two decades, the team scheduled an annual ski trip to West Virginia. As the years wore on, the women did less and less skiing, but more drinking and more laughing. Eventually, they bowed to reality. They still made the trip, but skiing was not on the agenda.

The second team Debby joined disbanded after one season. She didn't know the team was folding until the night before

British Ladies' Football Club in 1895. Nettie Honeyball is second from the left in the top row.

You mean a <u>woman</u> can open it ?

Alcoa Aluminum advertises its new HyTop twist-off
bottle cap in 1953.

Soccer teams compete in their first season, circa 1977.
Courtesy of Joan Liston

Virginia women feed lunch to RNMCB-23 (Sea-
bees) during grading at Pine Ridge, circa 1985.
Courtesy of Ruth Walton

The author inexpertly traps the ball, circa 1983.
Courtesy of Peter Horvath[1]

One of several women on the field playing with
a knee brace during an over-50 tournament.
Courtesy of Harald Buchholz[2]

Teammates are wearing pink ribboned breast cancer
awareness soccer socks for Christine Nolan (center).
Courtesy of Robin Peterson

Determined women fight for the ball.
Courtesy of Harald Buchholz

Women hustle on hot, humid day. The
high temperature of the artificial turf, estimated at 120F to 140F, melted shoes.
Courtesy of Harald Buchholz

Goalkeeper Dawn Cole (center front) and teammates
celebrate gold at the 2016 San Diego Senior Games.
The game was decided in a penalty kick shootout.
Courtesy of Dawn Cole

Lois Kessin with Seamus Malin
at their induction into the New
England Soccer Hall of Fame
Courtesy of Jacob Franke[3]

Some of the participants in Women's Over-70 competition at the 2017 Las Vegas Friendship Tournament
Courtesy of J. Tyge O'Donnell[4]

spring registration forms were due. Debby scrambled to find a place to play and at the last minute begged her way onto a team. It wasn't a good fit, and she again had to find a new squad. Debby played for two additional teams before settling with the PW Rebels. Debby didn't much care for the Rebels, but at least they let her play: fullback, midfield, or "wherever they could hide me" so her lack of skills did not hurt the team.

Friends and family repeatedly told Debby she was crazy to play soccer and warned she was bound to get hurt. Her mother was among her critics. However, her parents and her children attended one of her soccer matches at Glasgow Middle School on a rock-strewn, clumps-of-grass-and-dirt field. Debby played fullback. While near the half-field line, she booted the ball down the field toward the opposing goal, hoping a teammate would get the ball. Instead, the ball bounced a few times before slowing and rolling on the hard-as-nails dirt. The ball's path would skew at every encounter with a small rock. Perhaps it was even redirected by a wayward tuft of grass as it evaded the goalie, slipped by the post, and rolled into the goal. A garbage goal, but it proved to be the game-winner. Embarrassingly, Debby's parents wanted to celebrate her achievement and took her to dinner.

Scheduled to play in a tournament, the PW Rebels found itself in a bind when the goalkeeper canceled at the last minute. The coach told Debby she was playing goalie, a position she'd been trying to learn but had never played. It was a disaster. "I screwed up four goals. I let one go between my legs. I looked away. I got distracted. I was under so much pressure because these women were serious. They were out for blood. I totally screwed up."

Resolving that she wouldn't let that happen again, Debby attended a soccer camp where she learned how to play goalkeeper. Months later, she was vindicated. Playing goalie against several women who had seen her disastrous performance at the tournament, Debby was outstanding. Typically the Rebels would lose 5-0 against such a talented team, but Debby let in only a single goal. Only one of her opponents showed class and complemented Debby on her great play, but even she was demonstrably miffed that her team had not scored more goals.

The PW Rebels' coach from England had an uncontrollable temper. At various times, he'd been red-carded and thrown out of games, and been suspended by the league. Debby left the team, happy to go somewhere less volatile. Finally, the board of directors had enough of the coach and banished him from the league.

In the less-skilled women's games, goalies often stay close to their own goal, rarely straying outside the goalie box. Debby adopted a free-ranging style and was often found well up the field, sometimes as far as the midfield line. She'd played long enough that she knew which players could kick the ball over her head and into the goal from beyond the half-field line. There weren't many who could. She was beaten at times, but more often gave her team an advantage. Acting as another field player, she could beat opponents to the ball and turn the play around. One of her more nervous teammates screamed at Debby when she played outside the box, but she didn't care. Most of her teammates figured that if someone was willing to play goalie, that person could play the position any way she liked. "It's boring being goalkeeper if you just stand there," Debby said. "I wanted to do something."

At one time Debby played on five teams—three outdoor teams and two indoor teams—both in goal and on the field. She also played summer soccer, a glorified pickup game where one could play three one-hour games in a row. During an otherwise unremarkable summer game, Debby spotted a lobbed ball heading for the goal box. She came out to the top of the box to catch the ball, and while she had both arms up in the air and was unprotected, an opposing player crashed into her. Perhaps the woman was hoping Debby would drop the ball, but the play was acutely dangerous.

Although naturally competitive, Debby displayed a laid-back attitude on the field. Heck, they were all older women. There was neither money nor college scholarships at stake. Nobody was going to award them a one-of-a-kind crystal trophy. Why get upset over the game?

The audaciousness of a hit that could have broken her neck or back drove Debby over the edge. She was scared. And she was livid. She grabbed the ball and threw it as hard as she could at the woman's head. "I wanted to kill her. I really wanted to hurt her. It was so sick." The referee red-carded the woman, throwing her off the field. As for Debby? She had retaliated and could also be carded. The referee took her aside and explained he knew she'd been severely provoked. There would be no card.

For years afterward, Debby avoided the woman. She couldn't help feeling angry about the incident, and she couldn't forgive the recklessness. One day she spotted the woman wearing a protective face mask for a broken nose. Debby felt a sense of satisfaction. After all, there was a good chance the woman's rash actions had caused her injury.

After a dozen years of playing all out, Debby gave up the game, while she could still walk. "The early years, I never wanted to quit. I would say, 'I'm going to be playing soccer in a wheelchair. I'm going to play until I break every bone in my body. Never gonna quit.'" But her body quit on her.

During a match, when the goalie dives to stop a shot but doesn't control the ball, it can dribble away. While still on the ground, she must gather her legs underneath her body and push off again toward the rolling ball. When Debby failed to control a shot, she couldn't make the second push to reach the ball because her knee would collapse. She had worked in a job for nineteen years where she used her left leg and knee in operating heavy machinery. Add to that the wear and tear of soccer, and her knee wore out. After arthroscopy surgery on her knee, Debby's orthopedist said, "I'm not going to tell you not to play anymore, but there are only so many years on your knees. You can use them however you want." Debby's last few seasons had not been as enjoyable as previous years. She was having more trouble handling the heat and humidity. It seemed like the women's games were increasingly pushed into later and later time slots. In her younger years, Debby wouldn't think twice about heading out to play an 11:00 p.m. indoor soccer game. But now? Old teammates had quit because of injuries and illnesses, and the team was not as supportive as it once was. So she gave it up: the soccer, not the friendships. Women she met through soccer remain Debby's closest friends. "They would do anything for you."

Dolly

Dolly Scott is ninety years old. Rumor is that she gave up soccer at age eighty-two when she needed a pacemaker. It's not true. Dolly did have a pacemaker implanted, but she continued to play soccer and basketball.

Sports have intertwined Dolly's life. In high school in Pennsylvania, Dolly played basketball, field hockey, and ran track. While raising six children in California, Dolly played softball. When her son started playing soccer, she became a referee. And at age fifty she decided to step on the soccer field as a player.

When people speak of Dolly, of all she has done, the term irrepressible comes to mind. Not only is Dolly infamous across Southern California, but women in Washington state also know Dolly. Anyone who played in a sporting event with or against Dolly would be hard pressed to forget her voluble exhilaration.

Dolly played coed and women's soccer, competed in tournaments, founded leagues, refereed youth and men's games, and was enthusiastic throughout. At the California Senior

Games, she would play with her soccer team as well as compete for medals in track and field events, basketball, and free throw shooting.

Dolly and her basketball team, the San Diego Splash, won gold medals in the National Senior Games in 2009 and 2011. Afterward, Dolly quit basketball for a while but was encouraged to return by her teammates. "The first game I came back, this girl who was a very good basketball player pushed my arm. I knew it wasn't a foul, but I almost fell. I said, 'Stop the game. I'm not going to play anymore. I do not want to get hurt.'" Dolly had never had any problems with injuries, but recently she'd seen a number of her older friends fall and break wrists or arms. "I said, 'Do I want this? No, I don't think so.'" Mother of six, grandmother of nine and great-grandmother of five, Dolly walked away from both basketball and soccer that day. She was eighty-four years and nine-months old, and still going strong.

Joan Newton, Dolly's friend, noted that even after quitting soccer, Dolly would still come to watch her old team play and cheer them on. Only recently has Dolly stopped attending games, no longer confident in driving long distances. "She was fabulous," Joan declared. "A tough lady. The [women's] program wouldn't be what it is if it hadn't been for her."

Daisy

With golden hair and skin, sparkling hazel eyes, and enthusiasm for life, Daisy Atiles seems decades younger than her actual sixty-one years. An aura of pure joy surrounds her in and around a soccer field, and she is determined to continue playing the game, even though it could kill her.

Daisy moved to the Sacramento area as a young child when her parents divorced. She lived in "a very rough and drug-infested neighborhood that preyed on the new, the innocent, and the un-suspecting." With no other Puerto Rican families nearby, Daisy gravitated toward the Mexican community. "Mostly because they were all about family, protected their own, looked more like me, and spoke Spanish. My family had been fractured [and] I was frantically looking for some normalcy in my life." Perhaps more than most teenagers, Daisy felt the angst of not knowing who she was or where she fit in. In May of her junior year of high school, that changed.

"I had a Spanish teacher who took us to a Cinco de Mayo event. I was looking around, enjoying the food, and some women were playing [soccer]. I thought, 'Oh wow, that's pretty cool.'"

Her Spanish teacher's husband, Carlos, coached a number of the women who were playing. He noticed Daisy's interest, approached her, and asked if she wanted to play. Daisy's reply: "I don't even know what soccer is."

Despite her ignorance, Carlos gave Daisy a few basic instructions and put her in the game. What Daisy lacked in skill, she more than made up for in pure speed, and she proceeded to notch several goals. The goalie, known as *La Aranha Negra* (The Black Widow), was incensed that this first-time player had scored on her. How could that happen? When asked exactly how many goals she tallied in that first game, Daisy laughed. "Oh, gosh, I couldn't even tell you."

Since that day, soccer has been the passion in Daisy's life. "There's been a lot of turmoil in my life," she said. "Soccer gave me a whole new breath of air and kept me out of trouble."

It was 1973, the year after the passage of Title IX, and Daisy's high school Norte Del Rio offered soccer only for boys. But that fall in her senior year, Daisy and another girl tried out for and made the soccer team. She was elated, but it didn't last.

"The other teams didn't like me scoring on them. The boys didn't; it was a disgrace. My boyfriend at the time, my very controlling Mexican from Mexico, told me I couldn't play. So as a Latina, I obeyed ... I quit."

Daisy did play on a women's team. Following her display of talent at the Cinco de Mayo festival, Carlos had asked her to join his team, Maya, which played in La Liga Latina Americana, a local women's soccer league. Men in the area liked to bet on the outcome and on the players, notably who would make the most goals. Daisy was always among the top scorers with over fifty goals per season.

In the July after graduating from high school, Daisy began community college and, at age eighteen, married her high school sweetheart. He was still controlling, and still didn't like her playing soccer. Any soccer. But Daisy wouldn't give up playing with her women's team, even when he began manhandling her.

"He turned physically abusive after I had my first child. We went through a lot of arguing. Soccer was the only thing I did. I was pretty much confined to my home. At some point, he took over [coaching] the team so he could keep an eye on me. I played for him for a bit. But soccer was all I did."

It couldn't continue. At age twenty-three, Daisy had the marriage annulled and became a single parent of a young daughter. Her soccer skills contributed to her ability to support herself: she became a trainer, instructing others in how to play the game. A naturally gifted player, Daisy was also an astute observer of the game and a great teacher. Word of her capabilities spread within the soccer community and new students sought her tutelage.

Daisy lost her soccer team when La Liga Latina Americana was forced to disband; the park they used for games had been converted to a marina. Fortunately, Daisy discovered the Sacramento Women's Soccer League and found teams that wanted her capabilities. She proved to be a popular player and often was asked to join teams for tournaments.

Daisy married again, to a man who understood her soccer passion. He hired "someone else to help run our construction business while I trained, traveled, and played." Without his support, "there is no way that I could have achieved all that I have in the soccer industry."

In 1993, Daisy formed a women's team, Sacramento Select United, to compete in the Umbro National Championships. She contacted her old coach Carlos to help. Most of the players were over forty, but the oldest competitive tier was over-30. "We advanced through consolidated tournaments for the State Championship. Regional competition [was] against Washington, Nevada, New Mexico, and Utah, which we won." The National Championship games were in Dallas, Texas and with the team in good form, they bested the other regional champions and advanced to the final game.

Although she was a natural goal scorer, Daisy had become interested in the challenges of the goalie position. With the approval of Carlos, she not only trained with the team in her striker position but also participated in goalie training. "It was the night before the competition when Carlos was announcing the player's positions that he sprung on me that I would be the starting goalie!" Perhaps Carlos remembered how Daisy responded to the challenge the first time she ever played, or maybe he just wanted to shake up the team. "Surprised the heck out of me. I was petrified and felt horrible for Tania, the real goalie."

So Daisy's first ever game as the goalkeeper was for a national championship. In the second half, Tania minded the nets while Daisy returned to her normal position as striker. Sacramento Select United won convincingly, and Daisy was surprised at being named the Most Valuable Player. "I feel that we were all MVPs for bringing the first women's over-30 National Championship to Sacramento."

Also in 1993, Daisy was asked to be the assistant women's soccer coach at Cosumnes River College (CRC) in Elk Grove, California. "The head coach, Liz Belyea played in the Sacramento Valley Women's Soccer League. I probably played with her in a couple of tournaments; I don't even remember, but she knew of me and asked me if I would come by and check it out. And I did."

Liz was astonished that Daisy had not been certified as a coach. "She encouraged me to get my national coaching license. I didn't know anything about it at that time." Since she was knowledgeable about the game, Daisy skipped the preamble of obtaining her F, E or D license and signed up for a course to earn the C license. "The USSF [United States Soccer Federation] national licensing candidates consisted of fifty people from all over the world and I was one of five women attempting to [obtain a] license in a predominantly men's soccer world." A few years later she returned as one of three women vying for a USSF National B license. Again, Daisy was successful.

Daisy continued to coach at CRC through 1999. One year, finding the team short of players, the coach convinced Daisy, at age forty-two, to take courses at CRC and play on the team. She did, competing with and scoring against women half her age. The girls on the team voted her in as their captain.

Playing soccer for such a long time, Daisy has had her share of injuries. "My ACL on my right knee has been repaired three times," she said. "And I ended up having the total reconstruction of the patella tendon. So that is four [surgeries] on the right knee and one on the left knee." Daisy admitted the injuries stemmed from her "passionate and aggressive style of play: sliding tackles, bicycle kicks, sprints, and diving headers."

In 2004, Daisy was felled again. Not by a soccer injury, but by a pulmonary embolism in both lungs. Extensive tests confirmed that she had a genetic predisposition to forming blood clots. "I later found out that the embolisms were many and bilateral, making it even more dangerous to compete in a contact sport [like soccer]." The next five years were hell. "I was in and out of hospitals and in and out of death. It was pretty ugly. I gained forty-five pounds because I went from playing soccer four times per week to lying in bed 99 percent of the time. It was bad." One clot broke off and went to her heart. Even when Daisy felt better, her doctor advised she not play soccer as she could drop dead at any moment. Daisy was devastated.

Soccer was Daisy's passion, and without it, she became depressed. She sought out a pulmonary specialist and explained her situation. "I told him, 'I just want to play soccer.' And he said, 'You know, I have a lot of athletes like you. They have a passion for something and want to do it regardless.' He said, 'Daisy, go ahead and play. You could die tomorrow. All I want you to do is no more headers, no more slide tackles, no more bicycle kicks, nothing.'" A dark cloud rose from Daisy's soul.

Daisy returned to the field. Because of all the knee injuries, she no longer had the speed to burn by players, and with her medical condition, she certainly could not try going through them anymore. Daisy had to change her game completely. Instead of playing up front, she moved to the wing where she had the time and room to maneuver. From this position, she could survey the field and pick out a pass or a through ball for the forwards to run onto and, hopefully, score. Daisy admitted revamping her game was "difficult. But I didn't care because I was going to be on the pitch, so it didn't matter what I had to do."

Daisy was asked to play for Still Kickin', an over-50 team formed to play in tournaments, including the World Master's Cup. "The long travels [for international tournaments] would be too dangerous for me to attempt, so I helped, along with others, train the team." In the 2013 World Master's Cup in Turin, Italy, Still Kickin' finished second, earning Daisy a silver medal.

After forty years of playing, training, and coaching soccer, Daisy's love for the sport is undimmed. Her children absorbed her devotion to the game and like Daisy, have given back through coaching and training others. Daisy's ardor and experience led her in 2013 to a position with the Sacramento Republic FC, a newly formed team in the United Soccer League. In their first year of playing, the Republic won the league championship.

Daisy takes an anticoagulant and is regularly monitored, but each day could be her last. "I have dealt with this for almost seventeen years now and have been in and out of the hospitals, poked and probed, but I am still playing, and for that, I can only thank God. I have come to the conclusion that I have been put on this earth to teach and to learn. I will continue to do that until the Big Guy upstairs needs me there." As for soccer, it "will probably remain as part of my life until the end and for that, I am so grateful."

TEN
Camaraderie

For many women, the attraction of soccer is as much about the social interaction as it is about the sport. In that way, soccer teams replace garden clubs or book groups as an excuse to enjoy the company of other women and leave work and household responsibilities behind.

Though of disparate personalities, backgrounds, professions, and educational levels, each woman on Carrie Hood's San Diego soccer team was a tomboy in her youth and craved the opportunity to play sports. The women shared a passion for competing and a joy of being on a team. They christened themselves The Family, because of "the caring attitude we had towards each other. Not all teams were like that," Carrie said. After decades on the field, the women are no longer playing soccer, but The Family endures. They gather for important occasions such as weddings, birthdays, and funerals. Watching the U.S. women's team play soccer on TV provides an excuse for the women to meet up and catch up. Sometimes, they get together just because it's been too darn long since they've seen each other.

Soccer pals have become as important as family to Sharon Murray. She and several of her Sacramento, California teammates have formed The Adventurers Club and regularly meet up for hiking and other outdoor activities. When the demands of grandchildren or other obligations don't allow them the time for an adventure, they still make sure they get together, even if it is only for a cup of coffee, or two, or three.

Not all husbands understand or approve of their wives playing soccer and spending time with soccer friends. Anna Graham's husband more than once admonished her that, "If you play a sport, you are never going to get anything done around here. You'll let everything go." Anna didn't care. Housework bored her, and she was willing to live with a messy house. Besides, she had to play sports and, just as importantly, had to be with her friends. Her marriage didn't last, but her soccer friendships did.

In contrast, Gene Forsythe's husband has been supportive of her soccer mania. He has never played and doesn't entirely understand the infectiousness of the game or the camaraderie of the women, but is more apt to encourage Gene than complain. As with Carrie, Sharon, and Anna, Gene's teammates are like sisters, and Gene feels she is part of a large, extended family. "I have 200 or more women that I could hug and share stuff with whenever I see them. All ages, too. We play pickup games all the time. We spend fifteen, twenty minutes before every game just socializing, meeting up, how are you doing, what's happening with you. We've gone through births and deaths. We've gone through cancers and treatments, We've gone through every kind of possible thing, supporting everybody. We're all sistahs, soul sisters who love a particular sport."

At age seventy-five, forty years after first stepping on the field, Carol Watson still plays on the Go-Getters. Her team competes in an over-40 division, and Carol is one of the oldest players on the field. Many of the teammates she played with early in her career have given up the game, but they regularly get together for a walk, for biking, or for whatever strikes their fancy. Each year, about twenty of the women travel to Palm Springs for a girls-only vacation. Soccer brought them together, and the bonds of friendship forged over many years help to keep them young.

None of these stories are unusual. Many female soccer players note that their teammates, even those no longer playing, are present at significant life events, travel and spend time doing activities together, and just enjoy being with each other.

Rose Noga used to play six tournaments each year in addition to traveling extensively with her soccer sisters for non-tournament vacations. "They know me better than anybody. They love me unconditionally, and I love them unconditionally." She has experienced a closeness with these women that even surpasses her love for the game. Rose has advised her teammates that for her funeral—she hopes it's not imminent—she'd like her soccer friends from all the teams she's played on to wear their jerseys and be pallbearers or follow her casket. She'd like them to toss the medals and ribbons she has won on her casket. It would be, she said, "very cool."

Perhaps soccer friendships extend beyond the grave. One woman asked Christine Nolan, a former teammate who was dying of cancer, to save a place in heaven on her new soccer team. If she could just be on Christine's team, she would, "play any position, even goalie. Just not for the whole game."

A few years ago, Dawn Cole struggled with Hodgkin's Lymphoma. She could not play soccer due to the port installed in her chest to receive the chemo drugs. Her teammates, some of whom she's known for twenty years, rallied around by taking Dawn to chemotherapy when her family wasn't available. A few years later, one of her teammates was diagnosed with pancreatic cancer, and Dawn "went wig shopping with her. The team set up a meal train to provide meals to the husband when she was having treatment." Since Dawn's team frequently travels together for tournaments, when the women recruit new players they are as concerned about personality fit as they are about ball skills.

As the women age, it is a given that skills decline and at some point, a player will become a detriment to the team. On Dawn's team, the women want to stay around, even if they are a handicap. The team has devised a code for such a situation. The struggling player will be asked if she wants to coach. In other words, "it's time to hang up the cleats, but we still love you and want to have you around." Conceivably, the team could end up with a dozen or more "coaches."

Lynn Naftel's husband figured he was always behind soccer in his wife's affections. She denied it, but admitted that soccer was "way up there." When she lost her husband in 2013, soccer and soccer friends provided the support and comfort Lynn needed. For her, the game has been a vehicle for cultivating friendships far and wide. Tournaments are "one huge reunion where I get the opportunity to visit with ladies I have met coast to coast." Many of Lynn's teammates have become dear friends beyond the soccer field. She stays in touch with women up and down the west coast and eastward all the way to Virginia. Several years ago, eight team members decided it was time to quit soccer, but not to forsake their teammates. The women formed the Merry Mess. "Quarterly, two gals plan an activity; we all get together for hours of fun, reminiscing, and catching up on each other's lives." Lynn currently plays with other women in their seventies. They hold their own playing against women as young as forty-five. Lynn, too, speaks of these women as sisters.

Kathy Downer lived in Orange County, California for years. "I don't think I had a female friend since college. All my work associates were men, and I didn't socialize with them outside of work." Kathy jelled with her soccer teammates, staying with them for more than fifteen years. She and others started a weekday morning pickup game for all ages. It evolved to two mornings a week, frequently attracting up to sixteen players. Over time some of the women became empty nesters and returned to the workplace. To Kathy's dismay, the pick-up game struggled to survive. "I didn't realize what a huge thing it is to have female friends until my husband was dying. The emotional support I received was unbelievable. And the players from over the years showed up in force for the memorial soccer event for him." When she subsequently moved to San Diego, it was the friends she'd met through California soccer tournaments that helped her to adjust. The first time she stepped on the field with her new teammates, Kathy "felt right at home."

Playing at the Veteran's Cup in Wilmington, North Carolina, Janice Akridge met Belinda Crawford whom she describes as "a riot." Belinda taught Janice how to play pinochle. Less than two months later, Janice's husband passed away unexpectedly. He was only fifty-two. Janice was a basket case. Belinda called, offering to bring food, but Janice was already overwhelmed with food gifts. She asked Belinda instead to invite her and other soccer friends over for pinochle. "The four of us have been playing pinochle ever since. We try to play once a month. We're four very different people, but we have soccer in common, and we have a lot of fun."

As to be expected, life was very hard for Janice for a long, long time. She credits Belinda for making her laugh and picking up her spirits during that dark period. She and Belinda have become as close as sisters. Janice avowed that the soccer relationships mean more to her than the game. "We'll take care of each other. We might complain about each other on the field, but we'll take care of each other if anybody needs anything." And it's not just teammates who become friends. "It's funny how in soccer you go up against somebody on another team, and you can't stand them out there, you just don't like them. Then you see them in the grocery store, and you're best friends. It's just that on the field you're so intense." Janice noted with regret a time in her life when she was not happy and was super aggressive on the soccer field. Of one particular player, Janice said, "I just couldn't stand her, and I knew she couldn't stand me. When my husband died, she called me and told me how sorry she was. I was just shocked, and it had an impact on me. It brings me to tears even thinking about it. Now she and I talk … but we still don't like playing against each other."

Healing a Broken Heart

With the first game of the San Diego Senior Games tournament done, an exhausted Sarah Nash settled herself on the grass and began to talk about soccer, a sport she's played for over twenty years. Sarah loves soccer, but playing has also become therapy for her broken heart.

Sarah first took an interest in soccer while living on Okinawa with her husband and four children. Before the move away from the United States, the kids had been swimmers, and her daughters were active in gymnastics. However, there were no gymnastic classes available near their home in Okinawa. Amy, Sarah's second daughter, asked if she could play soccer with the boys. Sarah acceded. "She was a fantastic player." When the family returned to Virginia, the girls continued to play soccer. Sarah, age forty, also took up the sport.

Amy played on elite teams in Virginia. She attended Radford University on an athletic scholarship and became a standout on its Division II team. After graduation, Amy moved to California, played semi-pro soccer, and met her future husband. A few years later, she obtained her master's degree in occupational therapy to work with young children. In her free time, Amy ran marathons to honor young people with leukemia. With her two children in tow, Amy would attend her mother's soccer tournaments to cheer for Sarah and her team, just as Sarah had once supported her. From time to time, Amy would venture to offer her mother a little expert advice.

In 2013, Amy was diagnosed with a rare neuroendocrine gastric carcinoma.

Sarah's soccer friends were "super-supportive" in a thousand ways, big and small, including holding fund-raising events for Amy. When the Radford University soccer coach, Ben Sohrabi, informed his squad that a former Radford player was battling cancer, the women stepped forward to help with fund-raising even though none of them knew Amy personally. Amy had played at Radford. Therefore, she was family. Though she fought courageously, the cancer was merciless. An all too short seven months after her diagnosis, Amy Nash Touchet, wife and mother of two children, was dead. She was just thirty-three-years old.[1]

Sarah's eyes glistened and her voice faltered when telling Amy's story. Those within hearing distance shed tears. "It was a terrible, terrible thing. You don't get choices in life. My mom is in a nursing home. She had a stroke, and she's eighty-eight. She says to me, 'Amy's dead. Amy's not here. I don't understand: why am I here? Why Amy?' I say, 'Mom, you don't get choices.' No choices. But she loved life. Amy was a great kid."

With the love and support of her teammates, Sarah plays on. "Amy would want me to play. She would want me to play. She was number eight. Usually, I wear her number. It's my therapy. Absolutely the best therapy." Sarah gestured toward the field. "This is where my girl is."

Forever Teammates

Paula Hockster was among the women who founded the Great Lakes Women's Soccer League in 1980. Raised in Detroit, Paula attended Catholic schools whose "idea of sports was maybe you got to go outside on the playground on Friday if you were good all week." In high school, Paula tried out for field hockey at the suggestion of her gym teacher. She made the team but had a job in the afternoon so she couldn't play.

Paula later began her soccer career on a coed team. "After doing it for a while, we felt like the guys were not letting us play. We weren't incorporated into the game. If you happened to get the ball, you'd better do something [good] because you were not likely to get it again." She thought it would be great if she could play on a team with just women.

Paula heard about an effort by a woman in Lansing, Mj Wickens, to set up a woman's soccer league. Paula contacted Mj, they held several conversations by phone, and then met to discuss what it would take to organize an association. The two women began by holding a soccer tournament for women in the summer of 1979. Four teams participated from Ann Arbor (Mj), Huron Valley (Paula), Plymouth, and Toledo. During the fall and winter, Paula, Mj, and other interested women founded a league. It began operations the following May with five teams. Within two years the league had seventeen teams. When Paula moved away from the area in 1987, the Great Lakes Women's Soccer League included twenty-seven teams in three divisions.

Paula lived for nine years in Southern Virginia. There were few soccer teams, and she had to travel great distances for games. Paula chose instead to play volleyball, both beach and indoor. Having attained an associate degree when she was younger, Paula returned to school, attending Christopher Newport to obtain a degree in information technology. As a Division III school, Christopher Newport was allowed to field teams with players over twenty-five years of age. Paula became a walk-on to the women's volleyball team, where she played for two years. The year following graduation, she became assistant coach of the team.

In 1995 Paula and her husband moved to Pasadena, California and joined a coed soccer team. Paula played indoor soccer too, and founded a women's league for seven-a-side teams with no age divisions. A handful of Paula's friends from Michigan planned to come out for the 1999 Women's World Cup Final in the Rose Bowl and made arrangements with Paula, who lived within walking distance of the Rose Bowl, to meet, walk to the game together, and have dinner afterward. She didn't see them or speak with them again for another five years until one Friday night when she received a call from Rose Noga. "I'm in San Diego," Rose said, "and I know this is a weird question to ask you, but what are you doing this weekend?" Rose was in California for a soccer tournament, and her team was short players. The team organizer, a San Diego based player, asked Rose if she knew anybody who might be persuaded to join them at the last minute. Searching through her address book, Rose discovered that Paula lived within driving distance. So she called. Paula explained she had only been playing seven-a-side and was out of practice for the much larger field. Rose asked her to come anyway.

Paula drove down to San Diego that evening and was put up at the home of Rose's friend. "I played soccer with them," Paula said, "and became friends with all these women in San Diego." Since then the women have invited Paula to join them for tournaments across the country—presumably with more than a twelve-hour notice. Paula found herself in a similar position to Rose's a few years later when she was in Virginia Beach for a tournament. Paula called Mj Wickens who was still in Michigan. Mj flew down to Virginia and the women played soccer together for the first time in more than twenty-five years. Recently, Paula has not been able to join her San Diego friends for tournaments as her husband is fighting lung cancer. Her San Diego teammates call her regularly and offer her opportunities for quick weekend getaways. Paula's Pasadena teammates are likewise supportive. Most of them are twenty to thirty years younger than Paula and are very sweet to her. "Just really nice women," Paula said.

<u>Breaking Apart</u>

Anyone who has played team sports knows that camaraderie isn't automatic. As players' behavior ranges outside the norm of the group, they become more tolerated than liked. There are those who are chronically late to games and those who talk incessantly to themselves throughout the game. Some women play aggressively, but, like a spinning wheel, get nowhere. Finally, there are women who, even after years on the field, don't have a clue how to play the game and don't understand the rules. Some behaviors send teammates over the edge, like a woman who bitches and moans when she thinks she's been fouled, or a player who thinks she knows what everyone should do and yells instructions at her teammates both on and off the field.

Coaches who cross the boundaries of acceptable behavior likewise can destroy camaraderie. Tom coached his wife's team and left her and their four children for another player on the team. The group disbanded. Dick was so desperate to win that he brought ineligible players into the team. Many women quit the team in disgust.

Harriet coached a team that competed annually in a major tournament. She promulgated a rule that to be eligible for the tournament team, a woman must play with the league team for the spring season. The requirement ensured the women had adequate time together before the competition. Teresa, Harriet's wife and a long time member of the tournament team, chose to play with another team during one spring season. Nevertheless, Teresa was part of the tournament team and played. The fallout from this precipitated a few complaints and a significant reduction in playing time for several players. One player was appalled at the behind the scene intrigue that led to the disruption. "We are in our sixties and couldn't even talk about it." She took a season off from playing and is undecided whether to return to the team.

Fortunately, Tom, Dick and Harriet stories are rare. Through soccer, many women found teams they could play on for many years and soul mates with whom they could share their lives.

ELEVEN
In Sickness and in Health

MIA HAMM, ONE OF the best female soccer players of all time, played in the inaugural season of the WUSA professional women's soccer league while recovering from shoulder surgery. After a disappointing season for her team, Mia required surgery again, this time for damaged cartilage in her knee. In her own words: "Suddenly, I faced surgery, several months of painful rehab, and my first major professional hurdle: Would I be the same player I'd been before the injury? Would I be able to turn as hard, to run as fast? Soccer was my life … I was now presented with the possibility that I might not fully recover, and I wasn't sure that I had anything else to contribute to the world."[1]

Women injured playing recreational soccer face a similar uncertainty. While soccer is not a livelihood, for many a woman it is a significant part of her social life. The fear of losing precious moments with friends, the euphoria from playing, and the joy of being part of a team move these women to herculean efforts to return to the soccer field.

Decades ago Mary McCafferty needed a knee replacement. At the time, doctors recommended that following surgery one should avoid high impact sports like football, soccer, jogging, and basketball as these activities could contribute to the early failure of artificial joints. Mary didn't care; she wanted to play soccer. She rehabilitated her knee and, in her fifties, returned to the soccer field.

Years later, a study compared patients with knee implants who were model patients, and those like Mary who ignored their doctors' orders. Research determined that seven years after knee surgery there were no significant differences in wear or mechanical failure between the two groups. In fact, those that took part in the forbidden sports had better functionality with their knee implants than those who listened to their doctors.[2]

In 2016 and well into her seventies, Mary had a stroke. She's not revealed what advice she received from her doctor, but to the amazement of her soccer friends, she returned to play a few months later. Mary's only concession to her most recent health issue was to limit how far she'd drive to games. If she ever stops playing, the decision will be Mary's, not that of someone in the medical profession.

Penny Schulstad has overcome a host of knee injuries. In her forties, she tripped over the ball on a bumpy dirt field and blew out her knee. Her doctor would not do knee surgery on anyone her age. As a consequence, Penny spent six weeks on crutches letting the knee heal naturally. She vividly remembers attending a game during that period and, watching her teammates from the sidelines, being overcome with sadness at the thought that she might never play again. The experience was so painful that she didn't attend any more games. Penny lost significant muscle mass such that when she was able to walk without crutches, she spent months and months rehabbing her knee. Finally, her doctor agreed she could try jogging, and for the first time Penny believed that she might be able to return to soccer. A long year after her injury, Penny took the field, wearing a Lenox Hill knee brace. Her brace was a later version of one developed in the

1960s expressly for professional football player Joe Namath.[3] At the time of Penny's injury, the primary market for the product was the American football player. She found the brace was ill-suited to someone of her short stature. Because it provided inadequate stability, Penny eventually tore her ACL. This time she wouldn't settle for anything less than surgery. Penny recovered from the ACL tear and was playing soccer again when she tore her meniscus, requiring surgery. Penny was back on the field, playing with seemingly no problems when she experienced a second meniscus tear, which required yet another surgery. Eventually, Penny was given a new knee brace that has kept her on the field for the past twenty-two years.

Karen Sharpe's story is eerily familiar: she tore her ACL playing indoor soccer, thought she'd never play again, had reconstructive surgery, and spent a year rehabbing before returning to play. A few years later she tore her meniscus in two places and had more surgery and rehab. Karen also has sliced her face open—seven stitches—and fractured her toe, which has led to arthritis. Karen gave up playing indoor soccer, the site of most of her injuries. She continued to play outdoors on three teams each season and tore her meniscus yet again. Fed up with surgeries, Karen opted to undertake a vigorous exercise program to strengthen her quads and glutes to stabilize her knees and hopefully prevent injury. Quitting soccer was not an option.

Joan Hunter-Brody, seventy-nine and a trim 5'6" with short gray hair, is a quasi-bionic soccer player. Over an eighteen-month period beginning in 2012, she had both hips and one knee replaced. Her new joints are "perfect," she said. "Why not play? The team is so good to me. I just love them so much. Her decades-younger teammates are more than happy that Joan is on the team. Joan acknowledges that because of the surgeries she, "had to skip a few seasons, but now I'm happy I can do it."

On a Super Bowl Sunday, Janice Akridge shattered her ankle. "I was fifty-four. We were playing out at Dulles SportsPlex, indoor.

A girl did take my left leg out, but I don't know, I just landed funny on my right foot, and you could hear it breaking ... and pop. So I broke three bones and dislocated it. It was very painful." Janice's foot dangled from her leg, ninety-degrees out from its normal position. Lying on the floor with her foot up in the air—she dared not lower it—Janice knew the injury was severe. Her teammates who immediately called for an ambulance.

Like other indoor soccer facilities, the Dulles SportsPlex fields were rimmed with low walls. To exit the playing area, one would open a small door in the wall and step over the eighteen-inch-tall sill. Flat on her back with a non-functioning ankle, Janice was unable to exit the field of play. "I couldn't put my leg down it hurt so bad. I was literally spinning on the floor going 'Ahhhh!' This girl on the other team comes up to me and says [in a snitty tone], 'If you get off the field we can continue our game.' I looked at her and said, 'You aren't going to be continuing your game because I am not getting off this field until somebody can support my leg.'"

The medics arrived in due time, but according to Janet, they bordered on inept. One inexplicably started to untie her laces to take off her shoe. Good soccer players ensure their cleats are a snug fit to provide maximum control over dribbling and shooting the ball. The cleats are often one size smaller than one's street shoe size. Janet knew there was no way to take her shoe off without grasping and manipulating the position of her foot. "No, no, no!" she screamed. "If you want that shoe off you're going to have to cut it off." Another medic then commented that come to think of it, he didn't think they were supposed to remove the shoe.

The medics couldn't give Janice anything for the pain. She asked if they would provide a pillow so she could lower her foot. They complied and removed her from the field on a stretcher. Lucky for Janet, the hospital's emergency room was relatively empty and she was attended to immediately. The dislocation was reduced, and her foot splinted. The next day she had surgery. "Now I've got three screws on one side, and this [other] side is a plate. You can see all the screws. And I think I have five or six bolts. I always wondered what would make me quit. I always wondered how do you quit? My Mom was always on me, 'Why can't you play golf? Why do you have to play soccer?' I thought I was done."

For two years Janice didn't do anything athletic. A former teammate visited her at home and finding Janice sitting on the couch, told her she looked pregnant. Janice knew she was right; she'd gained a lot of weight and was out of shape. The friendly insult was the impetus Janice needed to return to soccer. "But that's not why I play," she said. "I don't play for weight management. I was just getting depressed, not doing anything." Janice admits she is now more cautious, apt to back off a bit rather than always challenging for the ball. She recently began to play indoor soccer again but refuses to play on the field where she broke her ankle.

Cathy Blum survived a painful bout with cancer to return to the field. Subsequently, she was playing in a soccer tournament and was smacked by a ball or an elbow. Cathy came off the field, complaining her side hurt and that she would sit out the following game. Still feeling sore, Cathy nevertheless played in her team's third game of the tournament. Teammates Debbie Greenslit and Rita Wilkie recalled that weeks afterward Cathy visited the doctor and was x-rayed for her rib pain. The photos revealed that she had broken three ribs during the tournament. "It just shows you how tough people are who have gone through cancer, what capabilities they have," Debbie said, shaking her head. Moreover, it demonstrates the devotion of these women to the game and their teammates.

Catherine Noonan, another one of Rita's and Debbie's teammates, had atrial fibrillation, an irregular heartbeat. Catherine had a stroke and developed blindness in one eye.

Passionate about soccer, Catherine continued to play. "She just had to be on the right side of the line ... she had to see from the left," Rita said. Debbie noted that even with her physical limitations, Catherine played on competitive teams and could make the moves to dribble past players and deliver on-target passes.

Sixty and seventy-year-old women who continue to play soccer after hip replacements, knee replacements, assorted broken bones, and other injuries might be considered a testament to the efficacy of modern medicine. Those who know them, however, will say it's the love of the game and sheer determination that bring them back. Ironically, a number of these women have daughters who can no longer play soccer because of injuries.

The daughters learned the game as children and, if they were skilled, joined competitive teams, trained year round, traveled to distant tournaments, hoped for college scholarships, and dreamed of representing the United States on the women's national soccer team. Unfortunately, an anterior cruciate ligament (ACL) injury occurs at significantly higher rates in young females soccer players than males.[4] An ACL tear became almost a rite of passage for these girls. Concussions, ankle injuries, and assorted broken bones were other common injuries. Eager to compete again, these youngsters would press to return to the field before they were completely healed. The stress of unrelenting play took its toll. By their twenties and thirties, the young women were hobbled by damaged joints and had to give up the game. They are envious of their mothers who, in aging bodies, can still experience the thrill of playing.

The Big C

Anne Ruth Potter discovered soccer at age thirty-seven. The team experience was new to her, and a great delight. In her second year on the team, Anne was tripped near the goal, fell awkwardly, and broke her collarbone. While examining the x-rays of her shoulder, the radiologist discovered a tumor. Subsequent tests revealed Anne had thyroid cancer. Since Anne recently had run a marathon and believed herself to be perfectly healthy, she took the news hard. Her teammates rallied around. While undergoing treatment, Anne had little to no stamina. Her teammates wanted her to know that she was still part of the team and encouraged her to come to games in uniform. They would sub Anne into the game for a minute or two, which was all she could manage, and then sub her out. "My soccer teammates were amazing," Anne said. Her spirits soared when she was able to play, even for a short time. During one game after Anne had gone in and out several times, the opposing team complained: Anne's team wasn't breaking any rule, but the frequent substitutions were annoying. The referee was aware of Anne's situation and, as Anne recalled with great satisfaction, put the whiners in their place.

Not surprisingly, Anne has been loyal to her team; she has played on Ocean Motion for twenty-five years. For over-60 tournaments, she and Ocean Motion teammates compete under the name Three Score Galore. With the removal of her thyroid, Anne has difficulty dealing with the heat. This condition curtails her time on the field, particularly during weekend tournaments that involve two or three games each day. It is something she manages but doesn't dwell on. Her philosophy in life as in soccer is that whatever happens, move on to the next play. Forget about the past. And she does just that with a smile on her face, surrounded by teammates.

In 1988, Judy Jones blew out her ACL. Since she was over forty, the orthopedist rejected the standard procedures, but noted, "There is something I can try, but I don't know I'm willing to do it if you just go back on the soccer field and blow it out again." Judy responded by saying that when she couldn't play soccer anymore, she planned to return to tennis. What she didn't tell him was that she had no intention of giving up soccer. Her doctor performed a procedure on Judy's iliotibial band, "leaving the iliotibial band attached to the base of the knee but notching out a section that he braided and then secured to the knee to give it more stability," Judy said.[5] He left the ACL where it could knit back together. If the surgery were successful, he planned to write a paper on the procedure. Judy was put in a soft, thigh-to-ankle cast with hinges at the knee and was instructed to put no weight on the foot. Her surgery took place at the end of the spring soccer season, and she wore the cast for six weeks. By fall, she was back on the field, wearing a brace but playing nevertheless.

A year later, Judy was diagnosed with breast cancer. Her soccer season was cut short and she underwent surgery in October. During her chemotherapy treatment, Judy played soccer, although her doctor did not recommend it. At the time the benefits of exercise during cancer treatment had not been studied, and Judy may have been the first player in the Fairfax Women's Soccer Association to play through chemotherapy. "The team was really great through all of that," she said. While her speed and stamina suffered, she did what she could. Being outside and surrounded by teammates was a significant boost to her energy and a motivator for her to battle back to full fitness. Other women followed Judy's example and now moderate exercise is recommended during chemotherapy.

During her long soccer career, Judy became adept at ignoring the advice of doctors. Following arthroscopic surgery on her knee, Judy immediately started to kick a soccer ball to get in shape for tournament team tryouts. A victim of regular ankle sprains, Judy studied sports medicine, learning how to effectively tape her ankles for games. She had arthroscopic surgery a second time on her left knee, and then messed up her right knee, the good one, in a car accident. Almost as soon as she could move, she was once again chasing a soccer ball.

Never Give Up

On a warm, September afternoon, women on over-60 soccer teams fought for a gold medal at the California Senior Games. Alice Moore watched the games from the sidelines, both knees swaddled in large bandages and crutches near at hand. A regular player in the tournament, this year she had traveled down from her home in Reedley, California with her friend Margaret Danner to watch and cheer on the women.

A few weeks earlier, Alice had been in Denver, playing goalie on a women's team in the 2017 Adult Soccer Fest (aka Veteran's Cup). Alice was holding the other team scoreless when she launched herself at an incoming shot. She managed to knock the ball away, but an opposing player running for the ball was hit from behind and piled into Alice. Her kneecap was knocked sideways, and Alice's meniscus, cartilage, and knee tendons were all torn. She counted it as good fortune that she had already scheduled an MRI for after the tournament because one knee had been giving her problems. The doctor, who was familiar with Alice due to her frequent knee issues, warned her that he might not be able to fix the right knee. Alice opted for surgery on both knees and now, weeks later, was on the road to recovery.

As Alice told her story, quite a few women from various teams strolled over to where she was sitting and inquired as to how she was doing. She would retell the story of her recent injury and confidently proclaim to one and all that she would be on the field again in a few weeks. They nodded knowingly; Alice is tough.

A few years earlier Alice had a particularly rough tournament. Excessive diving to make saves had taken its toll, and she could barely stand because of the pain. Alice's team made it to the championship game. At the end of regulation, the game was tied; penalty kicks (PKs) would decide the game. Alice begged for anyone else to go in goal for the PK shootout. There were other women on her team who had played goalie in the past, but they had damaged their knees and wouldn't go in. Alice was leaning up against a goalpost trying to stretch out and in tears because of the pain when her teammate Cathy and husband David walked behind the net. David noticed the tears and stopped to speak with her. Alice confessed that she didn't even know if she could move enough to save any penalty kicks. David said, "Get in that box, stand still with your arms outstretched. Just dive with your hands. Just use your hands. You'll be amazed how many you can knock away with just your hands." Alice followed his advice, saved a goal, and her team won. Alice, her knees badly swollen, collapsed after the game. She realized that as much as she loved her teammates, she had to find another team, one that could protect the goal. She couldn't keep killing herself playing goalie. "You can only take so much damage to your body."

Soccer is in Alice's heart and soul. It kept her going and provided an emotional and physical release for the ten years she took care of her mother when she had cancer. Alice also took care of her mother-in-law for the last two years of her life. Alice neglected her own health care and didn't go in for regular checkups. Nevertheless, Alice was lucky: the doctors caught her breast cancer in an early stage. Her doctor decided to rely on drugs. "They kept giving me medicine to stop the cancer. They'd tell my husband, 'Let's wait another month and see how we are doing.' It was killing me. I was losing weight, and I had no motivation, no strength, no nothing. Finally, after a year, my husband said, 'We're done.' They said, 'Well, why don't we wait another year.' My husband said, 'No. You just take those damn things now. She doesn't need them. That is not who she is. Just take 'em.' I was a very big woman. Double D. I wore two sports bras to play. He said, 'You just take them. This person here is the person we want back.' So they did." The plastic surgeon convinced Alice that for her self-esteem she should have reconstructive surgery. For nipples, Alice requested soccer balls.

Alice's teammates were her crutch while she endured repeated surgeries. They knew when she needed a hug, or a shoulder to lean on. Alice readily acknowledged that she wouldn't have survived had it not been for their love and support. After the initial surgery, she was subject to recurring infections, and it took nearly two years for all of Alice's surgeries to be completed. "I had the tube sticking out my side to drain. I went to Vegas, and I was supposed to play. I'm the goalie, and I was going to be in the box for our team. Because they wouldn't take this tube out, my coach would not let me play. I was very upset." It took two years for Alice to return to the field after her cancer diagnosis.

"Sports has been my lifesaver. The women on this field keep me out here. My team encouraged me to get back out there as quick as I can. When I'm not playing, I'm here on the sidelines cheering them on. That's why I'm over here on the line, trying to help them out. And everybody else I have played with because I've played with different teams. We all know each other because some of us have gone from team to team to team."

Alice currently takes care of a husband with failing kidneys. She manages their twenty-two-acre ranch by herself: cutting tree limbs, mowing, maintaining the house, and whatever else presents itself. Her best friend Margaret also takes care of an ailing husband. "We both have our plates full," Alice said. "Soccer is our release. This is our time to get out here with our friends and to let it all out. It's like you unload. The load is gone for that time. It may not sound like much to some people, but if you've ever been in that type of situation …"

In addition to cancer and knee injuries, Alice has had her ribs cracked, fingers broken, and fingers dislocated and bent all the way back past her wrist. And she's had two concussions. "Every so often I go in and get a cortisone shot to help me out because I get inflammation in my knees," Alice said. "As long as I can stand on that field they are going to have to drag me off; I'm not stopping."

Alice pointed out another woman watching the game. "That's one of those that lost her husband a couple of years ago to cancer. That's why we are all like we are. We all know each other and we've all been through it together. You know that the support system you have is the best damn thing you could ever have. Your family is there for you but sometimes they don't know what you need."

"One of the other girls just recently had a brain tumor and she's back out here. She came up and gave me a hug and said, 'I'm out on this field because of you, because you came out here after breast cancer. You gave me the encouragement to get back on this field and not quit.'"

Alice acknowledged that each woman has her own battle and sometimes she loses. Cathy, whose husband David encouraged Alice before the penalty kick shootout, died of a brain tumor. Her doctor encouraged her to play as long as she could. "We were right there with her and her kids were right there on the sidelines with her," Alice said. "She had a smile on her face. You can't replace that. You can't."

Already Gone

Christine Nolan was a long time player in Northern Virginia, and beloved by many. Her teammates looked forward to a big greeting from Christine when they arrived at the field. The social aspect was of more importance to her than the game. Frequently she'd dawdle on the sidelines, preferring to chat rather than to step on the field to start the game. Even in games where her team was outclassed, Christine would emerge with a smile as she observed, "We got our asses kicked."

In 1996 at age thirty-nine, Christine was diagnosed with breast cancer. She had none of the risk factors: not old, no family history, not overweight or sedentary, no increased radiation exposure, nothing that made her a candidate. It was a shock, but her treatment was successful. Christine returned to the soccer field with a new attitude. "I only want to play for nice teams from this point forward. It is not about winning. Winning feels good, but not at the expense of your or anybody else's body. Not at our age. I want to play the game and hang out afterward. That's what it's about."

In 2012, a mass was discovered in Christine's right breast: a rare form of breast cancer different from her first encounter. After an eighteen-month struggle with chemo and surgery, Christine was pronounced good to go. Before the start of the soccer season, she mused about other women who fought to return to the field.

"It's amazing to see how many of them, the minute they are mended, are back out on that field. I've seen women never stop, go through all their cancer treatments and be out on the field the whole time. Women going through divorces, heart attacks. I have seen women come back from multiple knee surgeries, broken bones, everything you can possibly imagine and they are back on that field because that is what makes them whole: soccer and their teammates. Once you stop playing, you miss it so much. You miss your teammates and you miss the game itself. Coming back means you are whole again, you've mended. That's the bar you set for yourself when you are injured or have cancer or whatever. If I can just make it back to the soccer field, then I know I'm well. Then I know I'm good. I've seen it so many times."

In the fall of 2015 at her six-month checkup, Christine's blood work was fine, but she asked her doctor for a scan. She had a gut feeling that all was not right. The ultrasound revealed metastatic breast cancer, which is not curable. As cheerfully and aggressively as she played on the field, Christine again fought cancer. She never made it back on the field. Christine died in October 2017.

TWELVE
Travel and Tournaments

A COOL BREEZE from the Pacific Oceans occasionally wafted over the sunburnt soccer field where the San Diego Senior Games were underway. The Olympic Game equivalent for adults over fifty years of age, the Senior Games are held annually at one or more locations in each state. In San Diego, competitors vie for medals in twenty-five events, including women's soccer. On this weekend, women had gathered on the fields of Miramar College in Mira Mesa. Teams from across California competed in the over-50 and over-60 brackets.

Two games were underway on adjacent fields while beneath the shade of a tent, Connie Bunch, Debbie Vasquez, and Sharon Murray sold T-shirts to raise money for their team. Laid out on a table were dozens and dozens of children's shirts in rainbow colors, emblazoned with "My Grandma Plays Soccer" or "My Grandpa Plays Soccer." The funds raised from the sales, which the women conducted regularly, were to be used to support the Still Kickin' trip to the World Masters game in Auckland, New Zealand in 2017. By the end of the tournament, Still Kickin' had sold nearly all the shirts.

"Some people think women are not competitive after they've had kids or when they are older," Connie Bunch said. "We're super-competitive. We're out there clawin' and scratchin' and winnin'. The fire is still there. It never leaves. Just need somewhere to put it. And now we have it." Connie played softball until she discovered soccer, which she's been playing for thirty-four years.

Debbie Vasquez also was a softball player. She majored in parks and recreation in college. For her senior project, she conducted a survey for the City of Sacramento to determine whether an opportunity to play soccer would appeal to female softball players. Fewer than 25 percent of those surveyed evinced any interest in trying the sport. Nevertheless, Sacramento forged ahead the following year and offered soccer for women. Debbie played for several years, but gave it up when she had children. A chance encounter in a Toy's 'R' Us store with Sharon Murray, a woman she'd met while playing soccer, brought Debbie back to the game and to Still Kickin'.

Sharon Murray is a soccer tournament junkie who has amassed an impressive collection of medals over the years. She proudly displays them on a hat rack at home. Her grandson is duly impressed. Approaching her seventieth birthday, Sharon claimed that the admiration of her grandson "keeps me going." Watching Sharon's aggressive play on the field, it is evident that she would continue to play soccer whether her grandson approved or not, or whether anyone approved. A retired teacher, Sharon doesn't want to tap the family budget for her tournament expenses so to raise funds she cleans lots and lots of houses.

Around 1990, Sharon and her husband accompanied her son's soccer team to Europe. The boys' U-19 team and an elite girls' U-19 were representing their club on a soccer tour. While playing in England, several members of the girls' team were injured, leaving them short of players. The girls turned to Sharon for help. They had learned from Sharon's son that she played. Would she play with them?

"I'm a mother!" Sharon replied. No matter, the girls had already obtained permission for Sharon to play. How could she say no?

Sharon and her husband went shopping for soccer cleats. The footwear salesmen were taken aback when they learned that Sharon, not her husband, needed the cleats. In her forties at the time, Sharon played with the girls and managed to hold her own. Perhaps she was more than a little disappointed when the injured girls recovered in time to play in the Netherlands, and she was relegated to the sidelines.

The Still Kickin' team had played in many domestic tournaments when their goalie and de facto team leader, Dawn Cole, suggested the women enter the World Masters Games in Edmonton, Canada. Modeled on the Olympics, the World Masters Games are held every four years in different cities around the globe for athletes over thirty.

Dawn had played in the previous World Masters Games in Melbourne, Australia as a guest goalkeeper. While participating in the 2001 San Diego Senior Games, women from a San Francisco-based team approached her to play for them at the upcoming Masters. Because she was such a good goalkeeper, Dawn was often asked to play in tournaments. However, she'd never before been asked to go to Australia and compete against teams from across the globe. She was "absolutely" ready to go. When the team left for Melbourne, Dawn only knew four of the players. Following the tournament, Dawn and her fourteen new friends traveled around Australia having a "ripping good" time. She was confident her Still Kickin' teammates would enjoy a similar opportunity. And they have. Still Kickin' competed in the World Masters Games in Edmonton, Canada (2005); Sydney, Australia (2009); Turin, Italy (2013); and Auckland, New Zealand (2017).

Dawn's husband accompanied her to the Edmonton games. She encouraged him to sign up for golf or softball, but he balked, not knowing what to expect. Instead, he planned to take in the sites and cheer for Dawn. As a result, Dawn's tournament credentials—pass to transportation, events and food outlets—read "Athlete" while his tag read "Paid Companion." Mercilessly teased by Dawn and others as a kept man, he signed up for golf at the following World Masters Games.

During the two-day San Diego Senior Games soccer competition, the commissioner soccer buzzed around—when she wasn't on the field—ensuring everything ran smoothly. Nona Marsh was an old hand at running tournaments. She had hoped to offer an over-65 bracket for the women at the Senior Games but did not garner the sign-ups she needed for the older age group. Instead, Nona grouped nine teams into the over-60 bracket. Nona and her teammates are well past sixty—some past seventy—and would have benefited from playing teams closer to their age. Nevertheless, they gave it their all, particularly Nona. Her friendly and easy-going demeanor as she performs her commissioner duties masks her highly competitive spirit on the field. Nona hates, hates, hates to lose.

Years ago, Nona roomed with a man who was quite knowledgeable about soccer. He graciously taught Nona the subtler points of the game. Once when Nona was ranting about losing in a tournament, he did his best to console her. "Nona," he said, "it doesn't count unless it is the World Cup." He was fortunate to escape with his life after such a remark. "Screw you," Nona retorted. "This is *my* World Cup." As Nona related this story, other women nodded knowingly. To them, tournaments are that important. On the field they vie for every ball, take every half-chance to shoot and score, and are upset when they lose. "You can't say that even though we are older, we're just playing for fun and friendship," one woman said. "Winning matters!"

In addition to teams from California, the San Diego Senior Games typically draw players and teams from as far away as

Northern Virginia. However, it is rare to see a team from California at a tournament on the East Coast, unless it is the famed Veteran's Cup.

In 1987, sisters Penny Schulstad and Shirley Metzger were on the first Fairfax County, Virginia team to travel to a California tournament. The women had lived in California before moving to Virginia. One of their California friends recently had joined a soccer team and invited Penny and Shirley to bring their Virginia team to a local tournament. Shirley laughed when describing how the team had traveled on the same flight, worn matching sweatshirts for the trip, stayed in the same hotel, and eaten meals together because that's what kid's teams did. Now when a team travels for a tournament, a spreadsheet with everyone's hotel and cell phone number is the limit of the coordination.

Penny, Shirley, and their teammates had a wonderful time at the California tournament and returned the hospitality by inviting the California team to the Fairfax Women's Soccer Association tournament held in mid-June. Perhaps that was a mistake. The Californians detested the Virginia heat and humidity. While the FWSA tournament does not always take place in a sauna, there have been times when the synthetic turf fields are so hot that soccer cleats melt.[1] On a warm, sunny day, artificial turf can reach temperatures fifty degrees higher than real grass.[2] Shoes fall apart, and the women are at risk of dehydration and heat stroke.

Penny believed that the California team she hosted warned other teams about East Coast conditions. Perhaps it was true, but the women in California, indeed across the west coast, do not need to travel great distances to get their fill of tournaments. From the Washington State Women's Soccer Association, through the Portland League and on down to women's leagues in Sacramento, the Bay Area, Orange County (LA), San Diego County, and inland to Las Vegas, tournaments abound on weekends from the spring through the fall. Texas is also awash in tournament opportunities and has a long and rich history of women's soccer. San Antonio's Fiesta Soccer Tournament is the oldest soccer event for women, having been held annually since 1979.

Martha Dinwiddie and her Dallas area teammates traveled to the first ever Fiesta Soccer Tournament. They returned for many years, winning their division each year, not necessarily by a wide margin, though. The final year her team competed, they faced girls between eighteen- and twenty-years-old in the gold medal game. Martha and her teammates were twice as old as the girls. "We were already kind of beat," Martha said. "This was not going to be pretty." Because earlier games that day had run long, the gold medal game was starting late and women were concerned about their travel arrangements. The referee offered to shorten the halves from forty-five to thirty minutes. The opposing captain agreed as did a grateful Martha. "At the end of the game we were ahead 2-1 and we were dying. They were fairly fresh." The other team tried to reverse the decision regarding the length of the halves, confident they could win the game with more time. But their protest was to no avail.

Martha played each year in Memorial Day and Labor Day tournaments, but the Fiesta Soccer Tournament is the only one where she traveled. "We always had fun in San Antonio and what happened in San Antonio, stayed in San Antonio. There were no husbands or boyfriends allowed."

The premier tournament for women in the United States is the Veteran's Cup. Founded in 1998 by the United States Adult Soccer Association (USASA), the competition is held over several days for players over thirty-years-old. Tim Busch, president of the Washington State Soccer Association, a founding member of the Washington State Referee Committee, and Commissioner of USASA, shepherded the development and the growth of the competition during its early years. The first Vet Cup took place in 1998 in Bellingham, Washington. Nine teams participated.

The following year the Cup was again held in Bellingham, and nineteen teams took part. In 2000, the event moved to Nashua, New Hampshire.

In the Boston area, Christiane Wollaston-Joury and Lois Kessin of the Eastern Massachusetts Women's Soccer League heard about the Nashua tournament and put together a team, one of thirty-nine teams that competed that year. Debbie Greenslit and Rita Wilkie were on that first Eastern Massachusetts team, and they have participated in fourteen of the last sixteen Vet Cup tournaments. For Rita, the competition "has been a blast." She revels equally in the soccer games and the social aspect of sharing a house for a week with teammates. As participation in the Vet Cup has grown over the years, additional age brackets have been added, including over-70 for men and over-65 for women.

Christiane, British by birth, has used the Vet Cup competitions as a way to see America. She and Lois make the trip every year and add an extra week for sightseeing. Despite fourteen years of playing in tournaments, Christiane did not win her first championship until 2016. She called it "a bit of a cheat" since her over-65 bracket only included four teams. Nevertheless, she is proud of her trophy. Years of making it to the semi-finals or finals and losing were finally behind her. Christiane openly displays her soccer medals, trophies, and ribbons. "In England, you never get trophies, so these are very precious to me."

Vet Cups have provided women with some of their most vivid soccer memories, such as the shoot-out in the 2001 semi-final game between a Washington state team, Copa di Vida, and a team from Hawai'i.

In tournaments, teams tied at the end of regulation play overtime. If at the end of overtime the game is still tied, a shootout ensues. A penalty kick (PK) shootout pits individual players against the goalkeeper, one on one. A player attempts to score by kicking a stationary ball placed on a spot twelve yards in front of the goal. Only the goalkeeper can stop her. The goalie stands on the goal line, and is allowed to move laterally, but cannot step forward from the line until the opposing player kicks the ball. The goalie tries to guess where the opposing player plans to shoot—left, right, center, high, or low—and lunges in that direction as soon as the shot is taken. If the opposing player doesn't miss the goal mouth, there is an 85 percent chance the goalie will not be able to stop it.[3] To resolve the tie, teams alternate taking up to five PKs. If they make an equal number of PKs, then they continue to alternate until one team makes theirs and the other does not.

Sue Boettcher remembered the game as if it were yesterday. "We ended up tying and went into a PK shootout. It was late in the evening, about 9:00 p.m. Now, we have the lights on the field. People are stopping to watch the game. The whole field was lined with people."

Copa di Vida scores on their first PK. The Copa di Vida goalie, Patti Cox, steps up to the goal line to face the Hawai'i player. "Patti Cox was one of those goalkeepers everyone looked up to and admired." Patti eyes the opposing player, takes a guess where the shot will go, leaps, and saves the shot. Her teammates erupt. A second Copa di Vida player takes her turn shooting and buries the ball in the net. Hawai'i's turn. Patti again is on the line and, as if she can read minds, she lunges and her outstretched hands push away the shot for a save. The field is enveloped in noise as the sidelines cheer her performance. A third Copa di Vida player calmly takes her PK and scores. The women are ecstatic; they will win if they make one of their next two shots, or if Hawai'i misses one of its three. For the third time, Patti takes her position between the posts. The ball rockets toward the goal and Patti makes the save. Copa di Vida is through to the finals.

"Patti says she was possessed. It was an incredible night." Sue recalled. "Everyone on that team remembers how phenomenal she was that night." Almost as an anticlimax, Copa di Vida beat Camp Springs, SC, the prior year champion, and took home the Vet Cup.

For many teams, the Vet Cup is a significant commitment. Gerihatrix from Northern Virginia plays in the cup every year. After the summer tournament, players enjoy the fall season, but come spring they begin training together for the Vet Cup, which is usually held in July. They hold practices and work on conditioning and skills. The commitment has paid off with the team bringing home many trophies over the years.

In the global soccer world, many of the great tournaments are Cup competitions: The World Cup, UEFA (Union of European Football Associations) Cup, England's FA (Football Association) Cup, and the Africa Cup of Nations among others. Winning the Veteran's Cup, therefore, carried a certain cachet amongst the players. In 2016, the U.S. Adult Soccer Association began marketing the tournament as part of its annual Soccer Fest. To longtime participants "Soccer Fest" sounds blah and many refuse to call it anything but "The Vet Cup."

Up until the 1990s, few soccer tournaments for female recreational players existed. It is theorized that at some point, tournament organizers realized that women of a certain age who play soccer were not tied down with children, had disposable income, and wanted to travel. Whatever the reason, tournaments blossomed in desirable locations across the United States and Mexico. Brackets were added for over-40 and eventually over-50, over-55, over-60, and over-65. Lois Kessin recalled traveling with teammates "to a tournament in DC. The coach said, 'Oh, God. Should we rent a bus?' And we all pulled out our credit cards and said, 'No, we'll fly.'" Lois laughed. "He was shocked because he'd been dealing with kids."

A favorite tournament for many women took place in Puerto Vallarta, Mexico. Its popularity stemmed in no small part to an opening ceremony that offered free drinks, enticing several to overindulge and jump fully clothed into a nearby swimming pool. Bev Vaughn called it "Spring Break for middle-aged women." Bev recalled one year she stayed in downtown Puerto Vallarta and the team took buses to the countryside. Waist-high, stone walls surrounded fields, and the calls of nearby roosters punctuated early morning games. Young men at the field grilled chicken, beef, and seafood all day long. Beer, if not free, was significantly cheaper than bottled water and became the beverage of choice for the hot, sweaty players. "It was a two-day tournament, and we would go for three or four days. We went horseback riding up into the hills, and we went out snorkeling one day, and we'd do some shopping in town, and there was this beautiful restaurant up in the hills: open air with a thatched roof. You're overlooking the ocean. Just the most beautiful scene." One year Bev joined a team that was very serious about winning the tournament: much too serious for her. Bev never returned to Puerta Vallarta.

For one of Janice Akridge's trips to Mexico, the team chose tie-dyed tank shirts with large white numbers pressed on the back. After the first day of games, the women washed out the shirts and hung them on the window ledge to dry. The next morning Janice's teammate, Diane, discovered her shirt had blown off the ledge and disappeared. The women were frantic: she couldn't play without a uniform and how would they ever find a matching tie-dye shirt in the town? On the way to the bank to get some money, the women spotted a local man selling his goods on the corner, wearing a tie-dyed shirt with a number on the back. Yes, Diane's number. After some bargaining, the man agreed that if the women bought him another shirt, he would give them the tie-dyed shirt. Like Bev, the Puerto Vallarta tournament for Janice was less about soccer and more about shopping, going to the beach, eating, and drinking.

Every year for ten years Lynne Clewell flew from Washington state to Puerto Vallarta to play in the tournament. But then,

Lynne typically participated in four to five tournaments per year. Noted for scoring big goals in tournaments, Lynne is less apt to talk of her heroics than about a special team at a memorable Veteran's Cup. In 2010 a team from Nkowankowa, South Africa, the Vakhegula Vakhegula (Grandmothers, Grandmothers) participated in the Veteran's Cup in Lancaster, Massachusetts.

In 2005 Beka Ntsanwisi, a South African, was recovering from her two-year battle with colon cancer.[4] During her time in the hospital, she became convinced that older women would fare better in the medical system, physically and psychologically, if they had the benefit of regular exercise. Accordingly, Beka introduced a light exercise program for older women in Tzaneen, a town in Limpopo province in the northern part of the country. Two years later Beka took the women onto a field to learn to kick a soccer ball, a move that drew the disapproval of many in a culture where soccer is a man's game and older women were expected to behave with dignity. Ignoring the stigma, the women persevered. They formed teams and competed, drawing curious crowds to watch their matches. A sufficient number of women took an interest such that a league was formed and games were played regularly on Saturday. News of these women reached the organizers of the U.S. Veteran's Cup who extended an invitation to the tournament. Herbalife, a sponsor of the Special Olympics and nearly 200 athletes, teams, and leagues worldwide, stepped forward to provide funding. A team of women ranging from ages forty-nine to eighty-four made the life-changing journey of eight thousand miles to the United States. For all of the teams participating, the tournament was an extraordinary experience. Cynthia Hale from Atlanta said, "It was amazing to watch them try to compete and play. The compassion the other teams showed them by letting them play, not just making it a walk all over them. That's the kind of people you have that are involved in some of these tournaments. It was great."

Wanda Rixon, an inveterate tournament player, is a natural organizer. Over a fourteen-year span, she consistently organized Virginia teams for a Las Vegas tournament and managed uniform, roster, local travel, player passes, accommodation, and other details. Then she stopped. When a teammate suggested assembling a tournament team, expecting Wanda to lead the effort, Wanda commented that it would be nice, just once, to be able to compete in a tournament where she didn't have to worry about the details. Her teammate took the hint. Wanda was able to play in the Las Vegas tournament with the sole responsibility of showing up to the field on time.

For some women, tournaments are attractive because of the opportunity to play on a decent field. Joanne Specht played for years in Virginia on "crappy fields" before moving to San Jose where she played on "more crappy fields." She was thrilled to play in a tournament on fields maintained by a college for their varsity team. Joanne could hardly believe how fast she could run and what crisp passes she could make when the ball wasn't bouncing around as if it were traveling over a heavily-mogulled ski run.

Women who play past age sixty find it more challenging to assemble local teams for anything other than top-tier tournaments. Often the over-60 teams include players from across the country. For example, a Prime of Life Tournament in San Diego on Memorial Day Weekend included an over-60 Virginia team with a third of the players from other states, including California. Some women just want to play and are not rigid about what organization they represent. Kathy Downer is one. She played in her first tournament in her mid-fifties and was hooked. Kathy has played in the San Diego Senior Games for the last fifteen years on so many different teams that she cannot recall them all.

Patti Storm discovered tournaments at the comparatively late age of fifty-eight. While attending the San Diego Senior Games to watch her husband play softball, Patti saw older women playing soccer. It piqued her interest, and she decided to try it. Known as Stormy to her teammates, Patti has played recreational and tournament soccer for the past thirteen years. During that period she attended the Huntsman World Senior Games, again to watch her husband's softball team. An international sports draw for men and women ages fifty and older, the Huntsman Games are held over a two-week period in Utah each October offering sports, health screenings, band concerts, and dances. Patti did not see soccer, so she approached the organizers and suggested the addition of women's soccer to the events. Now Patti attends the Huntsman Games every year with her team, Soccer Sisters.

In 2017, the Las Vegas Friendship Tournament offered an over-70 women's bracket, the first tournament to provide this age level division for women. As is oft the case with new ventures, there were a few growing pains. Organizers, not entirely sure of the physical capabilities of the women, proposed that the games take place on a half-field with eight players on each side and a small goal. Initially, there were to be no goalies. The night before the tournament started, the women talked with the organizers about changing some of the rules, including allowing goalkeepers.

Chris Hovind from the state of Washington was on one of the four teams that competed in the tournament. She discovered that with a goalie guarding a small net, "it was ridiculous to try and get a goal in." Nevertheless, one team managed to score, just not hers. The Washington team came in second. Despite the glitches, the women had a great time, and the organizers have promised a full field and eleven-a-side game for the next tournament. Chris and her teammates "are already compiling a list for next year of candidates to go down there and take the trophy!" Could an over-75 division be next?

THIRTEEN
A British Accent

JACQUELINE ELISE BAITY-BURT hails from England, the home of modern football. She was born in 1940 in Reddish, Cheshire, five miles southeast of Manchester, where two of the top English Premier League Football teams make their home: Manchester City and Manchester United.

From a young age, Jacquie hated soccer. "Half my family was for Manchester United, and the others were for Manchester City. Sunday get-togethers at my grandmother's were always fraught with arguments and sometimes ended with fisticuffs!" In 1958, a British European Airways flight crashed just after takeoff from the Munich Airport, killing twenty-three passengers, including eight soccer players from Manchester United.[1] Needing players, Manchester United extended a tryout invitation to one of Jacquie's cousins. His father, a die-hard supporter of Manchester City, warned his son of certain death should he even consider playing for United. The young man chose life and passed up the opportunity to play football in England's top flight.

Jacquie's grandmother and uncle raised her during World War II: Jacquie's father was away fighting in the war, her little brother had died in a bombing, and her mother had taken to her bed, overwhelmed by it all. It was through her uncle that Jacquie was first exposed to soccer. Too old for the draft and with engineering expertise needed on the home front, Jacquie's uncle stayed in England and became a member of the Home Guard. Each day he'd return from work, have his tea, and then gather up his flashlight, a gas mask, a flare gun, and Jacquie to patrol the surrounding area and look for "Jerries." Jacquie had no idea what they were searching for, but they often walked by a prisoner of war camp for Italians. Jacquie recalled that the men would wave and smile at her and seemed to be happy. Meanwhile, the prison guard lolled against the fence smoking a cigarette. When Jacquie first noticed the men kicking a brown ball around, she asked her uncle what they were doing. He explained they were playing football. Years later as her family fought over football games broadcast on the radio, Jacquie wondered why the prisoners of war she'd seen playing had been enjoying themselves.

In her youth, Jacquie played a myriad of sports, just not English football. At one time or another, she played kickball, beanbags, netball (similar to basketball), and rounders (akin to baseball). Additionally, Jacquie roller-skated, ran sprints, competed in the high jump and long jump for her track team, and skied. At the University of London Royal Holloway College, Jacquie was the bowler on the cricket team.[2] In this, she was following in the footsteps of her uncle, a well-known wicket-keeper. Jacquie played first home on the lacrosse team, scoring many, many goals. If that weren't enough, she fenced, swam the backstroke and the breaststroke, and subbed on the tennis team when she was available. In retrospect, she believes her father missed not having a son, and she became the next best thing. He encouraged her to try any and all sports that garnered her interest.

In 1965, Jacquie moved to the United States to marry her high school sweetheart. They settled in Solana Beach, California, an independent city in the San Diego Metropolitan Area.

Despite her years of hating soccer, when Jacquie's son turned five she signed him up to play because that's what his friends were doing. Her son's league had a shortage of coaches. League organizers, hearing Jacquie's prominent British accent, concluded that she must know a thing or two about the game. They browbeat Jacquie into becoming a coach and assigned her to a team of five-year-old girls. That first year, her team did not lose a single match. Jacquie's coaching abilities so impressed the league that it placed her with an older girls' team playing in a more competitive environment. As the league lacked qualified referees, officials also encouraged Jacquie to take an introductory referee course with Al Povey.

British by birth, Povey lost his family during World War II. He came to the United States as a young man to coach the Harvard rowing team. The cold and damp Boston winters reminded him too much of the English climate so he abandoned Massachusetts and moved to Southern California. With a background of playing and refereeing in England, Povey was a godsend for the referee-starved soccer leagues in his new home. In the mid-1960s, Povey began refereeing games in San Diego County and soon after that began offering referee-training courses. Over time, Povey became a powerful force in Southern California soccer, establishing the San Diego County Soccer Referees' Association and assisting in the establishment of numerous youth and adult leagues.[3]

Jacquie attended one of Povey's referee courses in the early 1970s. They hit it off immediately. Povey suggested to Jacquie that she try playing soccer. Given her athletic background, he thought she might enjoy the challenge of the game. The playing experience also would help her to become a sharper referee and better coach. Since there were no women's teams in the area, Povey and Jacquie built one.

Jacquie began by searching for women who displayed clear signs of soccer passion ... by yelling on the sidelines during their children's games. Jacquie would buttonhole the women and say, "Looks like you know the game. Have you ever considered playing or do you play?" Meanwhile, Povey ascertained the interest of female referees and requested them to recruit other potential players. The approach worked. Jacquie and Povey assembled enough women to form The Mudders, the first women's soccer team from North County (northern San Diego County). In that fall of 1975, there was only one place for the women to play: the Peninsula Women's Soccer League in San Diego, a relatively new league with just a handful of teams. From Solana Beach, Encinitas, Fallbrook, and other communities in North County, the women would meet up and carpool down to Pacific Beach for their games. Some days, by the time they'd played and returned as much as four hours had elapsed. More than one husband was disgruntled at having to watch his children for such an extended period. Since no one enjoyed the long commute, Jacquie borrowed the Peninsula Women's Soccer League constitution, rules, and regulations, and in 1976 the women formed a soccer league to serve North County. The team split into two, ensuring each new team had equal numbers of women at each position. Then each team recruited others to play. They discovered women living further inland who wanted to create teams. Consequently, the new league boasted four women's teams in its first season. Within a year there were eight teams and the two inland teams left to form yet another league, this one in the Scripps-Rancho Bernardo area. The coastal league continued adding more and more women. Reaching eighteen teams, the league offered four divisions based on playing ability. Women as young as eighteen joined the league, many of whom had been playing since their youth. Most of these young women played in the top division of the league. A few older players complained bitterly about competing with the young women. Over the objections of Jacquie and others, they implemented an increase in the minimum age for players. Cutting off the eighteen-year-old women severely damaged the pipeline of new players and league growth stagnated. Fed up with the situation, Jacquie abandoned the league she founded and joined a team in San Diego.

Jacquie was part of a cadre that created the San Dieguito Youth Soccer League to serve the towns of Carlsbad, Leucadia, Encinitas, Cardiff, Solana Beach, Del Mar and Rancho Santa Fe. When league officials realized they needed to foster a more competitive atmosphere for the elite players, Jacquie and others stepped forward to form the Surf Soccer Club. She coached and refereed for the Club for many years. Since its founding in 1977, the Surf Soccer Club has produced nine National Championship teams, twenty-four Regional Championship teams, and more than twenty U.S. national team players.[4]

Jacquie's family shared her passion for soccer. Her husband was a referee and coach, and all three of Jacquie's children became referees and played at a high competitive level. Jacquie's youngest son, now forty-six, still plays and coaches. Her daughter, a few years younger, regularly plays indoor soccer, manages three teams, and plays on two more teams plus a tournament team.

The Life of a Referee

In many of her early games as a referee, Jacquie found that parents were ignorant of the rules of the game, or rude, or both. Fathers were the worst, spewing comments such as, "Take him out. Go for his legs." Jacquie would show the parent a yellow card for unsporting behavior and tell him or her, "You make one more comment, and you're out of here." Those protesting that she had no authority to ban them from the game were immediately put straight. Until she left the field, Jacquie was in charge of players, sideline personnel, parents, and other fans. She had no compunction about using her power to keep order.

Jacquie recalled a game in which a team complained that a player on the opposing team was overage. The girl in question did indeed tower over the other girls on the field. Although Jacquie had glanced at the player identity cards before the game, she asked the opposing coach for the cards again so she could carefully check the girl's age. He gave Jacquie the card and pointed out the girl's parents. Jacquie verified the girl's birth date with the parents, returned the card, and signaled for the start of the game.

While the game was in progress, "The father starts berating me for questioning [the age of] his daughter," Jacquie said. "In Swiss-French." Jacquie was conversant with Swiss-French, having attended schools in Geneva, Switzerland. In addition to Swiss-French, Jacquie spoke Russian, Spanish, Italian, and German, the latter two of the Swiss variety. She ignored the upset father during the game but afterward confronted him. "In my best Geneva accent, I told him what I thought of him." The father took it well and, surprisingly after such a rocky start, his family and Jacquie's family were quite close for many years.

In children's games, the challenges come from the sidelines. In adult games, the challenger is in the referee's face. At times, the experience of refereeing men's games was reminiscent of being at her grandmother's house, with antagonists loudly denouncing each other. As often as not, ethnic tensions contributed to the animosity. Certain groups did not get along and their games frequently were punctuated by fights. Jacquie's most memorable experience occurred during a match between teams of Eastern European immigrants.

The men's games were assigned three referees. Typically one called the game and the other two ran the sidelines. When a referee did not show up for a (soon to be eventful) game, Jacquie and Al Povey divvied up the responsibilities. From the opening kickoff, tensions simmered and fouls were plentiful. It was no surprise to anyone when a fight broke out and fists flew. Al Povey attempted to intercede and was punched twice in the head. He crumpled to the turf, out cold. It could have been worse: in 2014, John Bieniewicz, a well-respected referee and president of the Metro Detroit Soccer Officials Organization, was punched in the head at a match and died.[5]

Al Povey lay unmoving on the field. The nearby school building was not open, no public phones were in sight, and no one carried cell phones at the time. Jacquie couldn't leave her fallen comrade. She wrote a note and gave it to one of the less belligerent players. With a mix of French, English, and every other language she knew—none of which the player spoke— she managed to communicate that he should run down the road to a shopping center where someone could read the note and call for help. Then she waited. The ambulance finally arrived. The emergency medical technicians attended to Povey and took him to the hospital. During all this time the players had been milling around. Jacquie, having done her duty by her fellow referee, abandoned the game and the field. As she walked quickly toward her car, she was followed by screams of outrage from the players. They demanded that Jacquie stay and referee the rest of the game. Despite this harrowing experience, Jacquie continued to referee men's games for many years afterward.

Being a referee did have its high points. In the 1970s, the North American Soccer League (NASL), a professional men's league, stimulated American awareness by attracting big-name soccer players to play on American soil. In 1975 the New York Cosmos signed the Brazilians Pelé and Carlos Alberto as well as the German star Franz Beckenbauer. Enthusiasm for the league grew substantially, and the Cosmos' average attendance increased from fewer than 4,000 per game to nearly 50,000 per game.[6] Big name stars Johann Cruyff (Netherlands), George Best (Northern Ireland), and Gerd Müller (Germany) were among those who joined other teams in the NASL. To foster greater interest in soccer, NASL assembled a team of stars to play exhibition games against local teams across the United States. Jacquie's home, San Diego, was a stop on the tour.

Jacquie was selected as one of the referees for the game. Rather than attribute the selection to her ability, she thinks many referees did not want to work the game, preferring to watch and enjoy the exhibition in all its glory. When working a game, a referee observes the game differently than a fan. She focuses on the men and the ball, not the evolving play, nor the off-the-ball runs, nor the individual skill of the players. The head referee for the game, Helmut Goebel knew Jacquie well as she and his son David often teamed as referees for high-level youth and men's games. He chose Jacquie and David as his linesmen.

"When [the NASL team] got to San Diego I think they had a bit of a shock," Jacquie said. "We had a lot of really good coaches and referees who had come from Europe and had grown up with the game. Several had been on Olympic teams. There were three Hungarians in San Diego who had been on the gold medal team in Mexico City."[7]

For the match, Jacquie worked the side the spectators were on. "It was a good game, and it was a friendly game. There was a lot of pushing and shoving because it was a men's game. But it was a clean game. I think there was one yellow card."

Franz Beckenbauer, one of the few international stars not past his prime, dominated play that rainy evening. With the score at 5-3 in favor of the international team, Beckenbauer latched onto a pass from a teammate that put him behind his defender. He shot, the ball flew into the net, and the audience roared. In the midst of the din and the celebration of Beckenbauer and his teammates, Helmut Goebel noticed that Jacquie, standing on the sideline, had raised her flag signaling that Beckenbauer had been offside when the pass was made. With thousands watching, Helmut ran over to Jacquie to confer. "Are you sure he was offside?" he said. Jacquie calmly replied, "I would not have raised my flag if he wasn't." The goal didn't count. Play resumed, but no one else scored, so the game ended 5-3 in favor of the internationals. As Jacquie, David, and

Helmut were walking off the field, Beckenbauer came running toward them. He shook hands with each of them and to Jacquie said, "Good game. I *was* offsides. I've never seen a woman ref before!"

Coaching

When Jacquie's daughter played competitive soccer, Jacquie was her coach. In one memorable game, they went up against an undefeated team from Escondido with a phenomenal player by the name of Shannon MacMillan. Jacquie knew that to win her team had to keep the MacMillan girl from scoring. Jacquie's daughter was her best scorer and her best player. She told her daughter that for this one game, she was not to worry about scoring. Her sole job was to "man mark" Shannon MacMillan. In other words, she was to shadow Shannon throughout the game, keep her from getting open to receive a pass. If Shannon did get the ball, she should not let her dribble and not let her shoot. With Shannon closely marked, the other team was unable to put the ball in the net. Jacquie was astounded when late in the game, her fullback—who never, ever, went past the half field line—ran down the field, took a shot from distance, and scored! Her team had won!

The opposing coach refused to shake Jacquie's hand after the game, but Shannon gave Jacquie a "good game, coach" and complemented Jacquie's daughter on her game. Jacquie developed a great admiration for the girl who had such presence, particularly when the coach was a jerk. Shannon MacMillan went on to play for the University of Portland, where she was an All-American and won the Hermann Trophy as the best female college soccer player in 1995. She had a storied career with the U.S. women's national team: winning the gold medal at the 1996 Summer Olympics, winning the 1999 Women's World Cup, and being inducted into the U.S. National Soccer Hall of Fame.[8] Jacquie, watching the success of the U.S. women's team, always rooted for Shannon MacMillan, a class act from a young age.

Jacquie coached both boys and girls. One year she coached a recreational team of high-school-age boys including a few she'd coached since they were five-years-old. Some of the players had the skill to compete on more competitive teams, but couldn't afford the expensive fees.[9] Jacquie decided to organize a soccer trip to Europe for the boys using her family connections to arrange games. Through the boys' car washes, raffles, other fund-raising activities, and the support of the pizza parlor where many of the boys worked, the team raised sufficient money for what became a memorable trip.

"We had two minivans and a small Volkswagen car. I drove the car to lead the way. I would zoom along with three boys in the car to the youth hostel—had to be there before 6:00 p.m., otherwise the hostel doors were closed—and get us checked in. I had a French-speaking kid in each of the vans: my kid and another boy whose mother was French. His father was Czech. He spoke French fluently because his mother would send him to France in the summer to stay with his grandparents. So we didn't have any problems translating or getting any place."

At the time, French law allowed sixteen-year-olds to purchase wine and beer and, as to be expected, the boys immediately took advantage of the opportunity. Consequently, most of them were hung over for their first game against a boys' choir. Barely able to focus, the boys played poorly and were creamed.

The next game on the schedule came through Jacquie's brother-in-law. He had a friend at a soccer club in Nice who made the arrangements. Unfortunately, something got lost in the transatlantic translation because the boys were pitted against a team of skillful adult men. They were creamed.

Jacquie and the team traveled in Italy and then drove up to Switzerland to play against Jacquie's old high school team.

Perpetual losers during Jacquie's time at the school, her high school team had just become champions of Switzerland. The result was predictable: her boys were creamed.

A small French village hosted the final game. Jacquie's team might have been able to win, but because the villagers had been so hospitable, the boys eased up a bit and settled for a tie. The town hosted a wonderful meal afterward during which Jacquie was asked why she was traveling with the team. The villagers had not quite grasped the concept of a female coaching a boys' team. "This is all in French, of course," Jacquie said. "I knew the word in French for coach was *entreneur*, so I made it feminine. 'I'm the *entreneuve*.'" Jacquie replied and was nearly deafened by the roar that followed the pronouncement. Her French hosts were almost falling out of their chairs, tears ran down their cheeks, and many were doubled over in hysterical laughter. Finally, a few were able to exert enough control to explain to Jacquie that *entreneuve* meant lady of the night. In the rare cases a woman coached, she was called by the masculine, *entreneur*.

Going Strong

Amidst all the soccer activity, Jacquie played other sports: league tennis, pickleball, and women's softball. She played on a women's lacrosse team for a time, only giving it up because of the long commute to Orange County. "I played cricket with a men's team, too," Jacquie said. The Rookis—Roo for kangaroos and Ki for Kiwis—included a cadre of technical experts from Australia and New Zealand in the United States on work visas. One of the coaches of Jacquie's women's team was the son of a famous cricketer from the Bahamas. He complained to Jacquie one day that his cricket team needed a bowler. "I said, 'Well, I bowled in school and at the University of London.' He looked at me and said, 'Do you want to come and see if it will work out? Remember these are men and they hit hard.' So I went to a game I was supposed to watch, but they needed a bowler against a Samoan team. I bowled this huge guy out, and he started chasing me with the bat. I had to run all the way to the parking lot while other people tackled him." Jacquie eventually quit the team, not because of irate batters, but because the games required extensive travel and she had too many other obligations.

In the summers Jacquie taught swimming. "The last two weeks in June when school got out, all the kids in our school district, K-6, could enroll in the Backyard Swim program, which was a Red Cross/PTA program—basic strokes and water safety—and free to all who enrolled, providing there were enough instructors and pools available. I taught from 9:00 a.m. to noon and would then go to Encinitas and teach kids who had severe physical impairments from 1:00 p.m. to 3:00 p.m. Solana Beach also had the only Junior Lifeguard program, so when our kids had done their years of backyard swim they could get into that program, and many did."

Since moving to Las Vegas a few years ago, Jacquie no longer plays soccer weekly, but still joins her friends for major tournaments. She's played in every Las Vegas Friendship Tournament from the beginning (1990), and every California Senior Olympics that has offered women's soccer. She noted that people are staying fitter later in life such that they can continue to play. However, it is becoming more and more expensive to travel to and participate in tournaments.

In 2017, Jacquie arranged for the Las Vegas Friendship Tournament to offer an over-70 women's bracket. Jacquie's team included players from Sacramento, Berkeley, LaVerne, Benita, Oceanside/Encinitas, and San Diego. Of the twelve players on her team, three (including Jacquie) were closer to eighty than seventy.

Jacquie doesn't know when, if ever, she'll stop playing. "My teammates have been the reason to go out and play. They are my best friends, my soul mates, and I'm proud to say, classy, colorful, hard working, joyful and cheerful in spite of what life throws at them."

FOURTEEN
Giving Back

FIND A WOMEN'S soccer league in San Diego County, and chances are Jany Staley is behind it. When Jany began playing in 1976, there were only six teams in the women's league. Since then Jany has been president and registrar, initiated a women's soccer tournament that reigned over the Thanksgiving weekend for twenty years, started an over-40 league, became president of an over-45 league, and served as Soccer Commissioner of the Senior Games in San Diego multiple times. Although many of her original teammates have retired from playing, Jany remains good friends with more than a half-dozen of them. At age seventy-two, she's not done. Jany is forming an over-55 division for her league and plans to play in it as long as she is able, or until an over-60 division is possible.

In conjunction with growing their leagues, women have supported the growth and operations of youth, men's adult, and coed leagues. They've served in administrative positions, coached, refereed, and expanded soccer into underserved communities. The stories below highlight just a few of the women who, like Jany, discovered the joy of playing soccer and the greater joy of helping others learn and experience the game.

Mary White first heard of soccer when her husband came home and announced he'd signed up their two oldest boys to play in Arlington, Virginia. Her response: "What's that? Never heard of it." Mary soon came to love watching her boys on the field and yearned to play herself. But then, Mary had been a tomboy and was willing to try almost any sport.

Mary had attended straight-laced, all-girls schools that didn't offer sports. Nevertheless, Mary biked, roller-skated, jumped rope, played kickball, and much more, almost exclusively with boys. Her "very structured" Catholic high school reined her in and the much tamer Mary ceased playing sports, for a time. She married and had four boys. It was through watching her sons play that Mary's athleticism was reawakened.

The Washington, DC area boasted a soccer team in the professional North American Soccer League. The original Washington Diplomats were formed in 1974 and played their games at the Robert F. Kennedy Stadium, then home of the Washington Redskins. In 1976, the Dips played home games at W.T. Woodson High School in Fairfax County, Virginia.[1] Mary attended many of their games with her family. At the time there was no women's national team and no soccer on TV. "That was all you saw compared to what you see now," Mary said. Eager to play the game, Mary placed an ad in the *Washington Post* looking for women interested in forming a team. Within the first month, she fielded over one hundred phone calls. Respondents included nineteen-year-old au pairs from Sweden, women who had played soccer in college, college-age athletes in other sports, and older women like Mary who wanted to try the game because their children played.

Aided by the Director of the Arlington Soccer Association, Mary put together several teams. In the fall of 1976, the teams played in the Washington Area Women's Soccer League, established the prior year for the few women's teams in the DC metropolitan area.

"We were driving all over the place. I thought we just needed to stay here in Arlington and play," Mary said. More ads, more phone calls, and more teams let Mary establish the six-team Arlington Women's Soccer League in 1977. Even amidst a declining population in Arlington County, the league quickly grew and in 2016 boasted 26 teams with over 450 players. After founding and nurturing women's soccer in Arlington, Mary stepped away from league administration.

Mary's sons attended the 1,100-student Bishop O'Connell High School in Arlington, which offered girl's soccer but only on a varsity level. The principal wanted to start a junior varsity girl's team and, knowing Mary played, asked her to be the coach. She accepted. The experience piqued her interest in coaching other teams. When a friend asked Mary to take over her daughter's travel team, she agreed. While coaching, Mary earned the U.S. Soccer Federation lower level licenses: F, E, and D. While that is as far as most coaches ever went, it wasn't enough for Mary. A relentless drive to improve led her to seek a C license, which required surviving a nine-day soccer boot camp.

Like military recruits, coaching license candidates at the U.S. Soccer Federation camp were awakened early every day and spent mornings and afternoons on the field. Candidates were instructed in various drills and then were expected to perform them. The theory was that a good coach must be able to show, not just tell. One by one, candidates were selected to run a short practice during which he or she would coach the others through drills on a specific topic. The outdoor sessions took place in all weather conditions with only one exception: lightning. Each night after dinner, training continued as attendees watched soccer films. In Mary's class, there were 120 candidates, ten of whom were women. Like Mary, most of the students were pursuing their C licenses, but about twenty were attempting to earn an A or B license, which meant being able to successfully execute all the drills, e.g., juggle the ball in the air using one's head or perform a bicycle kick.

Two complete days were devoted to testing. Mary was required to complete written tests and an oral examination where she was grilled by a panel of licensed coaches. She had never worked so hard in her life. At the completion of the grueling course, Mary was rightly proud of having earned the coveted C license.

Moreover, Mary obtained a National Youth License, a less onerous course geared toward coaches for players under age twelve. Mary also secured a referee's badge. At the time, there was such a shortage of female referees that she could almost immediately step into refereeing women's college games. However, Mary's primary interest remained coaching. She had only taken the referee course to improve her overall understanding of the game. During the soccer season, Mary typically coached two competitive—travel or high school—teams. Between coaching and playing, Mary's life revolved around soccer. She loved it.

Mary took her first girl's soccer team to England on a soccer tour. In London, the team stayed across the street from old Wembley Stadium, "the cathedral of football … the heart of football," in the words of Pelé and host to the most significant games in English soccer.[2]

The team had a bus and a driver who was familiar with soccer tours but had never driven a girls' team. Returning from one of the first practices, he informed the girls they had fifteen minutes to shower and change before the bus headed out to dinner. It was made very clear to him that with two appearance-conscious teenagers in each room sharing one bathroom, a fifteen-minute turnaround time was NOT going to happen!

After many years and many teams, Mary chose to step aside from coaching and attend to her ailing mother. Besides, the atmosphere was changing. In the 1970s and 1980s when soccer was new to the United States, most coaches were parents. As the sport became more popular, travel soccer became a big business. In highly competitive communities, such as the Washington, DC suburbs, many parents demanded top talent to coach their sons' and daughters' travel teams. Children began to train year-round, and many families (unrealistically) expected their children to earn soccer scholarships to college. Instead of letting teams or mothers of players choose the coaches, clubs began to hire professionals to coach: often former college players or young men from soccer-mad countries.

Without the commitments of coaching, Mary now has time to play in tournaments across the country. A highly regarded player, Mary has been recruited by teams as far away as Hawai'i and California for tournaments.

Throughout it all, Mary's husband has supported her. "He's been terrific, letting me do all these things without complaining," Mary commented. "But he said his next wife isn't going to like soccer."

In 1976, Sharon Murray was a teacher and mother of six-year-old twins in the greater Sacramento Valley. A gentleman offered to teach women soccer skills, so Sharon purchased a twelve-dollar pair of cleats and learned to play. Then she and three other women put their heads together and formed the Sacramento Valley Women's Soccer League, currently a nineteen-team league.

Although Sharon was not interested in becoming a referee, she obtained her referee certification. "If I'm going to play, I want to know the rules," she said. As a soccer player and teacher, parents assumed Sharon would be a good coach. She didn't disappoint. Sharon was a coach for a competitive boys' team that won the California State Championship two years in a row. She also coached high school soccer for many years. Sharon no longer coaches a team but enjoys the occasional session with her grandson and his team. When Sharon takes over a practice session with boys, she is met with their skeptical stares and unspoken thoughts of, "Who is this old woman?" That is until the boys realize she knows what she is doing. The boys' fathers are more dubious and repeatedly offer to help. She politely refuses. "I got it," she tells them firmly. "I got it." And she does.

Like Mary While, Sue Boettcher obtained her C License and coached Washington girls' teams at the club and high school levels. Sue is grateful that she was able to coach these girls during such critical years of their young lives. Many have kept in touch, celebrating with her the meaningful and joyful events of their lives: graduations, marriages, and the births of children. Knowing these girls has changed Sue's life.

Elizabeth, a multi-sport athlete and an A student, played soccer in high school under Sue. The spring of Elizabeth's sophomore year, she learned her dynamic and loving mother, a force in the local community, had brain cancer. During the summer her mother seemed to be doing well, but that fall she began to fade. At the end of the fall soccer season, on the first day of the playoffs, her mother died. The team rallied around Elizabeth, offering hugs, support, and tears. There was no chance of a postponement; they would have a play-off game that evening. Elizabeth was determined to play. "I have been grieving for six months about losing my mother," she told them. "You might not see tears in my eyes because I am already cried out." It was one of those cool, fall evenings that often follows a warm day. A light fog floated on the field. Elizabeth, playing on the wing, appeared as an ethereal creature flying up and down the field. She later said she felt as if her mother was with her throughout the game. "We all took away this wonderful feeling that life is precious," Sue said, "that Elizabeth's mother was with all of us. We embraced Elizabeth. We were a team experiencing one of the hardships in life, together."

Sue impacted the girls' lives too, sometimes without realizing it. Many years after coaching her in high school, Sue encountered a young woman who told Sue that she'd changed her life.

Sue had used team-building events to build spirit across the freshmen, junior varsity, and varsity teams. One such activity was the annual Mount Si hike, held at the beginning of the season. Mount Si is located in North Bend, Washington and the nearly eight-mile trek to and from the 4,147 feet summit is not for the faint of heart, nor short of breath.[3]

Katie, a freshman, had asthma and forgot to bring her inhaler. The varsity and junior varsity teams had gone ahead while Katie remained at the bottom, anxious about her ability to complete the hike. When she told Sue her problem, Sue responded that she'd walk with Katie. "I'm with you the whole way," she said. "All the way up as far as you want to go. If you want to turn back, it's okay. Whatever you do, it is pretty amazing." One step at a time they made their way up the mountain, slowly climbing as the other girls were descending. Katie plodded along with Sue by her side, chatting about this and that. Without the help of an inhaler, Katie reached the summit. Years later Katie told Sue that the experience taught her that she could accomplish anything in life. That knowledge sustained Katie through her high school years, and beyond.

Sue's involvement with Washington State Youth Soccer Association began with a chance encounter at a soccer field with a boy looking for a soccer team he could join. Jeffrey was thirteen and soccer fees in his home of Everett, Washington, were too expensive for his immigrant parents' meager income. Jeffrey had traveled thirty miles to the area where Sue lived, looking for a team. Sue stepped in to help. Her endless calls and emails finally produced a team in Everett that would cover most, not all, of Jeffrey's fees. To help him make up the difference, Sue hired Jeffrey to assist with yard work on weekends and vacations. Sadly, as Jeffrey began to play more, the parents of other children on the team who were now playing less became resentful of providing financial support. Jeffrey had to find another team. Each season Sue worked with him to find a place where he could play.

Sue tried to keep in touch and provide support, but Jeffrey fell in with the wrong crowd in high school and was expelled. When he returned to the straight and narrow, he was not allowed to play high school soccer. Sue knew he needed the lure of soccer to give his life purpose and to keep him in school. Her appeal for reinstatement denied, she found him a men's team. It was a blessing in disguise as a junior college coach saw him play and offered Jeffrey a scholarship. Jeffrey attended college—the only one in his family to do so—but quit after one year. He was unable to afford both college and food, even though Sue bought him groceries. Today, Jeffrey is gainfully employed. He has become like a son to Sue and thankful for all she has done. Knowing Jeffrey made Sue more aware of the plight of kids in poorer communities. She visited soccer clubs in the greater Seattle area and educated them on the need to provide financial help to those who could not afford to play. At the time, she garnered much less support than she had hoped for. Today she is thrilled with the outreach efforts of Seattle's professional men's (Sounders) and women's (Reign) teams to boys and girls like Jeffrey.

Peggy Ueda was one of the founders of the Eastern Massachusetts Women's Soccer League. In 1979, when her family moved from Cambridge to Brookline, she contacted the local recreation department and expressed interest in coaching. The director responded that her timing was perfect: Brookline was organizing their first girls' travel team, and they needed a coach. Peggy coached the under-12 team for their first year, and again the following year as they played U-14.[4] When other commitments precluded Peggy from devoting the time required for a travel team she coached recreational soccer.

Peggy also coached her daughters. Just eighteen months apart in age, they were on the same team every other year obliging Peggy to coach one or two teams each season. "My life was just full of soccer. It was wonderful." Her husband supported her completely.

Peggy did more than coach. "It drove me crazy," Peggy said, that every year, if not more often, children required new cleats for their growing feet. She established a cleat exchange at her daughter's elementary-middle school. Children bringing in a pair of cleats received a ticket that allowed them to select a pair of used soccer shoes. If they didn't have any cleats to turn in, they were allowed to buy a pair for eight dollars or less. Money made off the sale was given to the Brookline Recreation Department to be used for children who couldn't afford the fee to play soccer. Leftover soccer shoes were donated to soccer organizations catering to low-income children. One year the cleats were taken by a Brookline resident to South Africa. In a year when Haiti suffered a devastating earthquake, the shoes were sent there.

Peggy expanded the soccer exchange through all eight of Brookline's elementary and middle schools. It became so successful that the city recreation department took over the program. When Brookline instituted a Climate Week, Peggy organized 3R Depot (Reduce, Reuse and Recycle) and turned the soccer cleat exchange into a full sports equipment exchange where people could donate their unneeded sports gear and pick up what they needed for free at the 3R Depot. "It was wonderful to feel we created opportunities for people. Just fantastic."

In the 1990s, Peggy became teammates with Anne Strong, another woman who gave of herself to the benefit of the game.

Anne was raised in Westchester County, NY and discovered soccer in third grade, playing against boys in gym class and more often than not, beating them. "It didn't matter if you were a shrimp or really big and tall, for if you played through the ball, you could win the ball away from the biggest boy in the class. And it blew me away." No matter her talent, Anne was not allowed to play on the boy's team; she became "a frustrated female athlete." Although she played field hockey in college, it was a less than adequate outlet for her competitive instincts as few games were played against other schools. After all, competition among young women was not ladylike.[5]

Anne graduated from Smith College in 1966. She later married and divorced. In 1973, she moved to Cambridge and there raised her children, practiced law, cofounded and became president of Cambridge Youth Soccer, played soccer, and coached youth soccer. She was passionate about ensuring children were able to play. She organized carpools for children who did not have transport to and from practices and pushed local schools to encourage youth participation in athletics. Susan Ruff, Director of Cambridge Youth Soccer, said of Anne's commitment to the Cambridge youth. "She wanted everybody to have a chance." And she made sure they did. "If Anne had an idea about how things could go," Susan said, "she could sway a whole room about it."

Concerned that soccer had become a suburban sport and inaccessible to youngsters in the cities, Anne used her lunch hour to play pick-up soccer at an inner-city Boston school. The kids responded with enthusiasm, even skipping lunch for the opportunity to play. With the support of school staff, Anne recruited students from Harvard to help with after-school programs. The daily work of a lawyer, even one with her own practice, couldn't compare to the satisfaction of helping these children. Anne wound down her law practice to devote her energies and passion to making soccer available to underserved children.

In 1999, Anne founded CityKicks, Boston's first after-school soccer program for middle school children. More than just a soccer program, CityKicks stated objective was to "promote an active, healthful lifestyle among inner-Boston pre-teens, especially girls, by engaging them in an appealing recreational physical activity, whereby they become turned on to the exhilarating and contagious fun of regular active play and acquire the habit of frequent physical activity. In addition, their participation will be enriched by instruction and outreach to parents around healthy development and smart choices, to deepen their appreciation of the lifelong benefits of regular physical activity."[6]

In 1999, it was estimated that the youth of Boston had just one-third of the opportunities to participate in sports that were offered to children in the surrounding communities. Out of Boston's 100,000 school-aged youngsters, 84 percent were non-white. Five percent of all school-aged children played soccer and only 20 percent of these participants were non-white.

CityKicks started the first season with seventy-five girls on six teams in the low-income areas of Jamaica Plain, Roxbury, and Dorchester. There were no tryouts: girls participated on a "first-come, first-served basis." For $5 each season, a girl was given a uniform, transportation to and from games, and coaching. Within a few years, there were ten teams with enough girls for three more teams on a waiting list.

After managing CityKicks for ten years, Anne oversaw the merger of the organization with America SCORES, a similar program using soccer to combat the issues faced by inner-city youth. Anne became the director of programming for the New England affiliate, organizing games, volunteers, and equipment as well as raising funds. Today America SCORES encompasses more than 14,000 children in nearly 200 schools in major cities.[7]

When not involved with soccer, Anne played hockey, skied, and enjoyed sailing—a frustrated female athlete no longer.

Anne Strong died on April 4, 2014, at age sixty-eight. The City of Cambridge honored her with a bench in her name at Danehy Park, overlooking the soccer fields. She left behind scores of teammates and legions of inner-city girls with self-confidence and a sense of purpose.

FIFTEEN
Dream of Fields

IN THE LAST QUARTER of the twentieth century, the United States experienced a sea change in sports participation. Where fields were once the province of boys and adult softball teams, girls now were present in increasing numbers. Children began playing sports at younger ages, and many competed in multiple sports. Baby boomers, feeling their generation was exempt from the effects of age, also thronged the fields. Sports, such as baseball, that were once confined to a single season, now were offered nearly year-round. Local governments were faced with too few fields and what fields they had suffered from extreme overuse.

Squeezed in Virginia
In the mid-1970s Fairfax County, Virginia, had a population of 500,000 and burgeoning soccer programs for children. During the sign-up process for Braddock Road Youth Club (BRYC) soccer in the spring of 1976, several enterprising mothers recruited other women to learn the game their children were playing by trying it themselves. Women thus recruited were encouraged to

197

sign up friends and neighbors. So many women expressed interest that the organizers were able to form four teams: Red Hots, White Lightning, Blue Bombers, and Coyotes.

The women practiced and played each other on fields under the auspices of BRYC. As one woman recalled, "After the first week of practice, nearly half the players wore bandages on their upper right thighs, including me." Perhaps that is why their games consisted of four quarters of fifteen minutes instead of the standard ninety-minute match with a halftime break.

The following fall, the Fairfax Women's Soccer Association was established with six teams. Lynn Gaaserud, the first president of FWSA, was so gung-ho that she signed up friends and neighbors to play … without asking first. Ruth Walton, one of Lynn's tennis buddies, was among the conscripted.

Tall, willowy, and with an energy that belies her seventy-eight years, Ruth is delighted to talk with anyone about the joy of playing soccer. Born and raised in the southern United States, Ruth was taught that, "Once you got to a certain age, you were supposed to be a prim young lady." Playing soccer was an eye-opening experience. "The exhilaration, the feeling of being cheered on for doing something active and athletic and exuberant: it was such a surprise to me."

Despite being tennis-fit, Ruth and her tennis friends were not in shape for the rigors of charging up and down the soccer field. Many of them, including Ruth, sustained injuries during their first practice. Nevertheless, they persevered and at age thirty-eight, Ruth played in her very first soccer game. Ruth eventually hung up her racquet having concluded that for her tennis could not compare to the thrill of being on the soccer field.

By the fall of 1977, the six women's teams had grown to sixteen, divided into three divisions based on skill levels: White (recreational), Red (moderately competitive) and Traveling (highly competitive). Tryouts were held for a traveling team, which participated in WAWSL, the Washington Area Women's Soccer League. FWSA held their games on Saturdays and WAWSL on Sundays so players chosen for the travel team could play in both leagues. The following year, FWSA grew from sixteen to twenty-eight teams.

A survey of FWSA members conducted in 1981 revealed that a typical player was in her thirties, married with children, college educated, and employed full time. The primary reasons given for playing were fun and exercise. The majority of the women had never played a team sport prior to soccer but identified themselves as sports-minded, aggressive, and independent. Over 60 percent were fans of professional soccer, about half had read one or more books about soccer, and nearly one-third were coaching soccer teams. Although a majority noted they'd been injured in a game, the survey did not differentiate between minor afflictions—bumps, bruises, and twisted ankles—and significant injuries—cracked ribs, knocked-out teeth, and broken legs.[1]

During the formative years of the league, Fairfax County provided the women with fields for practices in addition to games. Many of these fields were on elementary and middle school grounds and were in poor shape. While players contended with the ill-timed charges, flying elbows, and wild kicks of unskilled opponents, the risk of injury was equally great from twisting an ankle or knee on an isolated clump of grass or falling on the rock-filled fields and cement-hard dirt. More often than not, the women found themselves on fields that canted from one side to another, or end to end, or both. This is not to say the women were assigned the worst fields. Fairfax County had not foreseen the explosion in soccer and the need for a large number of rectangular playing surfaces. As the county added fields, the resident population soared—from nearly a half million in 1976 to 800,000 in 1988—and the competition for playing fields intensified.

As early as 1979 a mere three years after the women began playing, the growth of the league was already being restricted by the lack of adequate playing facilities.[2] In the fall of 1980, Ruth Walton became the head commissioner of FWSA. When she heard about a public meeting regarding a vacant parcel of land that might be available for athletic fields, she pounced on the opportunity. Once the planned location for a high school, the forty-two-acre site was superfluous for that purpose and Fairfax County was receptive to athletic organizations using the land for playing fields. Ruth and a representative from Little League were the only public attendees. Together they formed the Pine Ridge Association for Little League and Soccer to build fields on the site. Little League spearheaded the effort to build ball fields while FWSA managed the construction of soccer fields. The women had no funds, so Ruth and others sought donations of material and labor from local companies. Holland Engineering developed a site plan for little remuneration. A prominent, local construction company, William A. Hazel, Inc., stepped up to provide free services and Reserve U.S. Naval Construction Battalion 23 (Seabees) graded the site as part of their weekend training.

The women added their sweat equity, gathering at the field on Saturdays and Sundays for "Rock Parties" to remove rocks and embedded asphalt. A particularly large boulder caught the eye of Cindy, one of the volunteers who was landscaping her yard. Cindy organized the other women to chain the rock, drag it across the field, and manhandle it into her station wagon. However, her free boulder came at the cost of a sizeable dent in her car from the attempt to load the heavy stone. The woes of another worker, Laura, were generated by a much smaller rock; a diamond from her wedding ring fell out at the field. A painstaking search miraculously discovered the stone and it was returned to Laura. Unfortunately, sometime after leaving the area she lost it again, for good.

The women raked the fields, took soil samples, spread mulch, filled low spots, erected silt fencing, and cut stakes to anchor the straw bales. However, with no water at the field, FWSA endured endless cycles of seeding and having the grass die due to dry conditions. Since the area was not fenced in, vandalism occurred regularly. Sand was poured into the gas tanks of the Seabee equipment, and on numerous occasions four-wheel-drive vehicles ran over the fields, tearing them up. This went on for years until the Fairfax County Board of Supervisors agreed to pay for fencing and the Fairfax County Park Authority installed irrigation. FWSA continued to be financially responsible for the remaining work. Nine years after the initial meeting about the unused school site, Pine Ridge hosted three new soccer fields.

"We played our first games in 1989," Ruth recalled. "The fields were gorgeous: flat, green expanses of lush grass." Ruth, as the driving force behind the development of the fields, was recognized years later when the county named Field #1 as the Ruth T. Walton Field.

Just a few years after the women began playing at Pine Ridge, the Fairfax County School Board proposed selling the property to developers. FWSA was outraged. Wanda Rixon, the FWSA commissioner at the time, led the fight for the site to become permanent parkland. Women soccer players attended and spoke passionately at hearings, signed petitions, wrote letters, and met with county officials.

Early on, Dr. Richard J. Ernst, the influential president of Northern Virginia Community College, supported a proposal for the State of Virginia to buy the land and use it for a nurse training facility. Ruth Walton recalled that Ernst was "very athletic himself, very involved with sports. Someone who knew him from FWSA told him that it was going to just destroy our league. He took it seriously." Ernst dropped the idea of the Pine Ridge location for the nurse training facility.

The battle continued for years until the Fairfax County Board of Supervisors arranged a real estate trade under which the property became part of the Fairfax County Park Authority. The women had won the battle but not the war.

Since 2000, Fairfax has installed artificial turf on fields across the county in response to growing pressures for playing space. Studies have shown that after the installation of turf, field use doubles. Whereas spring sports were often victimized by frequent rain-outs, teams could now play in any conditions, short of lightning or deep snow. In 2010, the Fairfax County Athletic Council recommended that one of the Pine Ridge fields be outfitted with artificial turf and lighting.[3] In conjunction, the Council recommended that the FWSA lose its preferential treatment to use the newly turfed field. Ironically, the field withdrawn from FWSA was the Ruth T. Walton Field. Having enjoyed the long-standing support of many officials in the county, the women were stunned. Pine Ridge, where most of the women would gather on Saturdays, would no longer be the home of FWSA. Ruth termed the Council, "a bunch of good ol' boys and football-oriented." The Council representative for women's sports was male. Immediately after the Board approved the Council recommendations, a football league attempted to claim Walton Field for Saturday use, citing a provision in county policy designating football as the primary fall sport. Fortunately, the field was given instead to a youth soccer league desperately short of playing space.

For a time the women were still allowed to use the remaining grass fields on Saturdays because the youth teams did not want them. That changed, and now the women are absent from Pine Ridge on weekends. With the support of the county officials who were aware of the fields' history, the women could still be found playing at Pine Ridge on weeknights, but only after 8:00 p.m.

In the past few years, the Athletic Council has taken further aim at adult sports by floating the idea that all fields in the county be reserved for youth activities until 9:00 p.m. The FWSA has lobbied against such a restriction, and while the 8:00 p.m. limit remains in place, there is concern about the future erosion of adult field use as newer county officials are unfamiliar with the FWSA role in building the fields. As it is, the women are indebted again to the Braddock Road Youth Club for having field space.

In 2006, the women were given rights to use another county field, Wakefield Park, because they paid part of the cost to install artificial turf. BRYC secured the loan to pay for the entirety of the work and allowed FWSA to pay it back in annual installments. A similar arrangement with BRYC and the Woodson High School Boosters Club allowed the women to gain access to the Woodson field, including on Saturdays. BRYC permits the women to use a BRYC-scheduled practice field on weeknights to conduct soccer clinics for new players, or players returning to soccer after long layoffs. BRYC allots one-half of a field to the "older girls" practice.

Over thirty years after first stepping on the field, Ruth retired from playing. At age seventy, Ruth played her last game during a tournament in Bellingham, Washington. "I scored a goal in my last game. That was a high for me. The next season, the first time I tried to run, the jolting just … I have scoliosis, stenosis in two places, arthritis, herniated disc, and whatever. I'm two inches shorter than I used to be!"

"I feel I was so fortunate to be right on the cutting edge to be able to do it. I don't know what I would have done with all this energy. One of the reasons I love it so much is that it's a game where anybody can come on the field and enjoy the very first time they ever play, unlike tennis where you have to be able to keep the ball in the court, and basketball where you need to be able to shoot or pass. The more you play soccer, the better, but beginners can come out on the field and say, 'Hey, I can kick the ball, and I can run. This is fun.'"

Ruth still registers with her team, Genesis, paying the registration fee each spring and fall season to support the league. Ruth's husband, Howard, coaches her old team and Ruth has become the FWSA recruiter, looking for new players, and still finding women even as old as fifty who have never played soccer but are eager to try.

At many an FWSA game, Ruth Walton can be found on the sidelines, cheering on her legion of soccer friends, and wishing she could be with them on the field. "I still dream about playing soccer."

Bad Fields and Worse Fields

Martha Dinwiddie was born and raised in Houston, Texas and played multiple intramural sports in high school and at the University of Texas. When Martha moved to Richardson, Texas, an inner suburb of Dallas, she and her husband discovered that soccer was a popular youth sport in the area. Her husband, thinking he would likely be called upon to coach his children at some point, joined a neighborhood men's soccer team. The wives, watching their husbands play, speculated that it would be fun to play and informed their spouses they were thinking of starting a women's soccer team. Many husbands responded to the idea with derision, adding fuel to their wives' resolve.

Martha and others posted signs around the neighboring area calling for interested women to meet at Richardson High School on a Sunday afternoon. Enough women showed up to form two teams. The boys' soccer coach at the high school volunteered to coach Martha's team. The women began practicing and soon heard that there was a women's soccer team in Plano (five miles northeast of Richardson) and another in Mesquite (eighteen miles to the southeast). "We got together, formed a little league, and played with those teams," Martha said. The women began playing in January, 1975. Following the recommendation of their coaches, the women played only thirty-minute halves that first season. A round-robin playoff was scheduled for the end of the season on a large field with a decided crown down the middle. For this inaugural tournament, the women played forty-five-minute halves. Each team played Friday night and during the day on Saturday and Sunday. During the daytime games, the thermometer reached one hundred degrees. "Why we didn't all have heart attacks or strokes and die right then I do not know. It was terrible," Martha recalled. She was not alone in her sentiments. However, the women returned for another season in the fall, and more teams joined. In two years the league grew to ten teams.

"The first or second season that we were playing, a TV station came out, took videos and interviewed women," Martha said. A reporter approached one of the husbands and asked how he felt about his wife playing soccer. His response: "I don't like it one darn bit. She comes home, and she's too tired for sex." That part was not aired. Within six years, The North Texas Women's Soccer Association had over one hundred teams and presumably a few more upset husbands.

Martha was the first league commissioner and was the scheduler for several years. Both the men's league commissioner and the men's scheduler were friends of Martha and her husband so for several years the Richardson's men's and women's teams were able to share the same field. As a result spouses and significant others were available to attend each other's games.

While soccer fields were plentiful in Richardson, they weren't necessarily good fields. In soccer, one should play with the head up to scan the area and determine the appropriate action with the ball: pass, dribble, or shoot. New players tend to play with their heads down, watching the ball until they become more comfortable with the ball at their feet. In the Dallas area, even as the women improved their skills they played with their heads down to avoid stepping in large cracks on the desiccated fields. Otherwise, twisted and perhaps broken ankles could ensue.

As in many leagues, teams were responsible for securing a field on which they could play home games. A new team on the south side of Dallas couldn't find an available soccer field and had to create one out of an open expanse. They lined the field, put up goals, and left a small tree growing happily on the designated play area. Apparently, since the area was only a temporary soccer field, the tree could not be cut down. Under the rules of soccer—not that they explicitly mention forests—the tree was part of the field of play, like a small rock or sprinkler head. Consequently, balls bouncing off the trunk or redirected by the branches were still in play and the game continued. The conundrum for a player, of course, was whether to play with her head down to protect her ankles or play with her head up to avoid a nasty encounter with the tree.

Eastfield, a community college in Mesquite, was one of the better fields, but on occasion presented a challenging playing surface. One time Martha's team was playing at Eastfield when the sprinkler system came on. The referee's decision was to "play on" even when a burst of water knocked the glasses off one of Martha's teammates. A nearby field was open and dry, but the women didn't have permission to use it. They continued their game, dodging the popped-up sprinkler heads and rotating streams of water.

Mary Pirnie began playing soccer in her late thirties in Boise, Idaho, which boasts a dry climate, averaging only twelve inches of precipitation annually.[4] A few years later Mary moved to Seattle, made a few phone calls and located a women's soccer team she could join. Although the mildness of the Seattle climate allows soccer to be played year-round, the dampness plays havoc with field conditions—Seattle receives three times as much rain as Boise and two of every five days contribute measurable precipitation.[5] "When we played at Grasslawn Field in Seattle," Mary said, "it was definitely slanted, and one of the goals was often under water." Mary recalled that a goalie diving for the ball would at times come up spouting water. But Grasslawn was not the worst field. That distinction belonged to a field covered with the artificial surface Centrex.

From a distance, a Centrex soccer field would appear to be covered in red dirt, not a blade of real or artificial grass to be seen. A close-up view, perhaps gained when one slid across its surface, would reveal that the material was red brick, crushed to the consistency of dust peppered with small rocks. Skinned knees, hands, elbows and faces were not uncommon. Used for base paths in baseball—the red looked gorgeous against the green grass—Centrex and similar materials were reviled for the torn uniforms and scraped skin that followed installation. When a Centrex field became muddy, the ground left permanent red stains on socks, shoes, and uniforms. If all that weren't enough, the Centrex field was a haven for Canadian geese that peppered the ground with their droppings. Stories abounded of players suffering open wounds that became infected from the parasites in the feces. Altogether an unpleasant and dangerous field.

Synthetic turf has been used for football fields since the 1960s, but only much later was it used for soccer. A harder surface than natural turf, the early artificial surfaces caused more frequent and more serious joint injuries than grass.[6] As turf technology evolved, sand was spread between the fibers to provide more stability and firmer grip for the players. Still, it was not widely adopted for soccer because sliding or falling on the surface produced painful abrasions. The latest generation of turf, which appeared in the 1990s, features a bottom layer of sand, a middle layer of rubber and sand, and a top layer of rubber bits mixed into longer fibers of fake grass. There is still a debate in the soccer community about the safety of this turf, although studies have shown it to cause no more injuries than grass.[7] Not in dispute is the fact that turf surfaces become extremely hot in warm weather. Like many areas with high demand for fields, municipalities in the Pacific Northwest have installed artificial turf on fields so they are usable in wet and rainy conditions.

Artificial turf is often eschewed for high-level matches partially because it is believed the cumulative effect of repeatedly running on the harder surface, as in tournaments, takes a toll on the players. Many older women have found that playing on the artificial turf puts a strain their backs thereby limiting their endurance. On the other hand, these women agree the synthetic surface is preferable to fields that are canted, under water, strewn with broken glass and rocks, fissured, or covered in crushed brick.

The women have long since learned, however, to be thankful for any field.

SIXTEEN
Barbarians at the Gate

WOMEN IN SOCCER, like children at Thanksgiving, have been seated at the little table, far from the real decisions and money. While there are men who have supported women's participation in the soccer hierarchy, the overall attitude of the governing bodies has long been to deny that women have any place in the management of the sport.

No Women Need Apply: Michigan Soccer Association
Before ever setting foot on a soccer field, Mari-jo Wickens was battling for the rights of women. In the mid-1970s, Mj was a volunteer in her community, responsible for checking on local schools' compliance with Title IX requirements. A short time later, divorced and back in college, Mj used her Title IX knowledge to badger the dean of a community college into providing sports opportunities for women, which up to then were nonexistent. He allowed the women to establish a softball team, which Mj joined.

Mj's boyfriend convinced her to try soccer, and she signed up for a new women's soccer recreational program in Ann Arbor.

After several sessions, she challenged Ann Arbor Community Education & Recreation to explain why the men played eleven-a-side soccer while the women were restricted to a smaller field playing six-a-side. She was told that if she wanted to play on the large field, she would have to prove there were enough women to field two full teams. To find additional players Mj approached the University of Michigan (U-M). Women's soccer at the time was not a varsity sport, but the University did recognize it as a club sport and provided fields for the women, albeit no funds. Non-students were allowed to join club teams, and Mj was able to recruit a sufficient number of women to field two teams. Rather than permanent teams, the woman chose to divide up at the beginning of each game. Although U-M colors are blue and gold, Mj noted that the women decided to wear blue or red jerseys "because we were mad" at not being given more support from the University. The women were soon bored with playing just each other. Mj contacted colleges in the area and set up a women's league for club soccer teams. The league provided much-needed competition and was the first step to women's soccer being recognized as a varsity sport by the University of Michigan.

Word of Mj's success reached the ears of Paula Hockster of Union Lake, Michigan, an hour northeast of Ann Arbor. Paula was one of several wives and girlfriends playing coed soccer with their partners. She loved the game but didn't like playing with men because they rarely passed the ball to women. Hearing about Mj, Paula thought of how marvelous it must be to play just with women. She called Mj. Several more calls and meetings later, Mj and Paula had organized a four-team women's soccer tournament, which was held in June 1979. Over the following fall and winter, they worked with others to draw up documents establishing the Great Lakes Women's Soccer League (GLWSL). Believing that only women should run the league, the constitution and bylaws restricted office holders to players—a stipulation that upset more than a few male coaches in the early years.

The GLWSL women took their sport seriously and ensured others did, too. When an article on Mj's team appeared in the features section of an Ann Arbor newspaper instead of the sports section, the women were furious. The team's goalkeeper, a physically imposing female attorney, strongly suggested to the newspaper that it reprint the article where it belonged. The paper capitulated and ran the article as a sports story.

GLWSL affiliated with the Michigan Soccer Association (MSA), the governing body for soccer in the state. In the first year of affiliation, Mj persuaded a large number of the women to attend the annual meeting. Under Mj's direction, the women voted as a bloc for and against various proposals. Up to that point, MSA had been the province of an old guard of foreign-born men. The presence of women at the meeting and, much worse, the bloc voting that swung the outcome on several proposals, caused a near riot. Shouting ensued, and some men stormed out. Since the women had adhered to MSA rules for voting, the men had to live with the results. Over the next few years, MSA enacted numerous changes to the voting rules. The men hoped these new procedures would lessen the power of the women. Astutely, the women adjusted to each new rule and continued as an influential voting bloc. In time Mj became the first woman—and in all likelihood the first native-born American—to sit on the MSA board. She encountered stiff opposition to her proposals. "Everything was a battle," she said, "a hostile environment." A number of the board members were of German extraction and would switch to their native language when they didn't want Mj to know what they were up to. Mj remained on the board for years, only making way when she was convinced the men were so thoroughly sick of her that they would welcome any woman who replaced her.

In addition to her work for the Michigan Soccer Association and Great Lakes Women's Soccer, Mj for years ran an international adult soccer tournament in Ann Arbor, Michigan with her husband. She obtained a B coaching license and was the first woman in Michigan to be paid as a high school coach for boys. At one high school game against a prestigious boys school, the opposing team refused to take the field against her team, Huron High School. The reason given was, "because you are a woman and that is against our rules: this is an all-boys' thing." With great difficulty, Mj held her tongue in check, although she did have to walk around the field before she could control her temper and her speech. She icily told the referees and the opposing coach that since the other school refused to play, she assumed that meant the game was forfeit, and the referees would declare the victory for Huron High. Realizing Mj had neatly boxed him into a corner, the opposing coach swallowed his principles and agreed to let the teams play. It was all the sweeter for Mj when her boys won.

The rapidly growing participation of girls and women in soccer led the president of the U.S. Soccer Federation to deliver a spiel at the annual meeting for more women to become involved in the organization. Mj stepped forward and became the Women's Coordinator for Region II, representing more than a dozen Midwest states. The first soccer tournament Mj played in after her appointment took place in Washington, DC. She enjoyed attending the competition not just to play, but also to be feted as "a somebody" that people wanted to meet. She was even invited to a dinner with soccer legend Pelé.

During tournament play, Mj was her usual competitive self: giving no quarter and contesting every ball. When the referee made some calls that were, in the estimation of Mj and her teammates, simply atrocious, she didn't remain silent. On the sidelines following the game, Mj and her teammates made comments amongst themselves about the referee. Their venting included a few pig snorts. Although she was unaware of it at the time, the referee duly noted the expressions of dissent and gave Mj a red card. She was prohibited from playing in the first game scheduled for the next day.

That evening Mj attended a reception for soccer VIPs at an embassy. While going through the receiving line, she came face to face with the head of referees for the United States Soccer Federation. Mj shook his hand and greeted him warmly. He responded to her greeting with a pig snort. Mj realized she was now known in the upper circles of soccer; she was indeed "a somebody."

One would think that building the league, working in soccer administration, coaching, refereeing both men's and women's games at all ages—she gave up men's games only after gunfire erupted at the end of one match—managing tournaments, and raising a family would have been enough for Mj. However, during the years she was active in soccer Mj earned her bachelor's, master's, and doctoral degrees from the University of Michigan.

Mj was elected to the Great Lakes Women's Soccer League Hall of Fame in 1988 for founding the league and continuing to improve women's soccer throughout the state. In 2010 she was elected to the Michigan Soccer Hall of Fame for "Outstanding contribution and dedicated service to the game of soccer." She has received numerous awards from the Michigan Special Olympics and still plays in the Great Lakes Women's Soccer League.

Mj will be the first to say that the success of Great Lakes Soccer rests on the shoulders of many hard-working, dedicated, and strong women. Julie Ilacqua is one of them.

Hallowed Halls: U.S. Soccer Federation

Julie spent her formative years on a small farm in Minnesota. In later years when her father struggled to understand how Julie and her sisters had become such ardent feminists, she explained to him that he was primarily responsible. As a youngster, Julie played 4-H softball on a coed team. Her father coached the team and believed in putting the best players on the field. That often meant that Julie and her female friends played while some of the boys watched from the bench, despite what it may have done to their egos. Around the family dinner table, Julie and her siblings were encouraged to venture their opinions—on any subject. Their parents challenged them at times, but never belittled their children's ideas. And when the siblings wanted to try something new and perhaps beyond their capabilities, they were never told they weren't good enough. Consequently, Julie and each of her siblings met the world head on and full of confidence in their abilities.

Julie met and married her husband when they worked for VISTA—Volunteers in Service to America, created in 1964 to help fight poverty. By the late 1970s, Julie had three boys, had moved to Wixom, Michigan, and was playing softball in an adult women's league. Her two oldest sons, nine and seven, joined soccer teams. The youngest one signed up too, but his team didn't have a coach. When no one volunteered, Julie said she'd coach. That was before she discovered she was pregnant. The day Julie came home from the hospital with her latest baby, she put her third son in the car and drove him to the soccer game, his newborn brother in tow.

Standing on the sideline during her boys' games, Julie would imagine herself in the game, contemplating what runs she would make and when she would shoot. She felt a longing to play. Serendipitously, Julie's husband enrolled in a soccer refereeing class where he met a woman who was working with Mj and others to establish a women's soccer league. He passed on Julie's name, and she was soon signed up for the inaugural year of the Great Lakes Women's Soccer League.

"When I started playing, I wasn't great at it, but I loved it," Julie said. She admitted that her home life went from crazy to chaotic: her boys played soccer at different times and in different places, Julie had her games, and her husband was busy refereeing. On the field, when her mind was fully involved in the game, Julie found relief from the stress of managing her brood.

Julie was drafted into coaching her youngest son's U-12 team. The boys were quite talented and won their division in the fall. However, in the spring many of the boys played baseball instead of soccer. The players replacing them were not great athletes, and Julie was challenged to produce a competitive team. One of the boys, Andrew, thought of himself as a defender and always played on the fullback line. However, Andrew tended to run through opposing players to get the ball, bowling them over in the process. The opposing team would be awarded a penalty kick, which all too frequently resulted in a score. This didn't make Andrew popular with his teammates. Julie couldn't let the situation continue so she had a serious chat with him. "I know you think you are a defender," Julie said, "but I want you to play center midfield. Your job is to get the ball and pass it to somebody who is open. If you make a foul out there, I don't care, and the other kids don't care." She convinced Andrew to move. He still knocked players over, but his teammates were no longer yelling at him, and his play improved significantly. After lopsided losses at the beginning of the season, the team as a whole began playing better and grew more confident. As the season neared the end, Julie asked Andrew if he'd like to play forward. "Oh no," he replied. "I'm a midfielder." In the last game of the season, Julie's team played well and beat the first place team. Afterward, Andrew's mother took Julie aside and said, "I just want you to know the impact you had on my son. Andrew is so much more confident in himself, he is much happier, and this has made a world of difference in his life." It was the high point of Julie's coaching career.

Julie's first and only experience in coaching girls came when she was asked to take over a year-old soccer program at Walled Lake Central High School. At the request of the school district,

Julie committed to coach for three years. "We were playing in the toughest league in the state," Julie recalled. "It was a real challenge to go into that league to coach." Her experience with the girls convinced Julie that if she had to have four children of one sex, she was darn glad she had boys. "The drama! The cliques that form! All that stuff with girls in that age group was crazy. I sat them down one day, and I said, 'I don't care if you are friends off the field. I don't care if you are friends at all. But in this situation, you are a team. If you are ragging on somebody, you are on the bench because I just won't have it.' My last year coaching, that third year, I had a girl who was a junior, and I put her on the varsity team. She said, 'I don't want to play on varsity if I have to play with Alexi.' I was dumbfounded! I had raised all boys. They don't care who they are playing with. They can duke it out [one minute] and be a team in the next minute. I said, 'Okay, but Alexi's the goalie so you can play JV, that's fine.'"

Like Mj, Julie became involved with the Michigan Soccer Association. "Mari-jo took me to my very first meeting with the Michigan Soccer Association. I sat there, I listened, and I learned. Then you'd go to the bar and have a beer. We'd talk about things. I said, 'Mari-jo, that's a lot of horseshit going on.' She said, 'Yeah, I know. That's why I wanted you to come.'"

One year the women voted for the only MSA presidential candidate who was willing to court their votes. When he won, some of the other leagues in MSA filed a complaint with the U.S. Soccer Federation claiming that the election was unfair because of the way the women had voted and carried the election. The leagues asked that U.S. Soccer void the results. Perhaps because of informal lobbying prior to the official hearing, the men were confident they would prevail. Julie, however, was not idle. She wrote up a defense demonstrating that the women—as usual—had followed procedure and that the men's leagues that had filed the complaint were in violation of the rule they accused the women of breaking. When it appeared the oversight board might not hear her, Julie informed them that if they refused to allow the women a say, she'd take the matter to the full council of the U.S. Soccer Federation. The board relented, heard her case, and voted to let the election results stand. Henceforth, Julie was known in MSA as "Dragon Lady."

A few younger men in MSA advised their elders that to counter the women the men also could vote in a bloc. But the men could never agree on an issue and organize around it. The women continued to hold sway in many meetings.

In the 1990s, the head of an ethnic eastern European league, the largest league the Michigan Soccer Association, asked Julie if she would run for president of MSA. At the time, Julie was in charge of volunteer services for the upcoming World Cup 94 games at the Silverdome in Detroit. Julie agreed to run, won, and served four years.

A coach, a player, and an administrator, Julie likely had her most significant impact on the game of soccer as a referee.

After Julie had been coaching for two years, her husband suggested she take a referee class. The youth league was chronically short of referees, and he believed she might like the role. He was right. Refereeing was a natural fit.

"I've always been decisive," Julie said. "I have a good brain and a good memory, so the rules were not difficult for me to learn. I also have the ability to let things roll off my back." As an example, Julie mentioned that more than once as a referee in a men's game, a player has called her a bitch or worse. If it is said softly such that no one else hears it, as when the player is running past, then Julie will ignore it. However, if a player yells the insult and others obviously hear him, then he is undermining her authority and Julie will eject him from the game.

Julie doesn't hold grudges, either. What's done is forgotten and not taken personally. But, she doesn't take crap either. Julie would hold her ground no matter who challenged her, something that happened from time to time in the ethnic men's leagues in Michigan. Being the first woman in so many areas, "you had to be straight up. You can't be namby-pamby. Sometimes you just have to lay stuff on the line. If you don't, you get walked all over," Julie said.

Early on, Julie predominantly refereed youth games but at times would act as an assistant referee at men's games. Carlos, an experienced referee, took Julie under his wing, watching her work and giving her pointers. When Julie reached a certain level of competency, he pushed her to referee a men's game, offering to be one of her assistants. Julie took up the challenge. During the match she issued a red card, throwing a man out of the game. Word got around. "Are you that little redhead who threw Danny Turner out of the game?" she'd be asked. With a reputation as a strict referee, Julie saw little egregious behavior and didn't have to give another red card for eighteen months.

Carlos encouraged Julie to become a state referee. The lowest level for referees, Grade 9, is given to adults and youths who are capable of being the center referee for U-12 games. A state referee is one who has attained Grade 6/5 and, in Michigan, is allowed to referee the Michigan State Premier Soccer League, Regional Leagues, and other higher-level games within the state. State referees have to pass a yearly fitness test. Julie took the tests, was assessed by veteran referees, and was certified as a state referee.

Julie and her husband sometimes refereed together at high school games. One night while driving home after a game, Julie's husband started listing the things he thought she did wrong during the game. Julie remained silent until he was finished, then said, "Now let me tell you a couple of little things you did wrong." They decided then and there that it would be better if they didn't work together again.

When Julie was coach of Walled Lake Central High School, she advised the parents that she knew every referee for the upcoming girls' games. "There will be not one referee who will try to screw us. So I don't want you yelling at the referee. Talking to the referees is my job." Those times the parents did get rowdy, Julie stood at the bottom of the bleachers and glared them into silence.

Some women felt unwelcome in the male world of soccer. Sue Boettcher noted that in her early days of coaching in Washington, she and other women "had to stand our ground against some men who didn't want us there. They didn't think we could coach, that we didn't have the skills. You'd walk into a room of mostly male coaches and nobody would reach out to you. It wasn't all welcoming arms."

Julie was fortunate to find men who helped her along in her refereeing career. She is unstinting in acknowledging their support. Steve Olson is one of those to whom Julie is indebted. A national referee since 1983 and a FIFA assistant referee since 1992, Olson refereed over twenty Olympic and World Cup qualifying matches in his career. Steve made it a point to attend Julie's games, assess her performance, and provide valued advice.

Fazi was another treasure and worked many games with Julie. Scheduled to referee back-to-back men's games one day, Julie and Fazi were forced to work without the third referee who failed to show up. For the game involving an Iraqi team, Julie took the center referee spot while Fazi ran the sideline. In the midst of the hotly contested game, Julie made a call that one of the players objected to. A very large, Iraqi man began to advance threateningly toward Julie. From the sideline came a yell from Fazi who rattled off something in Arabic. The player came to a dead stop, turned, and walked away. Afterward, Julie discovered that Fazi had forewarned the player that if he touched a single hair on Julie's head, he would never, ever play soccer again in Michigan.

In 1988 Julie Ilacqua became the first woman to officiate a Michigan boy's high school Class A state final. She attributes her selection in part to the support of a man who was involved in the referee assignment process and had seen Julie referee matches. In 1990 Julie was chosen to be the first woman to referee for the National Association of Intercollegiate Athletics women's soccer playoffs. Four referees were selected: Julie and three men. When the assignments were handed out, Julie was awarded the head referee position for the final match. Don Wilber, a highly respected referee from South Carolina and one of the other game officials, told Julie, "I am so glad you got the final, it's about time."[1]

The playoffs took place at Erskine College in South Carolina and the first night was unusually cold. Julie was an assistant referee (AR) for Don Wilber in the initial game. Her job entailed running up and down the sidelines and calling fouls, offside, and possession on out-of-bounds balls. To accurately spot an offside violation, an AR must stand on the sideline, even with the next-to-last defender, or even with the ball, whichever is closer to the end line. In the run of play, the AR executes sudden sprints to keep up with the field players who may be as much as two decades younger. During a ninety-minute game, an AR may equal or surpass the several miles run by players during the game. Don Wilber was impressed with the accuracy of Julie's calls and told her at the halftime break, "You are right on the money. I'm going with you every time."

Julie also was an AR for the second game that evening. The game ended in a tie in regulation and went into overtime. She barely survived. "I hurt so bad by the time I got done. I took a couple of Motrin, and I lay on top of a heater. I was in good shape: running fifty miles a week. But it was cold, and it was long."

Before the final game, Don once again expressed confidence in Julie's abilities. Eight minutes into the match Julie awarded a penalty kick. Pacific Lutheran University scored and led 1-0. After the PK, fouling was at a minimum. Berry College scored a tying goal and, at the end of regulation, the game headed into overtime: thirty more minutes would be played. Julie eyed the young athletic women on the field and told herself that no matter what happened, she would be the last person standing. During the overtime, Berry College scored two goals and won 3-1.

Despite all the support she received, Julie did face discrimination from the soccer establishment. Not just on the field as a referee, but in administrative situations Julie was subject to sexually demeaning comments. To the more suggestive comments she replied, "I'm happy to know at your age you can still dream." Then she'd go about her business.

As Julie's refereeing career progressed, she took on even higher profile jobs in the administration of U.S. Soccer. She was approached about taking a full-time position at U.S. Soccer headquarters in Chicago but declined at the time. The job would require her to relocate and her youngest son was still at home. Julie became the first female chair of the U.S. Soccer National Referee Committee, serving from 1996 to 1999. She was elected to the board of the National Association of Sports Officials and became chairman in 2001 during her fourth year as a member of the board. In 1999 with her youngest now out of high school, Julie was approached again about a position with U.S. Soccer. She and her husband moved to Chicago, and she became head of Membership Services and then Managing Director of Referee Programs for U.S. Soccer. In the latter position, she was responsible for overseeing the development of referees to service the game of soccer at every level of competition.

Julie counts herself fortunate to have worked at U.S. Soccer with another highly supportive man and excellent referee: Esse Bahamast. In 1998, Esse became the only American referee ever to take charge of two matches at a World Cup.[2] He was a genuinely gifted referee, a masterful instructor, and held in high regard in the global soccer community. "Esse is highly ethical …

an amazing human being," Julie said. "He and I established an awesome working relationship." Esse became Julie's right-hand development person and did all the international work.

Shortly before she moved to Chicago, Julie was diagnosed with autoimmune issues. Working for U.S. Soccer, it was not unusual for Julie to work for three weeks in a row without a day off. The lack of rest led to lupus flare-ups in the form of severe exhaustion, weight loss, fever, and anemia. Because of her ongoing health issues, Julie chose to retire in 2008.

Julie Ilacqua was inducted into the U.S. Adult Soccer Association Hall of Fame in 2007. In USASA Region II—which includes Michigan—the trophy for the women's over-30 championship was named for Julie.

When she was head of the referee committee, Julie convinced U.S. Soccer that it was time for a woman to referee a game in Major League Soccer. One of her mentors later asked, "Do you ever resent the fact you didn't get an opportunity to ref in the MLS? You could have done that job." Julie responded, "I don't even think about it because what I know about being the first in something is somebody has to crack the door and hold it open a little bit so the next person goes through. There always has to be somebody to crack the door."

As she reflected upon her soccer career, Julie said, "I loved playing, I loved coaching, and I loved refereeing. I loved all of it."

The Neanderthals of FIFA

Born in 1945, Linda Grant played semi-professional softball and basketball as a young woman in New England. She was hoping to be a coach but settled for an office job in Norwood, Massachusetts to be able to take care of her ailing mother. At a mere twenty-five years of age, Linda was beset with back spasms of such severity that she was out of work for a month and barely able to walk. After endless tests and doctor visits, she was told that her pain was due to muscle spasms from sitting too much. Her doctor recommended that Linda participate in a field sport requiring a lot of running.

Still playing softball and basketball at the time, Linda heard a spiel on the radio for Charles River Women's Rugby Club and thought she'd give it a try. Three nights a week she made the forty-minute drive from Norwood to Cambridge to play a sport where she felt she was neither big enough nor fast enough. When Linda heard another advertisement on the radio, this time for soccer, she decided to switch sports in hopes soccer would be easier on her body than rugby.

Linda joined a group of women assembled by Max Spector to play indoor soccer. She described the experience as "horrible," but with a hidden gem. Bob Friedman, an assistant coach at Harvard, worked as one of Spector's assistants. Bob was supportive of the women and encouraged Linda to contact Ellen Simons who was in the process of organizing some teams. Linda called and became one of the founding members of the Eastern Massachusetts Women's Soccer League (EMWSL). Linda joined the Charles River team and Bob Friedman became the coach. With Bob's nudging, Linda became manager of her team and then vice-president of the EMWSL. Again it was Bob who noted that a representative from EMWSL should attend meetings of the Massachusetts Senior Soccer Association (MSSA). Linda volunteered or was volunteered. As the only woman at the association meetings, it seemed fitting—to the men—that Linda take notes. She agreed, and for the next twenty years, served as registrar, secretary, and first point of contact for adult soccer teams and players from across Massachusetts. The association, like those in other states, expanded rapidly with the growing popularity of soccer.

In the early 1980s, Linda represented MSSA at U.S. Adult Soccer Association (USASA) meetings for Region I. One of four regions in the country, Region I encompasses thirteen states from Maine to Virginia. Once again she was the lone woman attendee. Linda was selected for an administrative position with Region I, which meant that she attended national meetings for USASA. It was at these meetings that Linda discovered the existence of women's leagues in other states and regions. The women formed a network of support, and when USASA established a Women's Committee, Linda became its head.

"U.S. Soccer was not supportive of women," Linda said. As early as 1978 U.S. Soccer had been approached about the need for a women's soccer organization. The administration actively thwarted attempts to establish a U.S. Women's Soccer Federation but did form a U.S. Soccer Ad Hoc Women's Committee.[3]

In addition to ignoring the women, Linda noted that U.S. Soccer "didn't care about the seniors [adults] at all: old, don't know what you are doing, pains in the neck, most of you aren't very good players. But what they did need were votes. They needed us. And we were pretty powerful that way because we could swing votes. I was a member of Mass Senior Soccer. Mass Senior Soccer, because it was fairly large, had [a strong voice.] We could swing elections, which we did."

Linda and the other women argued with U.S. Soccer to do more for adult women, observing that once the female youth players were out of college, they needed a place to play. Also, through league and tournament fees, women could be a significant source of money for U.S. Soccer programs. Despite years and years of pushing, Linda does not believe that the women have ever been heard.

In 1991, when the United States won the inaugural Women's World Cup in China, the FIFA Women's Committee was all male and included a Canadian representing the CONCACAF Region—Confederation of North, Central America, and Caribbean Association Football. Linda felt strongly that a woman from CONCACAF should be on the committee. U.S. Soccer was a mere spectator as Linda complained to FIFA and was put on the board as the new CONCACAF representative.[4] "It made me feel bad," she said, because the Canadian representative "was a peach ... but not that bad because I knew we needed to have a representative there."

For eight years she served on the women's committee, traveling to FIFA headquarters in Switzerland for meetings. Rarely were agendas sent out beforehand. They were distributed at the meeting, and when it was time to consider a particular item, Linda would learn that enough votes had been secured, there would be no discussion, and the item was approved. "FIFA was so incredibly corrupt and so incredibly political. It was tough because it was so political."

The pervasive rot in FIFA was an open secret. Lord David Triesman, former chairman of the England Football Association, said, "FIFA, I'm afraid, behaves like a mafia family. It has a decades-long tradition of bribes ... and corruption." The rot extended to the highest levels.[5]

In 2015 the world radically changed for FIFA when the United States indicted fourteen current and former FIFA officials and associations on charges of "rampant, systemic, and deep-rooted" corruption based on a three-year investigation by the FBI. The fallout has since claimed many careers. Yet Linda believes the corruption still exists. "Even now they are appointing women who haven't put in their time. We know what FIFA is all about."

The International Olympic Committee awarded the 1996 Summer Games to Atlanta. Marilyn Childress, a board member with Georgia Soccer, worked with Linda and others on a national campaign to include women's soccer as an Olympic event for the first time. Linda noted that the difficulty of garnering support was "awful, but we did it." The "we" did not include a U.S. Soccer organization that didn't bother lifting a finger to help. The women convinced Congressman Newt Gingrich from Georgia and eighteen other members of Congress from across the country to introduce a congressional resolution in 1992 that women's soccer be an Olympics medal sport. Both chambers of Congress approved the resolution. The women then petitioned the International Olympics Committee, which added women's soccer to the 1996 Summer Games. Linda was ecstatic. The Olympics provided women with "the opportunity to be exposed to an entirely new audience."[6] And indeed, the women delighted their new fans. In the semi-final game against Norway, Shannon MacMillan, the "class act" from California who had impressed Jacquie Burt, scored the winning goal to send the United States into the title game. In front of 76,000 fans at Sanford Stadium, Shannon MacMillan scored, Tiffeny Milbrett added a second, and the U.S. won the gold medal, defeating China, 2-1.

Linda served the interests of soccer in a variety of positions during the nineties. She was chairperson of U.S. Soccer's Women's Development Committee, part of a team staging the 1994 Men's World Cup in Massachusetts, and was a commissioner for the Women's World Cup held a year later in Sweden. Doug Arnot, managing director of venues and operations for the 1996 Olympics, was impressed with Linda's organizational skills and hired her to work for him in staging the Olympics in Atlanta. Furthermore, Linda was integral to the effort to stage the 1999 Women's World Cup in the United States.[7]

In addition to her administrative accomplishments in the soccer arena, Linda has contributed to the game on the grassroots level. She was part of the small group that founded Norwood Soccer League—a program now encompassing over eighty teams. She obtained a referee license and, in the early years, was the referee for all of Norwood's youth games on Saturdays. Linda coached her nephew's team from U-8 all the way through U-19. (Along the way, she helped found the Norwood Basketball Association for boys and girls.)

Several years after schools were directed to comply with Title IX, Norwood High School did not have a girl's soccer team. The school's athletic director didn't believe women should be playing sports and "didn't give a shit" about whatever Title IX mandated. Linda undertook a crusade for the girls. She obtained uniforms, arranged a schedule of games, and coached the team. And because she had a coaching license, the athletic director had to pay her. Linda created both a junior varsity and a varsity team, further enraging the director. Linda recalled that the team was "horrible. There were maybe four who had played soccer before; all the rest had never played." She recruited girls from the track team because the track season didn't conflict with soccer. Although the girls were fast and could blow by the opposition, they had almost no skills and sometimes ran right over the ball. Linda coached the team for five years.

In 1998, Linda Grant became the first woman inducted into the Massachusetts Soccer Hall of Fame. Although she has not played for years, Linda still meets up with old soccer teammates for dinner on a regular basis.

Old prejudices die hard, and despite the inroads of Mj, Julie, Linda, and their successors, women still are not treated equitably by U.S. Soccer or FIFA. Chris Hovind, a longtime board member of the Washington State Women's Soccer Association, aptly noted, "It's always a struggle to get some respect, but the female soccer community is a bunch of strong women; we're not going to just let it pass. We'll get there eventually. It's a long way and a slow journey." Indeed it is; Moses and the Israelites wandered a mere forty years for the Promised Land. The women have been kept in the wilderness much, much longer.

SEVENTEEN
Changes in the Wind

IT'S A TRUISM that older generations believe younger generations are not sufficiently aware or appreciative of the sacrifices of their elders. So it is with some older women who spent decades building women's soccer leagues only to see young women take the leagues for granted.

The women featured in this book were girls or young women at the time Title IX was passed. Their generation came of age when girls' athletic opportunities were limited and predominantly intramural. Generation Xers were the first beneficiaries of the changing sports scene in public schools. By the time Generation Y, the Millennials, reached high school—starting in 1995—2.4 million girls were participating in high school sports: 445,000 in basketball, 379,000 in track and field, 358,000 in volleyball, 305,000 in softball, and 209,000 in soccer. Other popular sports included tennis, golf, field hockey, cross country, and swimming & diving. Since then sports participation among high school girls has continued to grow with 3.3 million playing in 2016.[1] Little wonder then that the generations have vastly different attitudes toward athletic opportunities.

Years ago Lois Kessin was part of a Massachusetts club soccer organization that fielded women's teams at different age levels for a national soccer tournament. The under-30 squad for the club consisted of highly skilled women who were perhaps just shy of being national team caliber. Because they were elite players, these women for years had received free soccer uniforms, shoes, and bags from team sponsors. They owned multiples of everything, including cleats. Their last purchase of soccer gear may have been as pre-teens. Lois, who was on one of the older teams, mentioned in passing she was astounded that she had just spent more than $100 to purchase a good pair of soccer cleats. The younger players looked at her in disbelief. "What? You spent money on boots? They don't give you boots?" It never occurred to them that other women purchased their equipment. The next day, the young women brought little-used soccer cleats to a squad meeting and offered them to the older players. Lois appreciated the gesture but even now marvels at the gap in soccer experiences and expectations between the generations.

Decade after decade across the country participation in women's soccer leagues rose. Then it didn't. Ruth Walton, a longtime promoter of Fairfax Women's Soccer Association, recalled, "We had over 900 players, but then we realized our numbers were going down, particularly in that younger age group." Younger soccer players were eschewing the women's leagues for coed soccer. In 1971, the median age of first marriage was twenty-one for women and twenty-three for men. Today it is twenty-seven for women and twenty-nine for men. Coed soccer naturally appeals as a venue to meet members of the opposite sex. Ruth noted, "If we didn't do something to keep them involved, the league would ultimately disappear, and there are some women who don't want to play soccer with men. It's a different game." To boost their numbers, FWSA added preseason events, free clinics, and a development division for first-time players or those returning to the game after many years. Outreach efforts have added over one hundred new players to the league in recent years, but participation is still below the one-time peak.

Younger women are often underrepresented in league administrative positions. Christiane Wollaston-Jury noted, "The young people don't want to step up and do any of their responsibilities to the league." In many leagues, that means the older women can't step down. Or worse. In the Eastern Massachusetts Women's Soccer League men currently fill half of the positions on the board. "You give up, so the men step in and take over," Christiane said. "You get the wolves ruling the roost."

Lois Kessin agreed, commenting that the young women are not appreciative because the opportunity to play sports has been handed to them. And younger women are not as diligent in making the games. "I remember our Charles River team had an award for attendance at our end-of-season banquet," Lois said, "Ten people made every game!"

Alice Moore and Margaret Danner are often called to play on coed teams because the younger women players don't show up. In one tournament, Alice and Margaret had signed up to play with other women, but men they knew approached them about playing coed. None of the women who had said they would play on the coed team had shown up for the first game. Alice and Margaret didn't feel they could let the men down so after their match they trotted over to another field to play coed. "We were the only two women there to start the game," Alice recalled. "They had to play short men because they didn't have enough women. A few more women finally showed up, and we got two young girls out there." Nevertheless, the men's team remained short of women. Alice and Margaret spent the entire day going from a women's game to a coed game and back again. They played six games on Saturday and returned on Sunday to do it again.

"You get these younger coed teams where the women are not as dependable," Alice said. "The other girls show up [late], and they want to go on! It's amazing that the older people are the ones more committed to the sport, to get out there on these coed teams. Always the first out there."

Not all of the older soccer players feel the same way. One woman, now over sixty, said that she had become less dependable than the younger members of her team. "I never know when I roll out of bed in the morning whether I'll have some ache or pain that wasn't there the night before. When I was younger, I would play through anything. Not now. I can't remember the last season where I made more than 75 percent of the games."

The Washington State Women's Soccer Association was once the home of more than one hundred soccer teams. Now the spring season attracts between thirty and forty teams. The advent of more women's leagues and coed leagues is partially responsible. Additionally, women today can choose among a wider variety of athletic endeavors, such as Frisbee in various guises, lacrosse, and mountain biking. Long-time WSWSA member Wendy Fletcher said, "It's probably a good thing because there are more places for people to play. We used to be the only game in town for women. Nice it has spread out a little bit."

The growth of athletic opportunities has benefitted the older women, too. Lynn Naftel has played soccer since she was thirty-five. At the age of fifty-two, she was asked to play senior basketball. "I went to the National Senior Sports Classic in 1997. [The following year] the team moved to an upper age bracket. I was too young but wanted to participate in another National Senior Games as it was so much fun: opening ceremonies, the parade of athletes, uniforms, etc." Lynn was fast on the soccer field, so she decided to try track: 100M, 200M, and 400M. At a local high school dirt track where she went to practice on her own, Lynn had to ask a young man to show her how far 400 meters was. In her initial race, Lynn stepped on an all-weather track for the first time and was surprised to find that runners wore spikes. Nevertheless, in her plain running shoes, Lynn won all three distances in which she competed. One year later, Lynn smashed the national 800M record for a fifty-four-year-old woman, which had been standing for ten years. She missed beating the world record by less than a second. "At fifty-seven I added the 80M and 300M hurdles, setting a national record in the 80M and a world record in the 300M. Track improved my soccer speed, and soccer improved my track endurance. A win-win! I have been very successful in soccer and track with many first place medals." Lynn has run longer distances too, including 5K and 10K, even into her seventies. Her husband was participating in powerlifting and encouraged Lynn to join him. At fifty-seven, she began competing in the deadlift and bench press, setting records for her age/weight division. (She did not say whether powerlifting had helped her soccer.) About the only thing Lynn can't do is pickleball; she had to give it up at age seventy per doctor's orders after rotator cuff repair surgery.

Mary White noted that at a soccer tournament in Chula Vista, the California Senior Games were also taking place. She decided to compete in some track events. Leaving the soccer field after a game, Mary changed her shirt and shoes, ran the five minutes to the track, and joined the lineup for a 100-meter race. Never having practiced, she came in third. She was hooked and continues to participate in state and national events in the 50M, 100M, and 200M. Mary also picked up senior basketball, even attending a sports camp in Maine: the Not Too Late Basketball Camp. "I had the most fun I'd ever had in my life because I'd never been to a sports camp." Nine of every ten women at the camp had not played competitive sports while growing up.

Dawn Cole was one of the many Sacramento area softball players who quit to play soccer. A former shortstop, Dawn found playing goalie to be a natural transition. "The footwork is the same, the using two hands, the moving your feet to get in front of the ball, and the diving. I had no foot skills whatsoever and still consider it an adventure when they pass the ball back to me and I have to kick it with my feet. Plus I like the clothes too. The goalie clothes are flashier than other clothes." In 2008 Dawn took six months off from sports for chemotherapy to treat Hodgkin's Lymphoma and returned stronger than ever. Dawn subsequently joined a cycling team to raise funds for the Leukemia and Lymphoma Society. At age sixty-two, she rode her bike 100 miles around Lake Tahoe and another 100 for Viva Bike Vegas. At sixty-five, she put more than 4,000 miles on her bike while training and riding in events. Several years ago, Dawn's trainer formed a weight-lifting team for women, Sacramento Iron Maidens. Dawn has since set weightlifting records in the bench press and deadlift. Seemingly having energy to burn, Dawn then joined a team running half-marathons. Furthermore, Dawn is still playing goalie, including indoors in an over-40 league where the game is wickedly quick, and shots are fired from close range. Even at sixty-eight, Dawn is not done finding new sports in which she can compete.

For the women who lived and breathed soccer for decades, it has been difficult to watch their children and grandchildren express little interest in the sport. Christiane Wollaston-Joury had a hard time understanding why her granddaughter was not immediately smitten with soccer. She began playing at age four. Even little pink cleats were not enough to overcome her loathing of the sport, formed in part because boys (yuck) played on the team. Christiane cringed to watch her granddaughter and other girls on the field chatting and picking daisies while the boys ran around, shooting and playing the game in earnest. "It was so horrifying to me," Christiane said. "Absolutely stereotypical."

Fortunately for Christiane, her boy-hating granddaughter returned to soccer and became quite a good player. Both grandsons play, one as a goalie like Christiane. Having instructed them in the subtler points of the game, she regularly admonishes the boys to, "Remember that *Grandma* taught you."

EIGHTEEN
Time to Say Goodbye?

NEARLY SEVENTY years old, Mary White is amazed she is still playing soccer. "If you'd asked me when I was thirty, when I started, if I'd still be playing at the age I am now, I would have said, 'You're nuts!'" Having said that, she has no immediate plans to give up the game. Hers is a prevailing sentiment.

Nona Marsh is on the far side of seventy and, although slower than she once was, still eagerly takes the soccer field, giving each game her all. "Play, you just play. I do a lot of hiking and biking now too." Soccer makes her "happy, happy, happy." Nona's mantra is to just "Keep on moving, keep on moving."

Lynn Naftel, over seventy years young, lives by a similar maxim: "You don't quit playing soccer because you get old. You get old because you quit playing soccer!" Lynn still competes on two indoor soccer teams and two outdoor teams. Lynn's husband often told her that he knew that soccer was first in her life and he ranked second. It was not true but now with her husband gone—lost to cancer in 2013—Lynn's soccer team provides support and comfort. Lynn doesn't know how she'd manage without the camaraderie and the physical and mental boost she experiences from the game.

Sixty-nine-years young Sharon Murray is emphatic: "I don't plan on retiring ever, as long as I can play. If I can't run, if I can't do justice to my team, I will step off." Sharon is addicted to the travel and stimulation that comes with competing nationally and internationally. She and her teammates have discussed what they will do when they reach the point of being non-competitive. Walking soccer is an option. And if that becomes too difficult, they've floated the idea of starting a league for women who use walkers or wheelchairs. Never will they stop playing.

A youngster at sixty-eight, Dawn Cole has years of soccer ahead of her although she has given up playing outdoors in Sacramento because the oldest division offered is over-30. Though she is a goalie and doesn't have to run with the younger women, Dawn believes competing with youngsters was ridiculous. "They are much more aggressive. If I got injured because I was trying to play against a thirty-year-old, how stupid is that?" Dawn still plays outdoor soccer with her tournament team. "I could get injured in my over-60 tournaments, but I totally accept it there." And to keep in shape between tournaments Dawn plays on an indoor team.

Since Patti Storm did not discover the joy of soccer until she was nearly sixty, she has no intention of giving it up any time soon. "I love the game and am so grateful that I am playing. I plan to play until I can no longer and once that day comes, and it will, I will be very sad." Patti has requested that her husband ensure her tombstone reads, "Patti wishes she had started soccer earlier in her life."

Gene Forsythe, barely over sixty, already worries about her quickness (both physical and mental) when playing in the over-50 division. A natural goal scorer, Gene has decided that she will continue to play with the younger women until she can no longer put the ball in the net, but she doesn't expect it to be soon. Recently her doctor said Gene was a candidate for a knee replacement. She replied, "Naw, that's for old ladies. I'm not doing that. I'm not going there." Gene quotes her sixty-eight-year-old soccer buddy Debbie Craig in affirming she'll play "until they carry me off the field."

At Andrea Wessel's first soccer game, one of the players wore two huge knee braces and a brace on her wrist. Andrea and her teammate Nancy, also new to the sport, commented that the woman must be crazy to be on the field with her banged up knees. She should just quit the game. Today, Nancy wears a knee brace, and Andrea plays with two ankle braces and sometimes a knee brace as well. "Now we get it," Andrea said. "You don't want to give it up. You do what you can to keep going."

Rita Wilkie once thought she'd play until she was sixty, at which point she expected her team to toss her aside. Sixty came and went, and she was still on the roster. Rita then thought to continue until her teammates and other players began to patronize her by giving her more time on the ball and cheering at every good move she made. The patronizing started a few years ago. Rita decided she could live with it. She is now over seventy and still plays. Her Boston Breakers teammate Debbie Greenslit once told Rita that she hoped she could still play at Rita's age—Rita was forty-four at the time. Debbie, now sixty-seven, declares she will play until someone cuts off her legs.

The wise do not ask Alice Moore about quitting soccer. "Why do I have to stop playing?" Alice plays with and against younger women and men. Recently Alice was out-hustling a man in his thirties who, worn out, called for a substitute. Later he was told of Alice's age and refused to believe that such an old woman ran him into the ground.

Alice is adamant that, "As long as I can stand on that field they are going to have to drag me off. I'm not stopping. My husband said I'd probably be buried in my soccer uniform."

The idea is not without precedent. One of Alice's softball girl-friends was killed coming home from a game. Her teammates put her uniform, her bat, and her glove in her casket and served as pallbearers. "She may need it where she is going because she is going to be playing. Probably has been playing. We made sure we brought that stuff and put it in for her. That was important to her." Just as important as soccer is to Alice.

Joan Hunter-Brody is the very senior member of her soccer team. A younger friend she brought to play with the team became the second oldest player on the team: she was sixty-years-old. Most of the women on Joan's team are in their forties. Then there is Joan, eighty years young. "Kind of a blob" and overweight growing up, Joan didn't discover soccer until she was in her mid-forties. Like many women, it was love at first kick. Decades later she doesn't have the stamina she once had so she subs in and out frequently. "Ten minutes at a stretch is probably my limit," Joan said. Her teammates love her and want her to keep playing with them. "Why would I want to quit?" Joan said. "I would give it up if I felt miserable enough, but I always feel terrific. It doesn't really matter what the score is. It's just a lot of fun."

Wanda Rixon has thought about stopping. "Then I look at somebody like … Mary McCafferty or … Ruth [Walton] who played forever and I'm thinking, I don't really need to stop right now. I'm only sixty-two." Wanda admits that she will likely play until she has "an injury so devastating that it affects the true quality of life for the rest of my life." Wanda optimistically believes that such an injury isn't likely "for another thirty years or so."

In a discussion of the future, Pia Parrish noted that when she reached seventy, she could return to indoor coed soccer because the men wouldn't be able to keep up with her. Diane Lieberman agreed but stated they'd have to find an over-70 league. If there were no over-70 league, the women would build one.

Nancy Patrick began playing in her thirties with the Violet Vipers, a name too "wimpy" to survive. When in her forties,

Nancy heard about the Senior Olympics where one had to be fifty to play. "I thought, 'God, if I live that long, wouldn't it be great to be able to play once.'" Now competing in an over-60 league in Orange County, Nancy participates in soccer tournaments with her long-time teammates under the moniker 3Score Galore. The "Score" stands not for a goal, but for twenty years as in the "four score" in the Gettysburg Address. Many years from now, she hopes still to be competing at four-score-years of age. "This really is a lifetime sport."

Cynthia Hale was among the founders in the early 1980s of the Greater Atlanta Women's Soccer Association. While other women critical to the development of the league have died, moved away, or retired from soccer, Cynthia plays on. Although she discovered soccer while her sons were playing, neither of them was interested in sports. Cynthia is the lone athlete of the family, playing soccer for over thirty-five years and still competing alongside one of her original teammates. For many years, Cynthia played on two teams in different age groups at tournaments. Two years ago, she played on an over-65 team and was a sub on an over-60 team. Ten minutes into the over-60 match the coach sent her into the game and she never came out. Subsequent games followed the same pattern. Cynthia has since confined herself to playing on one team per tournament, feeling that she can no longer do her best when she plays nearly constantly. She is still in high demand for tournaments but only says yes to the first team that asks. Cynthia plays indoor soccer two or more times each week throughout the year in addition to playing ninety-minute outdoor games. She'll continue to play, "As long as I can."

Near the End?

After decades of playing some women do find themselves beginning to contemplate life without soccer. Jean Jarosz, playing in an over-60 tournament judiciously noted, "We do have more yesterdays than tomorrows."

Also, life changes disrupt soccer plans. Tran Diem Kratzke, now sixty, is still enthusiastic about playing but fears she may have to give up the sport if she moves. Tran has two daughters and one son, none of whom live nearby. She would like to be near her grandchildren who live in Texas. She has already checked out the soccer situation. "They don't have a big field; when you play in Austin, it is six on six. If I move there, I might not play as much." No more soccer might be the price she pays for seeing more of her grandchildren.

For some women, the physical cost of continuing may be too high. Rose Noga for a time played in five or six tournaments annually and traveled to Veteran's Cups and World Masters Games. She has been thrilled to be able to share her passion with her family. Rose and her daughter have played on the same team for twenty years. At one game where her granddaughter was in attendance, Rose's team was short players and the opposing team graciously allowed her granddaughter to take the field. Rose and her granddaughter were forwards, and her daughter anchored the defense: three generations playing together! Yet Rose fears such days may not come again. Playing in Michigan, the outdoor season is limited to May through October; the rest of the year she plays indoors, which is hard on her knees. Rose needs a knee replacement, but the doctors have told her there will be no soccer afterward. She knows that women undergoing such surgeries in their forties and fifties have ignored the doctors and returned to the field. Rose may not be as fortunate; she's already sixty-six-years-old.

Jeanne Farris has lived and played soccer in California, Arizona, Kansas, and Virginia. She played on multiple indoor and outdoor teams for years and traveled to tournaments when she could. Now seventy-four, Jeanne feels the wear and tear. She has had surgeries to relieve spinal stenosis—abnormal narrowing of the spinal canal that may cause pain or numbness—and to fuse several discs in her back. She can still play soccer, but can't touch her toes. Jeanne now plays more often in goal than on the field and saves more shots with her feet than hands because of the difficulty of bending over. Past injuries include broken wrists, broken ankles, and meniscus tears. She attributes some of her arthritic issues to these previous injuries. Jeanne has been receiving hyaluronan injections—a fluid that is similar to that which surrounds the joints—in her knee.[1] The first treatment relieved the pain for a year, but the second lasted just nine months, and the latest only six months. When the injections fail, the next step is a replacement of the knee, and as is the case with Rose, it is unlikely Jeanne would be able to return to soccer. "I'd be eighty before I'd be back on the field," she said. Jeanne recently quit her team in the over-40 division and is no longer traveling to tournaments, noting that when over-65 teams play eight-a-side on a smaller field, the players have more ground to cover than eleven-a-side on a full field.

The importance of soccer for Jeanne is fading. While she is registered on multiple teams, she plays less and less, showing up to games but only playing if a sub is needed. "I'm not disappointed if I don't play. So I think that is a mental urge out the door." Besides, she has other interests: Jeanne bowls with friends in the winter and they golf together in the in the spring, summer, and fall. Soccer is no longer her number one sport.

Many of the older women, but by no means all, are happy just to play and care little about the final score. The ethos of many younger players is different: they badly want to win. They are more aggressive, both physically and verbally. Is this a generational difference, or do the older players not remember being quite as aggressive themselves? In either case, women who have played for decades find themselves walking away from the game, disillusioned by the on-field attitudes of younger players.

Janice Akridge, in her sixties, took a break from the game when drama within her team soured her outlook on the game.

She later returned to the field but is not sure she'll continue with the game. "I am playing golf and I don't want to have an injury where I can't play golf for the rest of my life. You start to wonder, when is the right time to quit? At some point, it's not as much fun … because you're not keeping up with skills and stuff, so it's exhausting. I dunno, I'm actually transitioning to golf; I'm enjoying golf."

To those for whom soccer has been integral to their well-being, their identities, and their social lives, quitting the game elicits feelings of profound loss. Carrie Hood's life dramatically changed when her daughter brought a flyer on soccer home from school. "Whoever knew the years of joy this game would bring to our lives?" Carrie said. She played for decades, and both daughters played. One went to college on a soccer scholarship. When her granddaughter was five, Carrie had a picture taken of the three generations of women in their soccer uniforms. It is one of her favorite photos. Today the soccer prowess of the granddaughter is attracting the attention of colleges.

Carrie was still playing when she attended her forty-fifth high school reunion. The husband of a classmate was condescending to Carrie when she mentioned she was on a soccer team. "He was out of shape and couldn't even walk across the field. I tried to explain that we played all of the same rules as any professional team, except slide tackling. Finally I said, 'When I put on my soccer uniform and my cleats, even my husband is smart enough to back off.'"

When Carrie became a regular babysitter for her twin grandchildren, she felt she couldn't afford to get hurt and gave up playing. "I see my grandchildren playing now and miss the game; however, at seventy-four-years-old, I hurt too much to play. I still play tennis, walk three miles a week, and ride my bike once a week." Carrie enjoys kicking a soccer ball with the twins and being a loud fan at their games. Although she hasn't played in years, Carrie stated, "I still have my cleats and uniform."

A woman who has surmounted ankle, hip, and knee injuries in her younger years sometimes reach a point where returning to the soccer field yet again is not possible. Or perhaps she still plays, but worries about the next injury and fears the loss of mobility that may follow.

Debby Bowman quit in her fifties when her knees gave out. She still finds it difficult to talk about the mental pain of quitting. "Soccer was the most fun thing I ever did: made all those friends, had all those parties. Leaving soccer is like grieving the death of a person. A loss. For years, when someone dies, you have to grieve the loss of that lifestyle." After a break from the game, Debby tried to return but played only a few games. She had trouble seeing in the dark and her knees hurt. "It wasn't the same," she said. Debby quit, but her teammates didn't understand how much the decision hurt. "People would beg me to come back. It's overdramatic, but it's like asking a paramedic to relive a bad experience. No, don't talk to me about coming back. I have to feel bad all over again." Twelve years after her last game Debby finally feels like she's through the grief process. "I still wish I could play, but I don't feel bad like I used to."

At age sixty-seven, Judy Jones needed both knees replaced. She scheduled the surgery to be done after she completed Avon's sixty-mile walk to raise money to fight breast cancer. Judy might have come back to soccer after knee surgery. After all, she'd made a habit of defying doctors' orders and expectations. However, Judy has windswept knees. An unusual condition in adults, windswept knees mean one leg is bowed while the other is knocked-kneed. As a consequence, both knees point in the same direction. In Judy's case, her body compensated for the misalignment of her knees and she developed scoliosis—lateral curvature—of the spine. The doctors were surprised that Judy had been able to play soccer and recommended she not continue, as the jarring of running would stress her back. For once, Judy listened and agreed.

Bev Vaughn has been an athlete her entire life. Ten years ago, she was having a lot of back pain. Exercises, ibuprofen, heat, ice, nothing seemed to work. Bev feared she would need surgery. Her physical therapist suggested that she give up all athletic activity for a time. It was a drastic step for Bev, but she did it. In a matter of weeks, her back problems receded. Gradually she returned to tennis and softball, but not to basketball or soccer. "I think the culprit was playing soccer on those horrible fields we used to play on that were so rough and uneven. I didn't want to take a chance of messing up my back again. So I just never came back to it, but I loved it. I loved it."

Judi Whitestone had never had knee problems and was surprised when she tore her meniscus (not while playing soccer). She'd already decided to have a last hurrah—one more season—but it was not to be. Her knee was slow to heal, and Judi worried about its durability on the soccer field. Her grandchildren lived nearby, and Judi wanted to remain healthy enough to be able to play with them. At age seventy, she gave up playing competitively, but she'll still get out on the field to kick the ball around with her grandchildren. On a recent family vacation, three generations of the Whitestone family took to the field, males versus females. Judi was elated to be playing again. Although she has tried other sports, she's not found one to replace the joy and camaraderie of soccer. Judi cheers on her grandchildren but finds it difficult to watch them play. She has never gone back to watch her teammates play. "I just couldn't do that. I couldn't watch them on that field having fun. I just couldn't go back." But sometimes she believes she is back on the field. "Everybody who leaves soccer says the same thing: they dream about it."

Appendix A
Soccer Basics

Anyone who can kick a ball can play soccer. One does not have to be big or tall, although quickness is an advantage. Skilled and unskilled can play together, as can young and old, male and female, and all nationalities. A standard game involves teams of eleven players, but as few as two can play. To play, all one needs is: an open area of grass, concrete, sand, or mud; sticks, shirts, bags or something else to mark the goal areas; and a ball, empty water bottle, or small item that can be kicked.

Field
- Also called pitch, the field is 100-130 yards long and 50-100 yards wide.
- The field can be grass, dirt, or artificial turf.
- Adult goals are 24 feet wide and 8 feet tall.
- Field markings include a penalty box 18 yards deep by 44 yards wide in front of the goal. Within this box the goalie may use her hands.

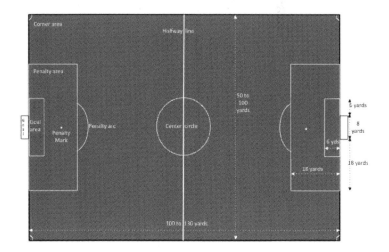

Positions

- Goalkeeper, also called goalie or keeper. May use her hands only inside the penalty area.
- Defenders, also called fullbacks. These players are primarily responsible for defense, although the right and left fullbacks may at times join the attack. Most teams play with three or four defenders (left, right, center). Sometimes the two central defenders play one behind the other (instead of alongside) and are called stopper and sweeper.
- Midfielders, also called halfbacks. Play both offense and defense, usually running the most of any players. Teams typically play with three or four midfielders.
- Forwards, also called strikers or wingers (if on left or right). Their primary mission is to score goals. Most teams play with two or three forwards.

Referees

- The head referee calls the game and is the final decision maker in matters relating to the play. She enforces the seventeen Laws of the Game, which include prohibitions against kicking, tripping, pushing, holding or jumping into an opponent.
- The assistant referee (AR), also known as a linesman, judges when the ball has left the field of play and which team is responsible. ARs also note when fouls happen out of sight of the head referee, and when an offside has occurred.
- Referees may yellow card (caution) a player for unsportsmanlike behavior, arguing with the referee, excessive fouling, or delaying the game.
- Referees may red card (expel) a player for receiving two yellow cards, committing a dangerous foul, violence against another player or the referee, bad language, or deliberately preventing a goal by pulling down another player or using her hands to redirect the ball.

Offsides

A player is deemed to be offside when

- She is involved in the play AND
- There are not two players (one of whom is typically the goalie) between her and the opposing goal *at the time the ball is passed* to her.

A player is not offside when

- She is not involved in the play or
- She receives the ball with one or no players between her and the goal provided there were two when the ball was passed or
- The pass by her teammate is backward or
- She receives the ball from a throw-in, corner kick, or goal kick or
- She is on her own half of the field.

When a player is called offside, the opposing team is given the ball at the point of the infraction.

Appendix B
The Players

Last Name	First Name	Location	Chapters
Akridge	Janice	N. California/Virginia	7, 8, 10, 11, 12, 18
Atiles	Daisy	N. California	9
Blum	Cathy	Massachusetts	11
Boettcher	Sue	Washington	6, 12, 14, 16
Bomar	Kathy	Virginia	7, 8
Bowman	Debby	Virginia	9, 18
Brown	Sue Pratt	Virginia	8
Bunch	Connie	N. California	7, 12
Burt	Jacquie	S. California/Nevada	13, 16
Carey	Kathy	N. California/Hawaii	4
Clewell	Lynne	Washington	6, 12
Cole	Dawn	N. California	10, 12, 17, 18
Craig	Debbie	S. California	18
Danner	Margaret	N. California	9, 11, 17
Diem Kratzke	Tran	Washington/Virginia	7, 18
Dinwiddie	Martha	Texas	8, 12, 15
Downer	Kathy	S. California	10, 12
Eddy	Kerry	Hawaii/N. California	2
Farris	Jeanne	California/Arizona/ Kansas/ Virginia	8, 18
Fletcher	Wendy	Washington	6, 17
Forsythe	Gene	S. California	7, 10, 18
Gaaserud	Lynn	Virginia	7, 15
Graham	Anna	S. California	10
Grant	Linda	Massachusetts	5, 16
Greenslit	Debbie	Massachusetts	11, 12, 18
Hale	Cynthia	Georgia, Missouri	12, 18
Hellyer	Janice	Oregon/Arizona	6

Hockster	Paula	Michigan	10, 16
Hood	Carrie	S. California	7, 8, 10, 18
Hovind	Chris	Washington	12, 16
Hunter-Brody	Joan	Massachusetts	11, 18
Ilacqua	Julie	Michigan	16
Jarosz	Jean	S. California	18
Jones	Judy	Virginia	1, 7, 8, 11, 18
Kessin	Lois	Massachusetts	5, 12, 17
Lauzen	Liz	Alaska/Washington	6
Lieberman	Diane	S. California	7, 18
Mahoney	Suzanne	Virginia	2, 7
Marsh	Nona	S. California	12, 18
Matalon	Wendy	S. California	2, 7
McCafferty	Mary	Virginia	11, 18
Metzger	Shirley	Virginia	8, 12
Moore	Alice	N. California	7, 9, 11, 17, 18
Mowry	Debbie	S. California	8
Murray	Sharon	N. California	10, 12, 14, 18
Naftel	Lynn	S. California	8, 10, 17, 18
Nash	Sarah	Virginia/S. California	10
Newton	Joan	S. California	9
Noga	Rose	Michigan	7, 10, 18
Nolan	Christine	Virginia	1, 7, 8, 10, 11
Noonan	Bernadette	Washington	6
Noonan	Catherine	Massachusetts	11
Parrish	Pia	S. California	2, 7, 18
Patrick	Nancy	S. California	18
Pirnie	Mary	Washington/Idaho	15
Potter	Anne Ruth	S. California	11
Quinzani	Joan	Massachusetts	5
Rixon	Wanda	Virginia	12, 15, 18
Ryan	Pat	Virginia	8
Schulstad	Penny	Virginia	8, 11, 12

Scott	Dolly	S. California	9
Sharpe	Karen	Virginia	1, 7, 11
Simons	Ellen	Massachusetts	5, 16
Slausen	Janet	Washington	6
Specht	Joanne	Virginia/N. California	12
Spencer	Sue	Texas, Massachusetts	5
Staley	Jany	S. California	14
Storm	Patti	S. California	12, 18
Straight	Kathy	Virginia	8
Strong	Anne	Massachusetts	14
Surowiecki	Maj	Washington	6
Teal	Lisa	Colorado/S. California	2, 7
Thorpe	Sandy	Virginia	1
Trader	Joyce	Washington	6
Ueda	Peggy	Massachusetts	5, 14
Vasquez	Debbie	N. California	12
Vaughn	Bev	Virginia	2, 7, 12, 18
Walton	Ruth	Virginia	7, 8, 15, 17, 18
Watson	Carol	S. California	10
Wessel	Andrea	Virginia	7, 18
White	Mary	Virginia	14, 17, 18
Whitestone	Judi	Virginia	8, 18
Wickens	Mari-Jo	Michigan	10, 16
Wilkie	Rita	Massachusetts	8, 11, 12, 18
Wollaston-Joury	Christiane	Massachusetts	9, 12, 17

NOTES

A Whole New World

1. Mayo Clinic, "Deep Vein Thrombosis (DVT)," https://www.mayoclinic. org/diseases-conditions/deep-vein-thrombosis/symptoms-causes/syc-20352557.

Title IX And All That

1. Theodore Caplow, Louis Hicks, and Ben J. Wattenberg, *The First Measured Century: An Illustrated Guide to Trends in America, 1900–2000* (Washington, DC: American Enterprise Institute Press, 2000), http:// www.pbs.org/fmc/book/2work8.htm.

2. Nina Stoneham, "Women's Roles in the 1950s," https://1950s.weebly. com/womens-roles.html.

3. For a nice summary of Babe's accomplishments see Don Van Natta, "Babe Didrikson Zaharias's Legacy Fades," *New York Times*, June 25, 2001, http://www.nytimes.com/2011/06/26/sports/golf/babe-didrikson-zahariass-legacy-fades.html.

4. Ellen W. Gerber, "The Controlled Development of Collegiate Sport for Women 1923-1936," *North American Society For Sport History Proceedings And Newsletter*, 1973: p. 27-28, library.la84.org/SportsLibrary/NASSH_Proceedings/NP1973/NP1973s.pdf.

5. Richard C. Bell, "A History of Women in Sport Prior to Title IX," *Sports Management, Women and Sports*, March 14, 2008, http://thesportjournal. org/article/a-history-of-women-in-sport-prior-to-title-ix/.

6. Women's Basketball Hall of Fame, "Women's Basketball Historical Timeline," http://wbhof.com/Timeline.html.

7. Katherine Switzer, "The Girl Who Started It All," *Runners World*, May 2007,http://www.runnersworld.com/runners-stories/kathrine-switzer-runs-the-boston-marathon.

8. The National Federation of State High School Associations has tracked sports participation since 1969. All statistics regarding high school sports are from this source. See http://www.nfhs.org/ParticipationStatics/ ParticipationStatics.aspx/.

9. U.S. Bureau of the Census, "CPS Historical time Series Tables on School Enrollment Table A-6: Age distribution of College Students 14 Years Old and Over, by Sex, October 1947-2016," https://www.census.gov/data/tables/time-series/demo/school-enrollment/cps-historical-time-series.html; and National Collegiate Athletic Association, *Sports and Recreation Programs of Universities and Colleges 1957-1982* (NCAA).

10. "Title IX and Sex Discrimination," U.S. Department of Education, https://www2.ed.gov/about/offices/list/ocr/docs/tix_dis.html.

11. Karen Blumenthal, "The Truth About Title IX," June 22, 2012, https://www.thedailybeast.com/the-truth-about-title-ix.

12. "Gender Equity / Title IX Important Facts," http://www.ncaa.org/about/resources/inclusion/gender-equity/title-ix-important-facts.

13. Longitudinal studies by R. Vivian Acosta and Linda Jean Carpenter, Professors Emerita, Brooklyn College contain excellent data and analysis on the impact of Title IX on women's roles as college sports participants, competitors, coaches, and administrators. www.acostacarpenter.org

14.The Association for Intercollegiate Athletics for Women (AIAW) was founded in 1971 to govern collegiate women's athletics.

15. Chelsea Janes, "The girls who fought for the right to play in Little League look back, 40 years later," *Washington Post*, August 13, 2014, https://www.washingtonpost.com/sports/othersports/the-girls-who-fought-for-the-right-to-play-in-little-league-look-back-40-years-later/2014/08/13/f86e4c88-2234-11e4-8593-da634b334390_story.html?utm_term=.d4ebb338db1c.

16. Kelly Bastone, "The History of the Sports Bra," https://www.ladiesonlysports.com/sports-bra-history/.

Not A Game For Ladies

1. Han Dynasty forebear of football was called Tsu' Chu and it consisted of kicking a leather ball filled with feathers and hair through an opening, measuring only 30-40cm in width, into a small net fixed onto long bamboo canes. "History of Football-The Origins," https://www.fifa.com/about-fifa/who-we-are/the-game/index.html.

2. Much of this section relies on this excellent book: Tim Tate, *Girls With Balls: The Secret History Of Women's Football* (London: John Blake Publishing Ltd, 2013).

3. "Ladies International Soccer Match," *Glasgow Herald*, May 9, 1881, http://donmouth.co.uk/womens_football/1881.html.

4. "Association football," https://en.wikipedia.org/wiki/Association_football.

5. Ben Dowell, "The origins of women's football to be explored in ITV drama Honeyballers," http://www.radiotimes.com/news/2015-07-02/the-origins-of-womens-football-to-be-explored-in-itv-drama-honeyballers/.

6. Deborah A.K. Brobst, "Women Munitions Workers in Britain during the Great War," *Theses and Dissertations*, Lehigh University, 2006, Paper 956, http://preserve.lehigh.edu/cgi/viewcontent.cgi?article=1956&context=etd.

7. The story of these remarkable women is best told in a wonderful book: Gail J Newsham, *In a League of Their Own! the Dick, Kerr Ladies 1917-1965*, (UK: Gail J. Newsham, 2014).

8. Ken Aston Referee Society Football Encyclopedia Bible, http://www.kenaston.org/football-encyclopedia/Carmen-Pomies.htm.

9. Boxing Day is a holiday celebrated the day after Christmas. It is a popular day for football matches.

10. "Pre 1991 Women's Soccer," Soccer Politics, https://sites.duke.edu/wcwp/tournament-guides/world-cup-2015-guide/history-of-the-womens-world-cup/pre-1991-womens-soccer/.

11. "France Women's National Football Team," https://en.wikipedia.org/wiki/France_women%27s_national_football_team.

12. Gertrud Pfister, "Must Women play Football? Women's Football in Germany, Past and Present," Football Studies, Volume 4, Issue 2, October 2001, library.la84.org/SportsLibrary/FootballStudies/2001/FS0402f.pdf; and https://en.wikipedia.org/wiki/Women%27s_football_in_Germany.

13. "Fútbol femenino," https://es.wikipedia.org/wiki/Futbol_femenino.

14. Sérgio Oliveira, "Futebol Feminino no Brasil – A História," *Última Divisão*, fev 8, 2011, http://www.ultimadivisao.com.br/futebol-feminino-no-brasil-a-historia.

RIDING THE WAVE

1. Marijane Nelson, "Island Pilot: Jane Kelley," *The 99 News, Official Publication of the International Organization of Women Pilots*, Volume 4, Number 1, January-February 1977: 16-18.

2. Phil Wright became the Director of Coaching and President of the San Juan Soccer Club. He was Chairman of the U.S. Soccer Club, which was dedicated to fostering the growth and development across the USA of club soccer programs. Wright also was chosen as the National Youth Soccer Coach of the Year.

NOT TO BE DENIED

1. http://www.usyouthsoccer.org/media_kit/keystatistics/.

KICKING IN THE RAIN

1. Soccer aficionados in Seattle, Washington vigorously dispute this claiming Seattle, not Portland is the true capital of soccer.

2. Information on Bernadette from interviews with WSWSA members plus: Harvey Araton, *Alive and Kicking,* (New York: Simon & Shuster, 2001); and Mark Trumbell, "In Seattle Women Play Soccer in Droves," *Christian Science Monitor*, August 12, 1994, https://www.csmonitor.com/1994/0812/12111.html.

3. Information on Mike Ryan from the following sources:

Joshua Mayers, "Mike Ryan, perhaps the 'principle pioneer' of Seattle soccer died last week at age 77," *Seattle Times*, November 25, 2012, http://blogs.seattletimes.com/soundersfc/2012/11/25/mike_ryan_perhaps_the_principa/;

Joshua Mayers, "Prep Soccer: New kicks for an old shoe," *Seattle Times*, October 9, 2007, http://old.seattletimes.com/html/highschoolsports/2003935020_mayers09.htm;

Frank MacDonald, "10 Questions with Mike Ryan," https://www.soundersfc.com/post/2008/03/18/10-questions-mike-ryan;

"Mike Ryan, The First Coach of the U.S. WNT Passes Away at 77," November 24, 2012, http://www.ussoccer.com/stories/2014/03/17/14/04/mike-ryan-passes-away-at-77; and

Paul Kennedy, "Obituary, Mike Ryan (1935-2012)," *SoccerAmerica*, November 25, 2012, https://www.socceramerica.com/publications/article/49341/obituary-mike-ryan-1935-2012.html.

4. Tom Farrey, "What a Kick: World Cup in U.S. Thrills Immigrant Who Boosted Soccer," *Seattle Times*, June 14, 1994.

5. Information on Janet from interviews with WSWSA members plus: Harvey Araton, *Alive and Kicking,* (New York: Simon & Shuster, 2001); and http://www.usadultsoccer.com/news_article/show/851309?referrer_id=971559-news.

6. Video at https://www.youtube.com/watch?v=SW-M9-s7z3c.

FINDING THE GAME

1. Bruce Chadwick, "Soccer-Loved and Ignored," *Sports Magazine,* July 1984, http://www.kenn.com/the_blog/?page_id=238.

ALL THE WRONG MOVES

1. Adam Hurrey, "Double trouble: why aren't there more two-footed footballers?" *Telegraph* (UK), June 20, 2015, http://www.telegraph.co.uk/sport/football/babb/11680631/Double-trouble-why-arent-there-more-two-footed-footballers.

2. Michael Wilbon, "Blues Rule Women's Soccer," *Washington Post*, July 10, 1979: D1.

CHARACTERS, CRAZY AND OTHERWISE

1. "Purple Haze" was written in 1966 and became the signature song of Jimi Hendrix.

PHOTOGRAPHS

1. Peter Horvath photos available at https://petermhorvath.smugmug.com

2. Harold Buchholz photos available at www.digitalnostalgia.biz.

3. Jacob Franke photos available at https://jaep.smugmug.com

4. J. Tyge O'Donnell photos available at www.theneoncity.com.

CAMARADERIE

1. "Amy Louise Nash Touchet," *Mercury News*, March 1, 2014, http://www.legacy.com/obituaries/mercurynews/obituary.aspx?pid=169904207.

IN SICKNESS AND IN HEALTH

1. *O, The Oprah Magazine*, August 2004. http://www.oprah.com/spirit/mia-hamms-aha-moment.

2. "A sporting chance for active total knee replacement patients," American Academy of Orthopaedic Surgeons, March 14, 2010, https://www.sciencedaily.com/releases/2010/03/100312071800.htm.

3. M.M. Gagne, "Joe Namath's Knee Brace," *Sports Illustrated*, June 25, 2014. https://www.si.com/2014/06/25/nfl-history-in-95-objects-joe-namath-knee-brace.

4. Kevin G. Shea, MD, Ronald Pfeiffer, EdD, ATC, Jo Han Wang, BS, ATC, Mike Curtin, MD, and Peter J. Apel, BA, "Anterior Cruciate Ligament Injury in Pediatric and Adolescent Soccer Players: An Analysis of Insurance Data," http://www.academia.edu/7067560/Anterior_Cruciate_Ligament_Injury_in_Pediatric_and_Adolescent_Soccer_Players_An_Analysis_of_Insurance_Data.

5. The iliotibial band is a sheath of connective tissue that contributes to stabilizing the knee and is constantly in use during walking and running.

Travel and Tournaments

1. See for example: Errol Nazareth, "Blazing heat burning shoe soles on Toronto's turf fields," *CBC News*, Aug 10, 2016. http://www.cbc.ca/news/canada/toronto/summer-heat-turf-1.3714351.

2. C. Frank Williams and Gilbert E. Pulley, "Synthetic Surface Heat Studies," Brigham Young University. aces.nmsu.edu/programs/turf/documents/brigham-young-study.pdf.

3. http://www.scienceofsocceronline.com/2009/04/penalty-kicks-by-numbers.html.

4. For the story of the grannies see: Robyn Dixon, "They kick like grannies, proudly," *Los Angeles Times*, June 21, 2010, http://articles.latimes.com/2010/jun/21/world/la-fg-soccer-grannies-20100622; and William C. Rhoden, "For the Love of Soccer and a Lasting Sisterhood," *New York Times*, June 6, 2010, http://www.nytimes.com/2010/06/07/sports/soccer/07rhoden.html.

A British Accent

1. http://www.history.com/this-day-in-history/man-united-players-among-victims-of-plane-crash

2. For an understanding of the game, see the twenty-page overview offered by Purdue University: https://www.cs.purdue.edu/homes/hosking/cricket/explanation.htm.

3. http://sdcsra.com/theassociation.aspx.

4. http://www.surfsoccer.com/about/.

5. "Report: Michigan referee punched during soccer game dies," *CBS News*, July 1, 2014, https://www.cbsnews.com/news/report-michigan-referee-punched-during-soccer-game-dies/.

6. https://en.wikipedia.org/wiki/New_York_Cosmos_(1970–85)

7. Hungary won the Olympic Gold Medal at the 1968 Summer Olympics in Mexico City.

8. https://en.wikipedia.org/wiki/Shannon_MacMillan.

9. Annual fees for club soccer can easily exceed $2,000 plus costs for uniforms, extra training, soccer camps, and soccer cleats. Boys on Jacquie's team worked paying jobs to help their families.

GIVING BACK

1. https://en.wikipedia.org/wiki/Wilbert_Tucker_Woodson_High_School.

2. http://football.wikia.com/wiki/Wembley_Stadium_(1923).

3. https://www.alltrails.com/trail/us/washington/mount-si-trail.

4. In Brookline, recreational and travel teams were divided by age into two-year groupings. Larger soccer communities often divide by each year. Children sometimes will play up a year or two in age, e.g. a 13-year-old playing on U-15 or U-16 teams.

5. Information on the life of Anne Strong from: Tzivia Gover, "Soccer in the city," *Smith Alumnae Quarterly*, Winter 2004-05: 18-20; and Michele Richinick, "Anne Strong; lawyer enabled girls to play soccer in Boston," *Boston Globe*, May 4, 2013, http://archive.boston.com/news/local/massachusetts/2013/05/03.

6. http://users.rcn.com/jlrobles/mission.html

7. http://www.americascores.org/

DREAMS OF FIELDS

1. *FWSA 10 Years*, Stephanie Shank, editor.

2. Jeanne Coughlin, "It's Better Than Playing Bridge," *Fairfax Journal*, August 22, 1979.

3. The Fairfax County Board of Supervisors appoints and is advised by the Athletic Council.

4. https://www.usclimatedata.com/climate/boise/idaho/united-states/usid0025.

5. https://www.usclimatedata.com/climate/seattle/washington/united-states/uswa0395.

6. Mark Drakos, "Artificial Turf: Does it Increase the Risk of Sports Injuries?" Hospital for Special Surgery, https://www.hss.edu/conditions_artificial-turf-sports-injury-prevention.asp.

7. Laird Harrison, "The Truth About Artificial Turf Injuries," http://sportswithoutinjury.com/truth-artificial-turf-injuries/.

Barbarians at the Gate

1. Don Wilbur served as a referee coach inspector for decades, first for the U.S. Soccer Federation and then for FIFA. He evaluated referees for the NCAA, Major League Soccer, CONCACAF, and FIFA. Wilbur held the role of National Coordinator of Officials for NCAA soccer and was inducted into the National Soccer Hall of Fame in 2004.

2. Esse Baharmast is best known for giving a late penalty kick to Norway in minute eighty-nine of their World Cup game against Brazil. Norway converted the penalty and won the game 2-1. Broadcast TV footage failed to support his call and he was vilified by millions of fans and the press. Colleagues knew Baharmast wouldn't make such an egregious mistake and one discovered video on the Internet from a Swedish TV station that clearly showed the foul. In 2016, *Referee Magazine* called it one of the eighteen best calls in officiating, across all sports. https://issuu.com/refereemagazine/docs/the_18_best_calls_in_officiating_hi/2.

3. Eileen Marie Narcotta-Welp, "The future of football is feminine: a critical cultural history of the U.S. women's national soccer team," http://ir.uiowa.edu/etd/2125.

4. The indifference of U.S. Soccer to women extended to the U.S. women's national team. The women that won the 1991 World Cup were paid ten dollars per diem and received room and board. Their uniforms were hand-me-downs from the U-20 men's national team, which they washed themselves.

5. João Havelange, FIFA president from 1974 to 1998, was widely believed to have profited handsomely through bribery, yet never faced prosecution. In Switzerland, the headquarters for many sports organizations including FIFA and the International Olympic Committee (IOC), bribery or payment of 'commissions' to obtain business was not criminal; it was in fact tax deductible. Havelange was also a member of the IOC for forty-eight years. He did not resign his IOC position until 2011 when he was under investigation for corruption in a then markedly changed Swiss legal environment.

6. Narcotta-Welp, "The future of football."

7. Winning the Women's World Cup in 1999, the women's bonuses were equal to those of the U.S. men who finished dead last in the 1998 World Cup.

CHANGES IN THE WIND

1. High school sports participation study, see note 8 under Title IX And All That.

TIME TO SAY GOODBYE?

1. https://www.drugs.com/mtm/hyaluronan.html.

67031530R00155

Made in the USA
Middletown, DE
17 March 2018